FUNDAMENTALS OF ECONOMICS FOR ENVIRONMENTAL MANAGERS

FUNDAMENTALS OF ECONOMICS FOR ENVIRONMENTAL MANAGERS

William F. Barron
Robert D. Perlack and
John J. Boland

Q

QUORUM BOOKS
Westport, Connecticut • London

Library of Congress Cataloging-in-Publication Data

Barron, William F.
    Fundamentals of economics for environmental managers / William F.
Barron, Robert D. Perlack, and John J. Boland.
        p.   cm.
    Includes bibliographical references and index.
    ISBN 1–56720–159–8 (alk. paper)
    1. Managerial economics.   2. Environmental management.
I. Perlack, Robert D.   II. Boland, John J.   III. Title.
HD30.22.B367   1998
338.5′024′658—dc21   97–41001

British Library Cataloguing in Publication Data is available.

Library of Congress Catalog Card Number: 97–41001
ISBN: 1–56720–159–8

First published in 1998

Quorum Books, 88 Post Road West, Westport, CT 06881
An imprint of Greenwood Publishing Group, Inc.

Printed in the United States of America

The paper used in this book complies with the
Permanent Paper Standard issued by the National
Information Standards Organization (Z39.48–1984).

10 9 8 7 6 5 4 3

In order to keep this title in print and available to the academic community, this edition
was produced using digital reprint technology in a relatively short print run. This would
not have been attainable using traditional methods. Although the cover has been changed
from its original appearance, the text remains the same and all materials and methods
used still conform to the highest book-making standards.

To

Pragmatic Visionaries

M. Gordon Wolman of The Johns Hopkins University
who believes environmental managers can and should be
eclectic without being dilettantes

and

Christine Loh (Loh Kung Wai) of the Citizens Party of Hong Kong
who believes public decisionmaking can and should be
open and participatory

Contents

Preface

This text presents the major elements of environmental economics, focusing on its applications to environmental decisionmaking. It provides an overview of the theoretical foundations of economics, emphasizing the underlying assumptions and typical focus of analysis and illustrating these through environmental examples. It is intended for environmental scientists and engineers, environmental policy students, and other non-economists with an interest in, or a need for, a basic understanding of what economics can contribute to environmental assessment and policy analysis.

This text may be used in several different ways. It can be used to support a one or two semester graduate level course in applied environmental economics or environmental policy analysis. Such a course would likely be found in a multi-disciplinary program in environmental management or in environmental studies. The book may also find use as part of courses offered in environmental engineering or science. It is also appropriate for short, intensive, professional development courses for environmental managers and others with environmental responsibilities (e.g., energy system planners, industrial managers). In such cases, the short course would likely focus on one or, at most, a few chapters. When used in this way, it is important to note that while a familiarity with the points covered in chapters 2, 3, and 4 is needed to fully appreciate the points made in later chapters, only a general familiarity with the theoretical foundations is essential in order to follow the points being made. Finally, the text may be used as a basic reference book for environmental managers who occasionally must direct or assess the work of economists.

It is assumed that readers are broadly familiar with environmental problems and management options. Detailed knowledge of these topics or of environmental policy may be helpful, but is not required to make effective use of this book. No previous training in economics is assumed; nor are mathematical skills beyond elementary algebra and graph reading necessary to make effective use of this text.

In the end, it is expected that serious readers of this text will develop a broad understanding of what economics may contribute to environmental assessment and decisionmaking. The reader will also come away with a recognition of the limits of economic analysis and where the line between the science and the art of environmental economics tends to occur.

Acknowledgments

Many threads lead to the writing of this book. Among these were those begun by Peter Kroll through his appreciation of an intuitive approach to economics, by Maria Hills who simply said "why not write your own," and by Jamie Allen with his timely advice and assistance with regard to publication.

A number of people commented on some of the basic ideas presented here as well as on draft chapters. Among those we would like to explicitly mention are Milton Russell, William Reilly, Joseph Liu, and Gordon Ng. Our graduate students provided a critical audience for much of the material presentation in this book.

On the actual work level for producing the manuscript we wish to thank Aileen Wong for her initiative and effective supervision of final text preparation. Megan Reilly, who served as an editor, and Jeanne Ng who served as a copy editor for the preliminary draft helped move the development of the text forward at crucial times. Mary Kwok and Carlene Van Toen patiently worked to iteratively generate the graphics as the authors envisioned them. Nils Steinbrecher provided invaluable software troubleshooting. Rosemary Barnes and Lynn Suter generously helped with the proof reading. Our thanks also go out to Frances Lam, Sheena Lam and the other staff of the Centre of Urban Planning and Environmental Management of The University of Hong Kong for their consistent spirit of enthusiastic cooperation which helped so much when faced with an impending deadline.

We also wish to acknowledge the support and understanding of BJ, Amy, Anna, and Nita.

1

An Economics Perspective on Environmental Management

Economics is the art and science of efficiently allocating scarce resources to meet needs and wants. *Efficiency* means attaining the greatest value of output using a fixed set of inputs, or minimizing the value of inputs used to attain a specific output of goods and services.

Economic theory is usually presented in a formalized manner, through mathematical representations, rules for optimization, and generalized presumptions about human behavior. These formal treatments help to delineate specific implications of the underlying principles of economics. They also make the application of these principles to particular situations more rigorous. Yet, at the most basic level, the underlying principles of economics simply constitute common sense approaches to assessment and decisionmaking. The common sense of a number of the most important points in an economics approach is briefly illustrated below.

Comparing Benefits and Costs at the Margin

Often, we face not only a choice between whether to fully engage in some activity or to completely refrain from it, but also at what level to participate. When this is the case, we can determine the appropriate degree of participation by comparing the benefits and costs associated with each incremental (in economists' terms, *marginal*) increase in the level of the activity. We would continue to increase our participation until we reach a point where going on to the next level would mean adding more costs than benefits. This is a rule most of us follow every time we decide on what and how much to eat, and it is the rule that economists stress should be applied to deciding the level of pollution control.

Considering Opportunity Costs

When deciding whether to use a resource—for instance, time, money, or gas—in a particular way, we need to consider not only the benefits and costs of putting the resource to a specific use, but also the *foregone* opportunities. That resource might have provided an even greater benefit if put to another use. For example, when considering whether to go to the cinema, we would normally weigh the benefits of enjoying that particular movie against the costs required in time and money. We might also consider whether there was some better use for our time and money, such as going to another movie, or staying home to unclog the kitchen sink. Similarly, when determining an air quality standard, in addition to weighing the benefits and costs of reaching that standard, we need to consider whether some or all of the resources necessary to clean the air might be better employed toward another goal, such as nature conservation or education.

Internalizing Externalities

Many of our commonplace actions produce unintended side effects, which impose costs on others. In most minor situations, either custom or the law does not require us to offer compensation to the affected parties for our impositions. These unintended side effects are called *externalities*, or effects external to the market decision, because they are conventionally excluded from an individual assessment of the benefits and costs involved in an activity.

For example, someone who is cutting his lawn with a faulty, gasoline-powered lawnmower on a Sunday morning may disturb neighbors having a relaxing breakfast with friends on their porch. In this situation, the impact of the noise (an unintended side effect) is treated by the one mowing his lawn as external to his own assessment of the benefits and costs involved in deciding whether to cut his lawn, at what time, and with what sort of machine. This might be particularly likely in a setting where neighbors are strangers to each other or where custom makes it unlikely that they would voice their concerns.

It might well be the case that the level of harm unintentionally imposed on others in this case is greater than the costs of avoiding or reducing it in the first place, perhaps by waiting until a less intrusive time or by fixing the machine. From the standpoint of the neighborhood as a whole, the existence of the externality reduces total welfare if the cost of reducing or avoiding the activity is less than the value of the damage caused by pursuing the activity. And just as the welfare of the person wanting to mow his lawn, combined with that of his neighbors, could potentially be improved if they were to negotiate a reduction in the externality, so might society's overall welfare be improved if previously uncontrolled municipal wastewater discharges are reduced or eliminated. In the latter case, a reduction in the discharges would generate greater net benefits than allowing them to continue unabated, if the loss of fishery and other aquatic resources in the water body receiving the discharges is valued more highly than the costs of wastewater treatment.

Moreover, the appropriate level of sound reduction (or postponement of the activity) in the first situation, and wastewater treatment pollution in the second, can be determined by comparing the benefits and costs associated with each incremental step in reduction of the externality. In each case there is a net welfare gain associated with some unspecified level of reduction. But reducing the externality too far may incur associated costs that result in a net loss.

For example, one incremental improvement in the situation involving the noisy lawnmower might be to ban the use of gasoline-powered lawnmowers on Sunday. A more comprehensive measure might require that everyone use manual or electric lawnmowers. This would succeed in making the neighborhood quieter, but would provide little additional benefit, since noisy lawnmowing only disturbs the neighbors when they are having brunch outside, which they are likely to do only on Sundays. Moreover, such a more inclusive measure would impose a higher cost on the neighborhood at large (i.e., by further limiting personal choice).

Likewise, it is possible that going beyond primary to secondary and tertiary municipal wastewater treatment might provide little additional environmental protection while imposing considerable additional costs on the community. In short, when an externality is internalized, it should not necessarily be completely eliminated.

More on the Common Sense of Environmental Economics

As illustrated above, each of us applies basic tenets of economic theory as we go about the business of daily living. This text aims to help readers develop a firm intuitive grasp of economics as it applies to environmental management. As you read this text, it is useful to consider how economic concepts apply to the way you manage your own personal activities, including those that may have a harmful effect on the environment, and your willingness to change your behaviour in order to mitigate those impacts.

Each of the important concepts dealt with in this text should be understandable in terms of, and compatible with, the logic applied to the large and small decisions we as individuals make every day. With that noted, we must also recognize that while the basic principles may be the same, decisionmaking at the *collective* level tends to be more complicated, because of the need to reconcile alternative value judgments. And much of environmental management is concerned with collective choices based on differing and evolving values. In other words, the logic may be rather straight forward but the actual decisionmaking may be quite complex.

PUTTING A VALUE ON THINGS

At the heart of economics is the matter of value. In contrast to what many probably think, economics is not about money. Rather, it is about *value*.

If money appears to be the focus of most economic assessments, it is simply because values expressed in money are easier to deal with than those that are not. As illustrated throughout this text, economic analysis is just as relevant to environmental values, for which it is often difficult to assign monetary values, as it is to market transactions.

Particularly in its policy applications, economics attempts to weigh costs against benefits. One useful way to define a *cost* is anything of negative value, whether input or output, while anything of positive value is called a *benefit*.[1] Costs, as well as benefits, often include more than just monetary considerations. For example, a decision about what type of home entertainment system to buy is likely to be a matter of more than simply treating its technical features as the benefit and its purchase price as the cost. A high level of complexity involved in operating a home entertainment system may be a relevant (though unpriced) cost to a potential buyer, while that same prospective buyer may consider the aesthetically appealing design of a particular system as one of its benefits, separate from the benefit of sound or picture quality. Similarly, the risk of losing biodiversity as a result of destroying the only known remaining habitat of a certain species may be a highly relevant (though traditionally unpriced) cost associated with the clear-cutting of a particular forest. And as noted in Chapter 9, the economist as well as the environmental manager needs to consider ways to account for risks not defined in monetary terms when assessing management options.

When conventional prices, in dollar terms, are unavailable, it is often possible to put a surrogate monetary value on certain types of costs and benefits, by estimating a community's willingness to pay for them. When we can do this, it makes decisionmaking potentially that more precise. However, even where we cannot confidently put a price on a previously non-monetized benefit or cost, clearly such unpriced factors may remain important to the decision-making process. Indeed, the implicit values given to non-monetized costs or benefits will sometimes be great enough so as to prompt a reversal of a decision made originally on the basis of monetized measures of value. For example, the perceived risks of nuclear power plants effectively limited the nuclear electric industry in many countries in the 1980s and 1990s. This happened despite arguments from the industry that the benefits of nuclear power outweighed its costs. Of course, the industry was focusing on the monetized benefits and costs, while the public tended to focus on non-monetized costs, particularly the risk of a catastrophic accident.

The point here is not that the decision to limit nuclear power was correct or incorrect. It is rather that the public made its decision on the basis that the perceived (and perhaps only vaguely understood) total costs of nuclear power were greater than the perceived benefits, after taking into account the non-monetized impacts. In other words, in making public policy, as well as many personal decisions, not all components of the benefit-cost streams are necessarily precisely defined, let alone specifically valued. And yet, we make decisions. As discussed in Chapter 8, this point is particularly important when it comes to the environment, because invariably certain aspects of the environment will not have, and cannot readily be given, an explicit monetary value. Without a price, it is difficult for those aspects to be directly incorporated into measures of a project's net benefits.

The Intrinsic Role of Values Assigned by Humanity

While some argue that the natural environment has inherent rights and absolute values that transcend those assigned by humans, the economist tends to see the natural environment as a set of resources whose worth depends on how people use and otherwise value them. In this sense, the environment is treated much like other economic resources, whether natural or man-made. However, with this noted, we also stress that an economics perspective is not incompatible with a strongly environmental perspective. The scope of economic analysis should be broadly defined so as to encompass the process of estimating appropriate values for environmental protection. For example, in a benefit-cost assessment of a project that might lead to contamination of a municipal ground water supply, it is simply common sense (and good economics) to incorporate the economic value of the aquifer, and the risk that additional costs might be incurred in developing alternative supplies.

In principle, the perspective of economics can go much further. As long as people are willing to explicitly or implicitly value such things as the continued existence of whales, or the preservation of biological diversity (either for its own sake or to ensure a broad genetic heritage for humans to exploit), such values can and should be incorporated into economic analyses. Hence, while economics stems from an anthropocentric perspective, it may take into account virtually any matter about which people are concerned.

The Changeable Nature of Value

Perhaps the most basic principle of economic analysis is that values are rarely fixed or absolute. The worth that an individual or a society assigns to an automobile, a certain type of food, the continued existence of a species, unpolluted air, or almost anything, is largely a matter of circumstances and value judgment. In part, the value we put on a thing may depend on how we perceive its intrinsic merit. Yet our perception of value typically is heavily influenced by the perceived usefulness of things to humanity, and our preferences and desires for those uses. Clearly the value we place on things, including environmental impacts, may change from person to person, place to place, and time to time.

This presents a challenge in making policies, particularly those with long-term implications. What one group believes to be appropriate policy may be thought foolish by other groups with different values. And what is deemed reasonable today may seem inappropriate in the future on the basis of additional information.   Hence, in environmental management, as with nearly all activities, policymaking is rarely "once and for all." It is, instead, an iterative process that must be carried out intermittently as values evolve.

MEASURES OF WORTH

As noted before, the basic subject matter of economics is the efficient use of resources to meet human needs and wants; efficiency means getting the most value out for what we put in.   The common perception that economics is primarily about money stems from the fact that much of the economics literature focuses on markets, and in markets it is monetized values, expressed in prices, which provide a readily measurable common denominator.

Prices

The most significant distinguishing feature of environmental, as opposed to conventional, market economics is the extent to which analysts rely on unregulated market prices as the primary indicator of value. Obviously, prices are one very useful indicator of value. Market prices tend to be set through a combination of factors which reflect (*i*) the value of the inputs required to produce a good or service, (*ii*) the value placed by consumers on that good or service, and (*iii*) the competitive conditions of the market. Market prices vary over time when supply or demand conditions change.

Supply conditions may vary as a result of factors such as technological development, the discovery of a new source of supply or the exhaustion of an existing one, or a change in the level of competition. Demand may change because of rising or falling consumer income, the emergence or disappearance of substitute goods, or a change in consumer preference. The competitive structure of markets depends on such things as the number and size of suppliers, and the number and demand levels of consumers. Prices arising from uncompetitive markets, where full and broad economic participation is somehow limited, may set prices that do not reflect appropriate measures of value for the goods and services offered.

Administered prices, or prices determined by public agencies rather than the free market, may be set so as to recover the costs of production, to encourage or discourage demand, to reflect the presumed intrinsic value of the good or service provided, or to generate maximum revenue. Clearly, the appropriateness of any particular administered price as an indicator of society's value for something depends on how well the values of the government reflect those of society.

Although all money prices are influenced by many things and are not always reliable indicators of value, they nonetheless serve as very convenient summary measures. And because they are quantified and use a common unit of measure, prices allow direct comparisons of value among very different types of things; for example, jobs, food, and travel. Yet, for all their usefulness, prices, especially those that are unregulated, tend to systematically exclude certain important types of values, particularly those related to the natural environment.

More on Externalities

Economic activity typically involves unpriced side effects, or externalities, as discussed above, which result from market activity but are not included in the assessments of suppliers and demanders, because they do not require compensation. Pollution, the overuse of renewable resources, and the inadvertent destruction of environmental services provided by healthy forests or estuaries are common examples of environmental externalities. Much of environmental economics focuses on externalities and, indeed, much of environmental management may be thought of as the process of mitigating the effects of externalities or attempting to internalize them into decisionmaking.

When we mitigate the effects of externalities, our goal is to make the environmental impacts resulting from the externalities less damaging. When we attempt to internalize the externalities, we are indirectly aiming to lessen the environmental damage by making those responsible for causing the side effects to see the externalities as part of the benefit and cost assessment, so that they will take such effects into account in their decisionmaking. Yet, as illustrated earlier, internalizing an externality or mitigating its effect does not necessarily mean the damage is completely eliminated. Indeed, completely eliminating the damages in many cases would be highly inefficient!

BENEFITS VERSUS COSTS OF INCREMENTAL IMPROVEMENTS

Assessing Incremental Changes

Basic economic principles, and common sense, tell us that we should reduce environmental damage, and protect environmental services, when the value gained by doing so is greater than the value given up through the costs incurred to do so. When the value of a particular environmental impact is high and the cost of eliminating it is small to moderate, it would be economically inefficient to tolerate that damage. By the same logic, when we are faced with an undesirable but relatively minor environmental impact that would require a high cost to eliminate, from the perspective of efficiency, such damage is something that we should tolerate until we find a relatively inexpensive way to reduce or eliminate it.

As elaborated in Chapters 2 and 3 and illustrated throughout this book, in most cases a benefit-cost assessment should consider incremental reductions of the problem, in addition to the options of complete elimination versus inaction. While the value of the first increments of environmental improvement may be far greater than the costs incurred, the value of further increments might be less than the additional costs. Even when the total benefits of completely eliminating an environmental problem are greater than the total costs, an intermediate stage of reduction might result in greater net benefits, and thus would constitute a more efficient course of action.

Collective Versus Individual Choices

In the absence of prices, the value of externalities must be estimated indirectly. This leaves considerable room for differences of judgment. The process of valuation typically is at least as much an art as it is a science and compromise and persuasion have much to do with that art.

In the market, consumers individually exercise their judgments with their wallets, and they themselves bear the market-related consequences of their own decisions. Yet, an individual decision about whether to engage in an activity with potentially damaging effects on the environment may affect large numbers of other people (not to mention animals and plants) in ways beyond the benefits and costs accounted for in the market. And in many cases the seller or buyer may have little knowledge about the details of the situation.

While many of the most important environmental management decisions are matters of collective concern, typically they are made not by the society at large, but by specialized organizations and authorities. The individuals within these organizations are often forced to make their decisions in the face of incomplete information and divergent environmental values within society. On what basis should the collective decisions be made? A perfectly "clean" environment is physically and financially unattainable. So, how clean is clean enough, and who should bear the costs? Economic analysis can help us in evaluating the pros and cons of alternative answers to these questions, but often does not provide clear and unequivocal resolutions to environmental issues.

Opportunity Costs

Opportunity costs are values foregone when resources are put to one use rather than another. In environmental debates, decisionmakers as well as concerned individuals and groups often focus on each particular environmental issue in isolation. While we cannot include all contingencies in assessing a problem, it is just as inappropriate to treat every problem without reference to the larger context. In the real world of difficult choices and budget constraints, taking a segmented approach to assessment and decisionmaking risks maximizing returns in one area only to miss even greater net gains resulting from applying resources elsewhere.

For example, a stricter air quality standard for tropospheric (lower atmosphere) ozone might be justified in the narrow sense of the value we place on health benefits compared to the costs of such improvements. Yet, it might be that for every dollar spent on tropospheric ozone, a greater return could have been obtained from reducing the ambient respirable particulate levels. It is perhaps tempting to say that the budget considerations for different types of policy choices should be mutually exclusive, but in practice there is likely to be competition for available funds for environmental protection. It may seem that it is a matter of simple common sense to consider opportunity costs when setting priorities, yet acceptance of this principle is not always evidenced in debates about environmental protection. It may be that to some advocates with a specific agenda ignoring opportunity costs is a potentially effective negotiation tactic. However, if all parties to the negotiation fail to consider, as the poet Robert Frost said, "the road not taken," then society as a whole is unlikely to be well served.

Argument for Efficient Pollution

As noted above, consideration of economic efficiency in regulating the discharge of pollutants does not necessarily lead to zero discharge. In fact, it rarely does so. Assessment of the benefits and costs of incremental changes in the level of discharge will usually reveal a point where further reductions in the level of pollutant discharge would cost more than the value of the resulting benefits. While this result may be clear from an economic perspective, it is by no means widely accepted.

Environmental activists and many environmental scientists are likely to take the position that *any* reduction in pollutant discharge is desirable, regardless of cost. While they may accept some level of discharge because of technological limits, they may view appeals based on economic efficiency to go less far in pollutant reduction than is technologically feasible as simply rationalizations on the part of those unwilling to fully protect the environment.

Leaving aside for the moment the issue of the uncertainty that is inherent in most estimates of costs and benefits (a topic dealt with in Chapter 9), the argument for economic efficiency as a criterion for pollutant discharge should be carefully considered. Suppose that economic efficiency is not used as the criterion for determining the permitted levels of pollutant discharge and that as a result discharges are reduced to a point below that which is indicated in the economic analysis. This means that some incremental costs have been incurred which do not produce a commensurate incremental benefit.

This leads to several observations. First, following on the preceding discussion of opportunity costs, the excess costs could have been used for some other, under-funded, environmental protection activity that would have produced larger incremental benefits. Second, because some funds are wasted, the total amount of environmental improvement attained with our budget is less than it could have been. Third, excess costs are imposed on those residents or businesses who must pay for it. This increases the likelihood of unexpected external costs (e.g., loss of jobs). Finally, when the excess direct and external costs become noticeable to the public, the probable result will be a reduction in public and political support for environmental initiatives in the future. Taking these points together, the principle of economic efficiency is in no way anti-environment. On the contrary, when we depart from this principle, it is the environment that ultimately suffers.

PERSPECTIVES ON EFFICIENCY

Assessing "Optimal" Average Speed

Working with scientific data and information about the needs and preferences of government and citizens, the economist plays an intermediary role in the process of evaluating environmental problems and recommending solutions. The role of the economist is not to make decisions. Rather, his primary role is to help define and systematically compare the costs and benefits associated with environmental management options. To the extent that enough is known about the nature of things lost and gained, and the values society places on them, the economist is able to show the decisionmaker the efficiency implications of choosing one option over another.

In the sciences and engineering, *efficiency* is defined in terms of physical quantities of inputs and outputs. In economics, at least one of the variables with regard to efficiency is normally defined in terms of its actual or imputed value rather than in terms of its physical quantity. The major advantage of using value as one element in the calculation of efficiency is that when the value of different types of things can be put into a common unit of measure (the most typical one being units of currency), it is possible to combine and compare them. This allows the economist to incorporate a wider range of factors into his definition of efficiency than is usually possible in a strict engineering or biological analysis. The disadvantage of using values is, of course, that such values may be difficult or impossible to specify with much precision.

For example, in comparing the efficiency of ten workers using hand tools to that of a single worker with an automated tool, the engineering analysis might involve a comparison of the physical inputs and outputs involved in each option. In the economic analysis such additional considerations as wage rates, supervision requirements, and replacement costs could be incorporated into the calculation of which option is more efficient. Nonetheless, when some values are not readily quantifiable in money terms, the economic analysis becomes problematic.

Consider the question of determining the most efficient average speed for trucks deployed along a certain route. Suppose the relationship between average speed and fuel consumption looks like that in Figure 1.1. Strictly in terms of fuel consumption, an average speed of F (for highest fuel efficiency) kilometers per hour is most efficient, since that speed enables minimum fuel use per unit of distance travelled. Often, the job of the engineer, chemist, or biologist is to determine the nature of the relationship between two physical variables, as illustrated by the example of Figure 1.1. Now consider the question of the most efficient speed from the somewhat wider perspective of net

Figure 1.1
Fuel Efficiency

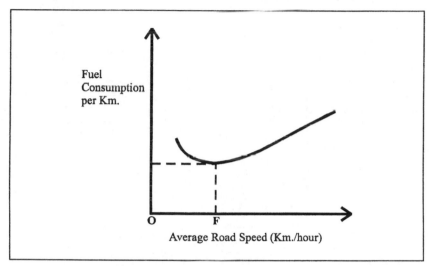

Note: F is the fuel efficient speed.

profit to the trucking company.   Suppose this is a long distance freight company, whose truck route faces competition from a freight train. Let us say that the trucking company determines that it can attract more freight business (and hence increase total revenues) by improving the time advantage of road travel compared to rail travel for a particular origin and destination. Further, let us say that the total revenue and total cost curves as a function of average road speed for the company's trucks look like those in Figure 1.2. The objective of the trucking company is to maximize profit, defined here as *net revenue*. As average speed increases past point F, the trucking company's costs increase since fuel efficiency is now going down. Yet, so long as an increase in the average truck speed results in a greater addition to revenues than it does to total costs, net profit increases as speed increases. Hence, profit is maximized by increasing average speed to the point at which any further increase would result in a smaller incremental addition to total revenue than to total cost.

Very small increments (in economic terms, *marginal* changes) in total revenues and total costs are indicated by the slopes of the respective curves. We can see in Figure 1.2 that at an average speed of F, the slope of the total revenue curve is greater than that for the total cost curve. We illustrate this by drawing a tangent to each curve to highlight the slope at that point on the axis showing speed. The tangent to the total revenue curve at F is steeper than that for the total cost curve at this same speed; hence, additional profit is gained by increasing average speed past that of level F.

We also can see that as speed continues to increase, the slope of the total

Figure 1.2
Economic Efficiency

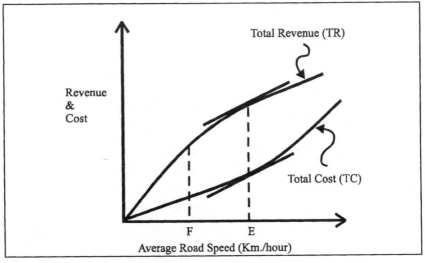

Note: E is the economically efficient speed.

revenue curve begins to level off while that of the total cost curve increases. This reflects the likelihood that delivery time is only one of the factors that influence customer choice in selecting the mode of transport. At an average speed of E (for economic efficiency) kilometers per hour the two slopes of the two curves are approximately equal; tangents drawn to the curves at this point on the speed axis would be parallel. Any further increase in average road speed results in a net loss in revenue, since the incremental costs outweigh the incremental benefits. Hence, from a profit maximization standpoint the most efficient average road speed is not F, but E kilometers per hour. This is efficiency considered from a wider perspective than fuel consumption alone.

Now let us bring in the regulators—in this case probably a government transport safety agency. Suppose that the relationship between average road speed for large trucks and the statistically expected number of accidents per year looks like that in Figure 1.3. Often the definitions of "acceptable" and "unacceptable" levels of safety will be highly subjective and change from time to time and from place to place. For our purposes here we might use the points at which the accident curve changes rather sharply (*inflection points*) to determine the range of greatest interest. For example, we might concentrate on average road speed between points L and H (for a relatively low and high number of accidents). Let us assume that for various reasons the regulator decides that an acceptable maximum number of accidents is M. Hence, the maximum safe average speed is S (for safety limit) kilometers per hour. Let us assume here that S falls between speeds F and E.[2]

Figure 1.3
Tradeoff of Speed Against Safety

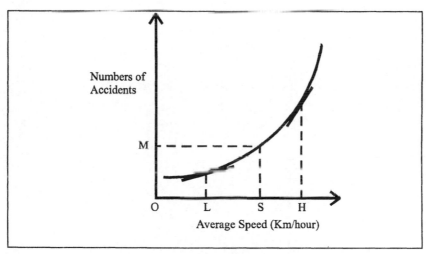

Note:
M is the regulator's view of maximum number of acceptable accidents.
L is the lower inflation point where accidents begin to rise significantly with increases in speed.
S is the regulator's assessment of maximum acceptably safe speed.
H is the higher inflation point where accidents increase greatly with even small increases in speed.

Since net revenues are increasing speed from F to E, the trucking company would increase the speed of its vehicles to the limit allowed. If speed S had been higher (i.e., in Figure 1.2, to the right of) speed E, it would not have influenced the determination of the most efficient safety-constrained speed from the profit maximization perspective.

In each figure (1.1, 1.2, and 1.3), the abscissa (*x* axis) remains the same: average road speed. Yet each different evaluator—the engineer, the economist, the safety regulator—attempted to determine the most efficient speed on the basis of a different variable on the ordinate (*y* axis)—fuel consumption, revenue and costs, and the expected number of accidents, respectively. Figure 1.4 brings together all this information. To sum up the results of this example, in a narrow sense of minimizing fuel consumption, F is the efficient average road speed. In the wider sense of net revenues to the trucking company, E is preferred. In the still broader sense of profitability tempered with a concern for public safety, the choice is S.

An essential feature of the preceding example is that in each of the analyses, different factors (variables) were considered. In the engineering analysis, revenues were external to the analysis as defined. In the economic analysis, safety was external to the calculations as defined.[3]

Figure 1.4
Summary of Figures 1.1, 1.2 and 1.3

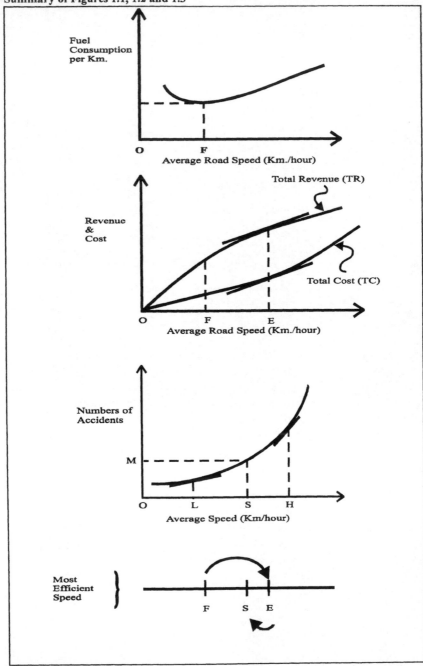

Designing a Sewage Treatment Plant

Although the previous example refers to transport, the same modes of analysis might apply to an environmental question, such as the appropriate design of a sewage treatment plant. An engineer assessing options for the treatment works might design it to provide a certain capacity, based on population levels, assumptions about per capita water use, and regional wastewater discharge quality standards. An economist might take a somewhat different perspective by also assessing options for reducing the demand for water in the first place, perhaps by increasing consumers' water charges and thereby stimulating greater efficiency of use.[4] The costs of programs to implement such *demand-side management*, as techniques addressing the demand component of a problem are termed, might then be compared with the benefits (in this case the avoided costs) of downsizing the capacity of the sewage treatment plant. An environmental protection officer charged with ensuring water quality for the marine waters into which the treated sewage would ultimately be discharged might have a rather different set of concerns. He might, for example, be particularly concerned about the impact on local fisheries and other marine resources stemming from the siting of the plant and the outfall point where the wastewater reaches the sea. Hence, even when the discharge is treated to meet quality standards, decisions about where to build the plant and to site its outfall are important in terms of environmental protection.

In each of these cases, the engineer, the economist, and the marine biologist see the matter of designing the sewage treatment plant in terms of rather different considerations. In this particular example, the engineer is the central player. However, his designs will be appropriate in the larger context only if he considers two factors. First, he must determine the size of the plant not only in terms of a fixed volume of wastewater throughput, but in light of the cost effectiveness of various possibilities for water conservation. Second, he must take into account the impacts of treated wastewater on particularly sensitive ecosystems and the losses incurred by society as a result of those impacts. He must compare such impacts against the cost required to avoid them by moving the plant, changing the outfall point, or increasing the discharge standards.

The Analytic Perspective

Obviously, the matter of analytic perspective is a vital one to consider in environmental management. Physical and biological scientists as well as engineers primarily seek to develop a better understanding of how the natural environment works and how it becomes disrupted, and ultimately to understand how to lessen such disruptions. Economists attempt to combine the insights developed by the scientists and engineers with information about how society values the resources involved. While economists might argue that conceptually any type of value might be incorporated into the economic analysis, in practice, certain types of values tend to be excluded and left to consideration within the broader social or political process.

In our two examples, some of the most important environmental impacts, such as road safety and the threats to marine ecosystems, were at least partly unpriced. While economists have various methods for imputing values in the absence of price signals, there may remain considerable differences of opinion about which, if any, method is appropriate for a given situation.

Sometimes it is easier to deal with certain environmental management issues in terms of what people would be willing to spend to accomplish a specific environmental objective, rather than attempt to determine a specific monetary equivalent measure of value places or an impact society. In such cases, the question of implied value is one of what we are willing to give up in terms of monetized values; for example, tax revenues or higher user fees, in order to protect our non-monetized values, such as human health or the integrity of a local ecosystem. Such a tradeoff does not tell us the specific value people place on the unpriced effect, but it does indicate the maximum and minimum extent of that value. In other words, if we accept some form of environmental tax—a charge levied on society for the purpose of protecting the environment—we are implicitly valuing the increased environmental protection at least as highly as the level of tax.

Implicit valuation of environmental impacts is generally undertaken in the context of the socio-political system, which includes government as well as influential interest groups, such as industry and social advocacy organizations. This is not meant to suggest that economists' estimates of the appropriate monetary value for sensitive environmental impacts are (or should be) necessarily put aside in favor of those that emerge through the political or social process. Rather, the point is simply that at some stage the valuation process tends to move out of the hands of specialists, in this case economists, and into a more broadly based assessment forum.

Advocates and decisionmakers in society often avoid addressing controversial questions of value. For example, an environmental advocate might argue that any amount of heavy metal in the sediments of a particular body of water is unacceptable. This same advocate also may refuse to discuss the question of whether people are willing to pay the costs of fully removing contaminated sediments and eliminating all future discharges. Likewise, a legislator might support a bill that mandates more stringent water quality standards without carefully considering the costs of attaining the higher standards. Meanwhile, an industry lobbyist might acknowledge that a factory's discharge of heavy metals constitute a health hazard, but argue that imposing environmental regulations will result in closing the factory. In so doing, the lobbyist is focusing the policy debate on the drastic alternative of closing the factory and the negative social impact of the resultant job losses. Clearly there might be a more moderate option that would incorporate some degree of environmental protection while keeping costs to a point that permits the factory to continue providing jobs and income.

One of the tasks of economists is to treat environmental values, along with the process of assigning and comparing such values, as explicitly as possible. For example, in the situation described above, the economist might address a question to the environmental advocate: if something is considered environmentally unacceptable, then how much will society consent to pay for specific measures to prevent it? The economist might attempt to estimate the costs of alternative strategies for meeting the higher water quality standard proposed by the legislator, and encourage him or her to consider the costs as well as the benefits when framing environmental standards. Finally, the economist might ask the industrial lobbyist to evaluate the costs of incremental levels of pollutant control within the context of the affected industry's overall cost structure, so as to determine the relationship between a range of pollution control levels and expected job losses. The economist might then provide this information to decisionmakers to assist them in evaluating the expected benefits in terms of human health and to the environment, and the costs in terms of losses in productivity and employment, associated with each specific incremental step in pollution reduction.

In trying to make explicit the tradeoffs among alternative environmental management decisions, the economist strives to move the decision-making process to dispassionate and well-reasoned grounds. Often, another role of the economist is to take a larger perspective and encourage decisionmaking that considers the interests of all groups in society—not just those of particular interest groups, such as factory employees or environmental advocates.

CONCLUSION

This chapter has introduced most of the major points that will be raised in the rest of the book. Hopefully, as the following ten chapters relate the principles of economic analyses to efficient environmental management, their basis in intuitive logic will come through clearly. To the extent that this text is successful, the reader should finish it with a good appreciation of how economics assists decisionmaking, and where it reaches its limits.

In the end, what we decide to do with our environmental heritage remains a matter of judgment based on personal and social values, which go beyond what any science, including economics, is able to tell us. The disadvantage of using values is, of course, that such values may be difficult or impossible to specify with much precision. The role of economics, then, is to provide a method that is as systematic as possible for incorporating assessment and comparison of values into our social decision-making processes. The following chapters describe in greater depth the way in which economists tend to view questions of resource allocation within the broad context of society and the more narrow field of environmental management.

NOTES

1. An alternative approach is to define all inputs (whether desirable or undesirable) as *costs*, while defining *benefits* as outputs of goods or services (again, whether these are desired or undesired). Under this set of definitions some costs may have a positive value. If not, consuming an input would lead to undesirable consequences (as in the case of recycling of hazardous wastes). Likewise, some benefits might have a negative value; environmental damage can be one output of a production process. In many situations this alternative definition of benefits and costs, if used consistently, would give the same results as the definition we use in the text above. However, for one measure of project attractiveness, the benefit-cost ratio (in which a project is rated good when the ratio is greater than 1), the choice of definition could affect the relative ranking among alternative projects. With this point noted, for the purpose of this text, benefits will be defined as things of positive value and costs as things of negative value.

2. One might say the regulator implicitly recognizes some acceptable tradeoff between speed and accidents, and therefore that the level of likely accidents need not be set at zero. While some people might object to any explicitly acknowledged acceptable number of road accidents, in practice virtually all systems are designed to reflect a level greater than zero tolerance for failure.

3. Of course, if the safety issues made it more difficult for the trucking company to hire willing drivers, or necessitated paying them a risk premium, then the total cost curve would need to reflect this by rising more sharply as speed increased. Likewise, the costs to the company of accidents and associated losses of goods, worker's compensation, and insurance premiums must also be reflected in the total cost curve if these vary with the average speed. For the sake of simplicity, we assume here that the regulator's determination of point S is to the left of an average road speed at which the trucking company's own costs for such safety considerations would be significantly affected.

4. The cost of sewage systems is largely determined by the volume of water flowing through them. While some level of waste loading is non-discretionary, the total volume of water used by households or industry generally is at least partly discretionary. Hence, the *throughput* on the system is not necessarily rigidly determined even when total population size is known.

2

Basic Concepts in Supply and Demand

We noted in Chapter 1 that even when prices are established through competitive markets, they often systematically exclude certain types of values, particularly values related to the environment and natural resources. Pollution is just one example of an excluded value, or what economists term *external effects* (or *externalities*).

Although much of environmental economics deals with externalities, which are both non-demanded and unintentionally supplied, the basic supply and demand framework of market-based economic analysis nonetheless provides crucial insights. We may use this competitive market model to illuminate how values tend to be assessed and compared at the level of the individual consumer and supplier and how individual decisions ultimately determine what is provided and at what price. With this understanding, we can better determine how environmental and other external values would be treated if they were somehow internalized into market decisions. Such insights may be used to help develop more appropriate environmental policies and effective ways to implement them.

In this chapter, the concepts of demand, supply, and the interaction of demand and supply are discussed. These concepts, and the principles that stem from them, provide the foundation for the discussion of marginal analysis in Chapter 3 and the application of these principles in subsequent chapters.

THE LAW OF DEMAND

The term *demand* has a distinct meaning in economics. Demand is a formal expression of the relationship between the quantities of a good, and the prices that consumers, including producers who require such goods as factors of production, are willing and able to pay at a particular time. Demand is a quantitative expression represented by a curve (graph), or equation, relating price to quantity. The particular point in time can be thought of as a short interval, such as one day or a week; the interval is kept sufficiently short so that other considerations, such as changes in consumer tastes, prices of closely related goods, and income, generally do not come into play. With these other considerations held constant, we treat the demand for a good or service as a function of its own price.

We can illustrate the concept of demand through an example. The demand curve in Figure 2.1 represents what an individual would be willing to pay for various quantities of some good, such as shoes or safe drinking water. This price-quantity information could be ascertained in a number of ways, but for this simple example we could ask the individual the question: How much of this good would you be willing to buy at price P? By varying P (i.e., the price) and repeating the question, we can trace the individual's demand curve. If we connect the individual price-quantity pairs with a line, the result is a demand curve looking something like the one in Figure 2.1. Note that the plot of our demand line is curved, rather than a straight line. This means that the changes in quantity Q demanded in response to changes in price are not constant. In this and other chapters, we will use the basic relationship of price (P) and quantity (Q) quite often. Whenever we use the y-axis (ordinate) label P, this will always stand for price. Whenever we use Q along the x-axis (abscissa), it will always stand for quantity (demand or supplied) at some price.

Figure 2.1
Demand Curve

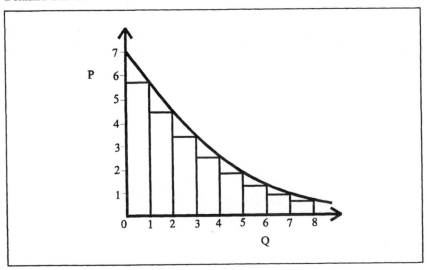

Note:
P is Price.
Q is Quantity.

For any given quantity, a point on the demand curve shows what the individual would be willing to pay for the last increment (*marginal* unit) consumed. Hence, we may think of a demand curve as a plot of the changing willingness to pay for each incremental unit. For example, as shown in Figure 2.1, if the individual is consuming 5 units, his willingness to pay for the fifth unit is a little less than $2. His total willingness to pay at a level of consumption of 5 units would be equal to what he would be willing to pay for the first, plus his separate (and presumably lower) willingness to pay for the second, and all the way up to the fifth unit. The sum of these willingnesses to pay is equal to the area under the demand curve. If for example the good in question is environmental quality, the area under the demand curve up to a given level of environmental quality is a measure of total benefits or value, and any point on the demand curve is what the consumer is willing to pay for that next unit of environmental quality.

Figure 2.1 illustrates the inverse relationship between price and the quantity of the good demanded. This is the law of demand: as price declines, the quantity of the good purchased increases. (The major exception to this general rule is the case of prestige goods, which are of only occasional relevance to environmental economics assessments.) The downward-sloping demand is based on two important factors:

* *Income effect*, which means that at some particular level of income, the consumer can afford to purchase more of the good as the price falls and less of the good as the price rises.

* *Substitution effect*, which expresses the likelihood that as the price of a particular good falls, the consumer may find it desirable to substitute this good for other goods and/or find new uses for the good. Similarly, if the price rises, the consumer will substitute other, less expensive goods for this one and its demand will fall.

The downward-sloping demand curve also holds for another important reason. As additional units of a good are acquired, the value of these units to the consumer falls; it is only at lower prices that the consumer is willing to pay to purchase more of the good. This relationship is directly related to utility theory and the law of diminishing marginal utility. This law states that although a consumer's total satisfaction generally increases from having an additional unit of the good, the additional (marginal) increment to utility from consuming the last unit is likely to be less than that from having consumed the previous unit.[1]

The law of diminishing marginal utility is important because it establishes that consumers are willing to pay more for the first units of a good and less for additional ones. Since consumers typically pay the last price for all units consumed, a surplus is generated for the previous units of the good consumed. Hence, most consumers pay less than their total willingness to pay. Economists term this *consumer surplus*, defined as the difference between the amount people are willing to pay and what is actually paid.

For example, how much are you willing to pay to purchase your first air conditioner? That depends on what specific use you intend for it, and how much you value that particular use. Will you put the air conditioner in the living room, your bedroom, or the dining room? The answer, of course, is that you will put it in whichever of these places where cool air is of the highest value to you. And if you then decide to purchase a second unit, where would you put it? Of course, you would place it in the next highest valued location. Note that by definition, the first unit was put to the most valued use. If that use is more valued by you than the use you have for the second unit, then presumably you would have been willing to pay more for the first unit than you did for the second. Further, you only would have purchased the second one if that second most valued use was worth at least as much as the second air conditioner cost you.

When you pay the same price for both units, then you obtain a surplus of value on that first unit. Likewise, if you need only one air conditioning unit and the price is lower than you would have paid, then you are also enjoying a surplus. Think about the surplus value you receive each summer and early fall when you purchase fresh local fruits and vegetables at lower prices than you are willing to pay in winter for food that is not so fresh. Graphically, we can show what we mean by consumer surplus in Figure 2.2.

Figure 2.2
Consumer Surplus

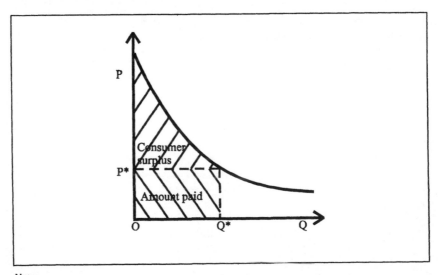

Note:
P* is the price paid per unit.
Q* is the quantity consumed.

Suppose an individual is consuming quantity Q*.   The marginal willingness to pay for Q* would be OP*. The amount paid for Q* would be the price OP* times the quantity OQ*. In other words, the amount paid would be equal to the area OP*AQ*. Recall that the individual would be willing to pay more for the first units consumed. Total willingness to pay is not only the amount actually paid, but what the purchaser would have paid (if he or she had to). This amount, the consumer surplus, should be added to the amount paid when calculating total willingness to pay or an estimate of total benefits. Assessing total willingness to pay is often important in estimating the full value to society of protecting the natural environment, since for many people the value they place on environmental protection may be greater than the actual cost of providing it.

Market Demand

The market demand for any good or service is defined as the quantities of the good or service that all individuals in aggregate are willing and able to pay at all relevant prices at a given point in time. To illustrate, we can add three more individuals to our example in Figure 2.1 and assume that these four consumers constitute our market. Again, we can ask a series of questions about their willingness to pay for the good. This information, along with that for our first individual, is shown in Figure 2.3. The market demand (the right-hand side of Figure 2.3) is simply the summation of individual demands. That is, we hold price constant and sum the quantities; this is called *horizontal summation*. The market demand is what all individuals in the market would buy at any given price. Of course, the market does this aggregation of individual demands automatically. (Unless otherwise stated, when we speak of "demand" we are referring to the market demand.)

Figure 2.3
Individual Demand and Market Demand

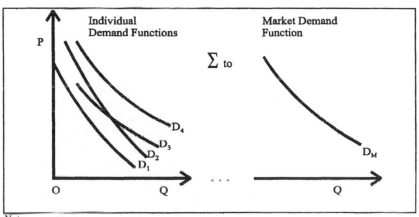

Note:
D_1, D_2, D_3, D_4 are individual demand functions.
D_M is the market demand.

As elaborated in Chapter 4, there is another class of goods that economists term *public* or *collective* goods. These goods are special in that they can be consumed by more than one individual simultaneously and no one individual has exclusive rights to their use. Many natural resources and certain aspects of the environment are public or collective goods. For example, a scenic vista in a national park is a public good. Any one individual cannot exclude others from enjoying the view and one's own enjoyment, within broad limits, does not diminish that of others. Since public goods can be used by more than one individual at the same time, we aggregate individual demands for a public good vertically. That is, we ask each consumer how much they would be willing to pay for the good and sum these amounts.

Movements Along a Demand Curve and Shifts in Demand

At the outset, we noted that demand curves are an expression of what consumers of a particular good or service are willing and able to pay at a particular point in time. When there is a sudden change in the price of a good or service, we generally assume that supply conditions, rather than consumers' preferences, tastes, and incomes, have changed. For example, when a drought prompts the price of a particular fresh vegetable to rise, consumers may reduce their vegetable purchases or substitute canned products in response. (In Chapter 3 we will consider why the price goes up under these circumstances, separate from any advantage being taken by producers). To consider another example, the opening of new facilities for manufacturing computer chips could lower the cost of the chips, and perhaps the price of computers themselves, thus making computers more attractive to consumers.

The important point here is that, in basic economic analysis, we assume for simplicity that the quantity demanded of a particular good is a function of its own price and this alone. In this type of situation, when supply prices change exogenously, changes in demand reflect movements along the demand curve. In contrast, over a longer time period, we often consider shifts in demand, such that the entire demand curve might rise or fall at every possible price. In the latter case, at any particular price we would see a higher or lower demand compared to that prevailing under the old demand curve. For example, new scientific data that links some product with cancer may cause a dramatic shift downward in the demand curve for that product. As explained in Chapter 4, this point of distinguishing movements along a demand curve as distinct from shifts in the demand curve is quite important to the distinction between externalities that have an impact on economic efficiency (technological or real externalities) and those which do not (pecuniary externalities). Figure 2.4 illustrates movements along and shifts in demand curves.

Figure 2.4
Distinguishing Movements Along from Shifts in a Demand Curve

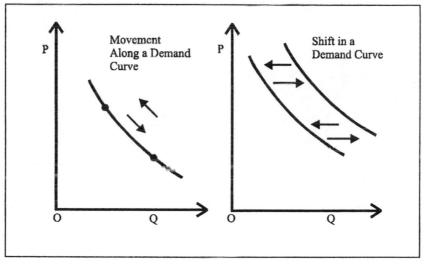

Elasticity

Often, we want to know more precisely how changes in a good's own price and other determinants affect the quantity demanded. Economists use the concept of *elasticity* to measure these changes. Elasticity is a measure of the responsiveness of the quantity sold of a particular good to a small change in any factor that affects demand. Functionally, it is:

$$\text{Elasticity} = \frac{\text{Percentage change in quantity demanded}}{\text{Percentage change in demand determinant}}$$

Typically, these determinants include the good's own price, consumer income, and prices of related goods. Elasticity is defined specifically with regard to which particular determinate we are considering. For example, price elasticity is the percentage change in quantity demanded divided by the percentage change in the good's own price.[2]

The demand for a good is said to be relatively elastic when a given percentage change in price results in a proportionately larger percentage change in quantity demanded. The price elasticity in this case would be greater than 1 (ignoring the minus sign). Conversely, demand is relatively inelastic when a percentage change in price results in a smaller percentage change in quantity demanded. In this case, elasticity is less than 1.

Price and income are both factors in determining whether the demand for a particular good is elastic or inelastic, but more importantly such a determination

Figure 2.5
Price Elasticity of Demand and the Closeness of Substitutes

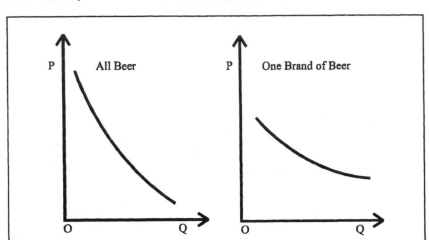

depends on the availability and price of substitute goods. The availability of closely related goods will typically mean that demand will be more elastic and therefore more responsive to changes in the good's own price.

Consider the overall demand for beer (Figure 2.5). This is probably relatively inelastic because there are no close substitutes. Now consider the demand for a particular brand of beer. This is probably relatively price elastic since there are now close substitutes (i.e., other brands of beer). The same logic is applicable to determining the elasticity of demand for natural resources and environmental goods. For example, in the United States, the demand for water for indoor uses, such as drinking, cooking, and washing, is relatively price inelastic. In contrast, the demand for outdoor water (seasonal summer use) tends to be more elastic because there is more discretionary consumption for purposes such as watering lawns and washing cars. Likewise, we might expect that the demand to camp overnight in a rare or unique natural area is less price elastic than the demand to camp in an ecologically common environment with readily available close substitutes. The point here is not that we can reliably predict the specific degree of elasticity *a priori*. Rather, we stress that when the price of a good or service changes, we are generally able to anticipate the direction and the approximate degree of the change in demand by considering such factors as the availability of close substitutes and their prices, as well as the significance of the price change relative to incomes.

Price elasticity is important in determining how revenues will change in response to a change in price. If a price change causes total revenue to move in the opposite direction from the price change, demand is elastic. That is, if a decrease in the price of a good causes sales to go up more than proportionately, demand is relatively elastic and total revenue (P*Q) will rise. Likewise, if a decrease in price causes sales to go up less than proportionately, then demand is relatively inelastic. To consider another issue, results of empirical studies indicate that summer demand is more price elastic than winter demand. This suggests that higher prices in summer could be used to curtail demand in the face of supply shortages.

Elasticity is also an important consideration with regard to pricing and sizing facilities, such as a centralized industrial waste treatment plant. If the demand to generate a certain type of waste is relatively price inelastic, for instance because such waste generation is inherent in the technology, then demand to use the facility is likely to be insensitive to price. In such a case, it may be relatively simple to determine the appropriate capacity of the treatment facility and to set prices so as to fully cover costs. However pricing policy may not be effective in controlling the level of waste generation if the demand to create the waste is relatively price elastic (e.g., because high levels of resource recovery and recycling are technically feasible), then it may be difficult to determine the appropriate size of the plant. Likewise, it may be difficult to set prices to cover costs unless the particular degree of price elasticity is known in advance. Yet when faced with a price elastic demand, pricing policy would tend to be effective in lowering the generation of wastes in the first place. Table 2.1 summarizes the relationship between price elasticity and total revenue.

Income elasticity of demand is defined in the same way as price elasticity, except that for income elasticity it is the relative change in demand with respect to a change in income at unchanged prices that is of interest. A basic difference between the price elasticity of demand and income elasticity of demand is that for most goods, income elasticity is positive rather than negative. Hence, as income goes up, demand tends to follow.

Environmental quality might be expected to be income elastic, since as incomes rise, people may tend to desire proportionately higher environmental quality. This might be particularly true if, as is often the case, the early process of economic development severely degraded the environment.

Table 2.1
Elasticity and Total Revenue

Direction of Price Change	Effect on Total Revenue		
	$e < 1$	$e = 1$	$e > 1$
Price Rise	Increase	Same	Decrease
Price Fall	Decrease	Same	Increase

Note:
e is elasticity.

It is also important to note that income elasticity can be negative for some goods. Consider the demand for charcoal as a cooking fuel in urban areas of developing countries. As incomes rise, people prefer more modern and convenient fuels such as kerosene, bottled or piped gas, and electricity instead of increased consumption of charcoal.

Cross price elasticity is defined relative to the price of some other good. That is, it is expressed as the percentage change in the quantity demanded of good A divided by the percentage change in the price of good B. With this measure of elasticity we can determine if goods are substitutes or complements to one another. For example, if the price of good A were to rise and the quantity demanded for good B were to rise as a result, the two goods are substitutes. If the price of A falls with a rise in the price of B, the goods are complements.

We might expect that the demand for access to a mountain park would rise along with the cost of going to ocean beaches, since these two types of environments are likely to be at least partly substitutes. Likewise, we might extend this idea by noting that the true full cost of using fresh air increases with rising levels of pollution; the fresh air may be unpriced but its impacts on our health and comfort constitute potential costs. In the case of air pollution, we would expect to see people switching to partial substitutes, such as relying on air conditioning even when the outside temperature is not overly warm.

THE NATURE OF SUPPLY

In addition to demand, supply is the other component that affects the determination of market prices. The supply schedule, or curve, shows the quantity of a good or service producers or sellers are willing and able to offer at all relevant prices at a particular point in time. In other words, the supply curve summarizes the producers' reaction to changes in market prices. However, unlike demand, supply is directly related to price. At higher prices producers are willing and able to supply more of a particular good or service, whether it is a final product or some factor of production.

The supply curve slopes upward because of rising costs of production as more units of the good or service are produced. The rising costs of production as quantity supplied increases may be due to such factors as shortages of certain types of labor, or the need to use lower grade resources. For example, increasing the production of tomatoes may require a farmer to move production to land that is less fertile, requiring use of more fertilizer or water. Increasing production also may require the farmer to bring more distant land into production, thus imposing higher transport costs.

Another way to look at supply is that at higher prices, and when the costs of production are low relative to the prevailing prices, more producers believe that they can profitably produce some particular good or service. Hence, higher prices attract new producers and motivate existing ones to increase production.

Alternatively, when production costs are high relative to prevailing prices, producers tend to curtail production and some less efficient producers will stop production. Virtually all mature production systems exhibit this rising cost behavior.

Production Costs and Supply

The supply curve shows the quantity of a good that a producer will place on the market at all relevant prices at a given time. Producers decide how much of a good or service to provide on the basis of market price and their costs of production. At any given market price only those producers with costs at or below the selling price will be able to stay in the market. And just as some consumers enjoy a surplus, so to do some producers, because their production costs are lower than the selling price. Hence, there tends to be a producers' surplus as shown in Figure 2.6.

Producers generally face two broad categories of cost: fixed and variable. Fixed costs do not change with changes in output in the short run. As an example, consider the farmer again. Fixed costs for the farmer include the cost of land rent, depreciation on equipment, insurance, managers' salaries, and property taxes. For a manufacturing firm, fixed costs are those associated with a given capacity of the production operation. The important point about fixed costs is that they must be paid regardless of how much output the firm produces in the short run, even if it falls to zero. We define the short run as a time period in which fixed factors or production or costs cannot be changed.

Figure 2.6
Supply Curve and Producers' Surplus

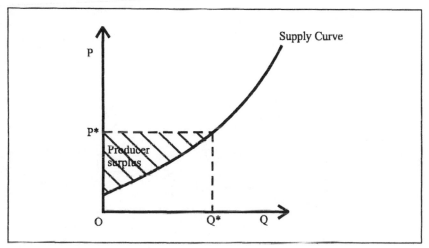

Note:
P* is the selling price.
Q* is the quantity sold.

In contrast, variable costs are directly tied to the producer's output decision. A farmer's variable costs might include seed, fertilizer, hired labor, fuel, and equipment repairs. Although variable costs change with output, they do not change proportionately. For example, we know that crop yield (output) will respond greatly to fertilizer at first; however, at a certain point, repeated applications of fertilizer result in declining additions to output per unit of fertilizer applied. The same applies to other inputs. This phenomenon is what economists call the law of diminishing return (similar to the *law of diminishing marginal utility*). This law says that as the amount of some factor of production is increased, with all other factors of production held constant, output will increase but successive increases will bring about progressively smaller additions to output.

Figure 2.7 shows the typical shape of a variable cost curve. At first it increases at a decreasing rate as production increases. This is perhaps due to economies of scale. However, the cost curve eventually begins to rise as diminishing returns take effect. To use an oft-cited example, this law explains why it is impossible to grow the world's food supply in a single flowerpot. When we combine fixed and variable costs we get total cost. As shown in Figure 2.7, at an output level of zero we incur fixed costs but no variable costs. As output increases, total costs increase by the amount of variable cost (this definition of cost includes a normal profit).

We can show fixed costs and variable costs as averages: average fixed cost, average variable cost, and average total cost. These average relationships are found simply by dividing by output. At low levels of production, average fixed costs are very high; however, as production increases, average fixed costs

Figure 2.7
Total and Variable Costs of Production

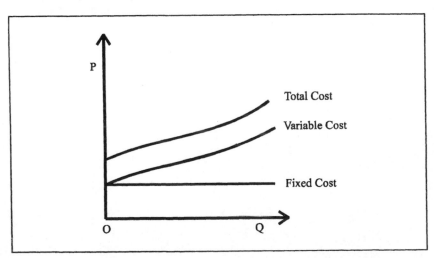

decline because these costs can be spread over many more units of production. Average variable cost and average total cost are typically U-shaped. These costs start high, because the producer is usually not efficient at producing very small quantities of output, and then decline as economies of scale are attained. As production continues to increase, diminishing returns eventually set in and average costs begin to rise.

It also may be the case that at relatively low levels of demand new industries are unable to make full use of economies of scale. Thus, it may be only over time, as demand grows exogenously (meaning that the demand curve shifts as potential consumers become more familiar with the usefulness of the new product), that production can reach the level corresponding to lowest average costs. Likewise, in an industry with rapidly evolving technology, production costs may fall and total output increase even as prices are stable or falling. Both situations characterized the supply of personal computers, especially in the early years. Yet as noted in this type of situation, rising output in the face of stable or falling prices, stems from the very immaturity of the industry. Once economies of scale are realized and the fundamental technological breakthroughs attained, the supply curve thereafter is one of rising costs. From this point on, higher outputs require higher selling prices.

Marginal Cost and Supply

Marginal cost is defined as the additional or incremental cost of producing the next unit of output. A producer considering increasing production will compare the marginal cost of the added output with the prevailing selling price, in order to determine if it is profitable to produce the additional unit. If the price is greater than his marginal cost of producing it, then it is profitable to make and sell the additional unit. Readers should note that marginal cost is not an average cost, since it does not include fixed costs. It consists of the variable costs associated with producing the incremental unit.

The marginal cost curve is U-shaped for the same reasons as the average variable cost curve. At low outputs, economies of scale typically provide relatively high output from additional inputs, while at higher levels of output, diminishing returns set in. That is, at low levels of output there may be synergy among the inputs, which would allow additional output to be greater than the sum of the additional inputs. At higher levels of output, it is likely that the simplest and most cost-effective uses of additional factor inputs have already been found, and additional inputs do not have the same impact on output.

The marginal and average cost curves have a definite, defined relationship as shown in Figure 2.8. Average cost is influenced by all the incurred costs, including those for the units produced up to that point. In contrast, marginal costs are only those associated with the last unit. Thus, if marginal costs are falling, average costs are above marginal costs because the average costs include fixed costs. When marginal costs begin to increase, the average cost soon begins to level off. The marginal cost curve always intersects the average

Figure 2.8
Average and Marginal Costs of Production

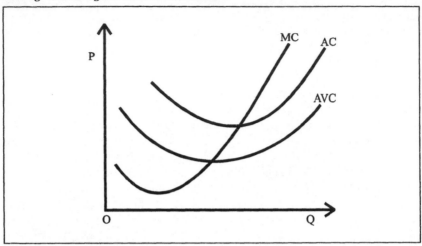

Note:
MC is the marginal cost curve.
AC is the average cost curve.
AVC is the average variable cost curve.

variable and average cost curves at their minimum, because when marginal costs are below average costs, they pull down the average cost curve. When the marginal costs are above average, they pull up the average cost curve.

The marginal cost curve is of fundamental importance in economics. A basic tenet of economics holds that every producer attempts to equate marginal cost with marginal revenue. Why should this be so? If we assume that the producer is too small to influence the market price, then what he sells or receives for the additional unit is the market price. Equating marginal cost with price ensures the profits will be maximized. For example:

If MC < P, then the producer can make more money by increasing output.

If MC > P, then the producer is losing money on the last unit, or units.

In effect, the portion of the marginal cost curve that lies above the average variable cost is the supply curve for the producer. Looking at Figure 2.9, if price P_1 is equal to marginal costs (and average cost), then all costs are covered at a production level of Q_1. Included in these costs is a normal profit. If price were to increase to P_2, the producer would not only cover all costs including a normal profit, but would make abnormal profits and would produce at the level of Q_2. In the long run, the presence of abnormal profits would encourage new firms to enter the market or existing firms to expand production, and eventually the price is driven back down.

Figure 2.9
Average and Marginal Costs of Production with Price Indications

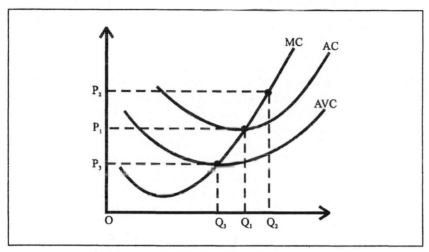

Note:
P1 is the price where marginal cost equals average cost (only normal profit).
P2 is the price where marginal cost is above average cost (excess profit).
P3 is the price where marginal cost equals average variable cost (loss since fixed cost not meet).

In contrast to the situation above, if price were equal to P_3, the producer would produce Q_3 units to cover the variable costs, but not all of the fixed costs. In the short run, the firm might continue to produce since a fraction of the fixed costs were being covered. However, in the long run production would cease if the selling price did not eventually rise sufficiently (i.e., to P_1) to fully cover cost. Of course, if price were to drop below average variable cost, the producer would cease operations immediately.

As elaborated in Chapter 3, these general relationships hold for the supply of many environmental goods. For example, if a firm faces a cost for each unit of pollution discharged (i.e., a pollution tax), it decides on the level of its pollutant discharge by comparing the value of avoiding the emissions tax with the cost of in-house pollution reduction, perhaps through such possibilities as materials recycling or increasing efficiency. While the first units of this emission reduction would likely be relatively inexpensive, eventually all of the no-cost or low-cost opportunities would be realized and further reduction in emissions would come at increasingly higher costs. At some point, it is likely that reducing pollutant emissions by one more unit would cost more than the level of the tax and hence it would be efficient for the firm to pay the tax on all remaining pollutant emissions rather than to reduce emissions further. We may view this situation as the supply curve for pollution reduction, in which the firm is supplying increased environmental quality (or, more to the point, less environmental degradation) and deciding on the level of output by comparing the marginal costs of production with the marginal benefits (in this case not having to pay the tax on that increment of pollution).

Determinants of Supply

As with demand, the supply curve summarizes the relationship between quantity and price with all other determinants of supply held constant. These determinants include the time period, the availability of the factors of production, the prices of inputs, and perhaps government policies. Changes in any of these factors may cause the supply curve to shift. A change in technology, such as the development of a new, higher-yielding variety of rice, may cause the supply curve to shift outward to the right. An increase in the price of fertilizer, or farm labor would cause an opposite shift in supply.

Just as we distinguished movements along from shifts *in* demand curves, so we should keep the same distinctions in mind for supply. With a given technology and resource endowment, an increase in price will elicit movements along the supply curve as shown in the left-hand part of Figure 2.10. In contrast, as shown in the right-hand part of Figure 2.10, when there are exogenous changes in supply (e.g., due to a new resource discovery or a basic technological breakthrough), higher output becomes possible at a wide range of prices.

Supply Elasticity

Price elasticity of supply is defined in the same manner as is price elasticity of demand: the percentage change in quantity supplied divided by the

Figure 2.10
Distinguishing Movements Along from Shifts in a Supply Curve

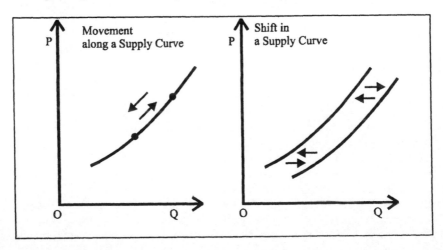

percentage change in price. However, unlike demand, the determinants of supply costs usually change more slowly, and a producer's decision to supply is often made well in advance of actual production. Supply elasticity is therefore often considered in terms of a time.

Consider a farmer's decision to sell vegetables on any given day versus the farmer's decision to plant vegetables at the planting season. On a given day, the farmer's supply of vegetables may be quite inelastic; it may be nearly impossible for the farmer to produce additional vegetables that day regardless of the price. However, if we look at a longer time period that encompasses an entire planting season, then the farmer's supply is much more responsive to price, or more elastic. We can extend the time period to assess the long-term situation, in which all factors of production, including the amount of land available to farm, are subject to change. We then conclude that the long-term supply of any good will tend to be more elastic than the short-term supply, and thus more responsive to changes in price.

Market Supply

The supply curve for an industry or for individual producers is analogous to that for consumers. Market supply is simply the horizontal summation of the supply curves of the individual producers comprising the industry. That is, price is held constant and all quantities offered at this price are summed horizontally. Consider in Figure 2.11 the four producers that comprise the industry for a particular good or service.

Figure 2.11
Individual Suppliers and Market Supply

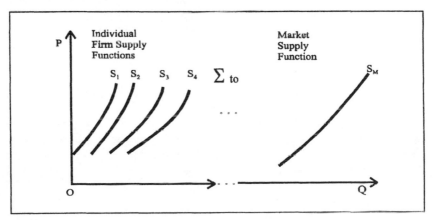

Note:
S_1, S_2, S_3, S_4 are individual supply curves.
S_M is the market supply curve.

Opportunity Costs

Market prices do not necessarily reflect all values. The same is true for costs. To be consistent with our measure of benefits, we need to broaden our definition of costs. Any factor or resource used in production has a cost, which may or may not be reflected in its price. The most basic way to regard costs is to think of foregone opportunities. *Opportunity costs* reflect what must be paid or given up in order to enable a certain activity to take place. Because resources have opportunities in other uses, an indication of their value is their next best alternative use.

For example, consider the cutting of a large tract of national forest. The opportunity cost of cutting the forest is not the cost of the goods and services that are used to harvest and haul trees, or the selling price of wood. Rather, it is the value of the standing forest as a place for recreation, a habitat for animals, and as a watershed protection. On the other hand, the cost of preserving the forest is the foregone opportunity to use the trees as a source of lumber, and to use the land for other purposes. As stated in Chapter 1, opportunity costs are values foregone when resources are used for one thing rather than something else.

Often there is no market price for many important environmental services. Analysts may try to value such services by attempting to determine the value of the foregone uses. The "cost" of keeping a wetland is not limited to its direct maintenance costs; it also includes the value we place on other potential uses of the land, if it is filled in. Indeed, by looking at the opportunity costs for keeping wetlands we could conceivably sketch out a supply curve for protecting wetlands. Likewise, the value lost when a wetland is filled in depends on how much we value the environmental services the wetland provided (e.g., flood control, aquatic system productivity, recreation, as a food source for migratory birds). In this way we could develop a supply curve for giving up wetlands, based on the foregone values stemming from the wetland. In each case, one important outcome of such an exercise would be to distinguish one wetland from another with respect to the foregone costs of keeping it and the foregone value of failing to keep it. If we think of any particular wetland as the incremental unit of supply, we could then compare the benefits to the costs of the next increment of wetland conversion or preservation. However, in doing so we need to keep in mind the matter of marginal utility and marginal cost. The benefits of preserving a particular wetland will in part depend on how many such wetlands exists in a given area. Likewise the opportunity costs of preservation will depend in part on the need for additional land for such proposes as agriculture or commercial development.

THE INTERACTION OF SUPPLY AND DEMAND: MARKET PRICES

When viewed separately, the demand curve (an expression of the marginal willingness to pay) and the supply curve (an expression of marginal costs) are functions of price. However, when demand and supply are viewed together, they determine a specific market price. In markets, whether for factors of production or for final goods and services, prices provide signals to individual consumers and producers. Low prices tend to encourage consumption and discourage production, while high prices have the opposite effect. In any given market at any given time, equilibrium prices are established at the balance between what producers are willing and able to supply, and what consumers desire and are willing and able to pay.

Figure 2.12 illustrates the interaction of demand and supply for a particular good. The point where demand and supply intersect determines the equilibrium price (P_e) and quantity (Q_e). At this equilibrium, the full quantity supplied by the producers is bought by consumers. At prices above P_e, there will be an excess supply of the particular good, meaning that producers will supply more than consumers are willing to pay. Only by lowering the price can the excess be eliminated. Conversely, at prices below P_e there will be shortages; consumers will demand more of the good than producers are willing to supply at that price. This description is, of course, one based on a model of effective competition, in fact one of perfect competition.[3] The market tends to come into equilibrium when a price is found that clears the market, equalizing demand with supply. Will this equilibrium be stable? Yes, as long as the demand and supply relationships remain stable.

Let us look at another example and see how a change in income might affect producers. Let us assume that the increase in income resulting from reduced taxes causes the demand curve to shift to the right. As illustrated in the

Figure 2.12
Demand and Supply Together Determine Price

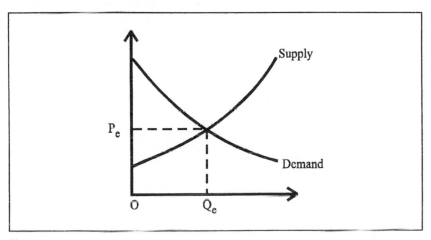

Note.
P_e is equilibrium price.
Q_e is equilibrium quantity.

left hand portion of Figure 2.13, a new equilibrium price and quantity are then established at P_2 and Q_2 due to the intersection of the new demand curve and the old supply curve. The increased price makes it profitable for the producer to expand output because, as we mentioned before, producers attempt to equate marginal costs with price. At the higher level of output and price, the original producers earn excess or abnormal profits. Other firms, seeing that excess profits are being earned will tend to increase their own production, or new firms will try to enter the market. As shown in the right hand portion of Figure 2.13, this causes the long run supply curve to shift outwards, driving the price back down to P_3 and expanding quantity to Q_3. The point here is that when one factor in the supply and demand changes, there will tend to be temporary price adjustments followed by a response in the other factors and over a longer period the establishment of a new equilibrium price and quantity.

CONCLUSION: APPLICATION TO ENVIRONMENTAL VALUES

As very briefly noted in Chapter 1 and elaborated further in Chapter 4, even when they are established in competitive markets, prices often do not include all values, particularly environmental ones. Moreover, value is not fixed. The amount people are willing and able to pay and the amount producers are willing and able to provide depends on a host of conditions, and these conditions are often subject to change. An appreciation of the changeable nature of value is crucial to environmental management, where price signals are often absent and thus much of the debate is over the value of particular levels or types of improvement in environmental quality. Unfortunately, this debate sometimes tends to be one of extremes. It is important to keep in mind the common sense evident in responses to changes in supply and demand as described above when considering environmental values.

Figure 2.13
Changes in Price and Eventually Supply with Changes in Demand

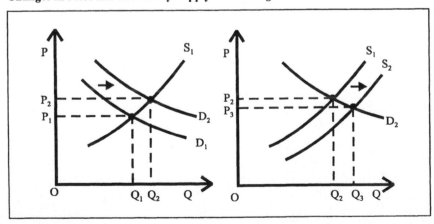

Some people say that a clean environment is essential: *all pollution must stop, and soon!* Others say that in a competitive international economy, environmental protection is a luxury to be addressed some time in the future, not something that can be dealt with now. In fact, there is a wide range of possible environmental quality. And there are demand curves and supply curves to achieve various levels of environmental quality. We may not necessarily be able to measure these curves with confidence, but we do know that, in general, the more costly something is the less that people are willing and able to pay for it. We also know that in many cases, such as that of reducing industrial pollution, as we attain higher and higher levels of environmental quality, each additional increment (marginal unit) of quality is likely to cost us more, directly as well as in terms of foregone opportunities to do something else.

It appears that the implied demand curve for environmental quality is shifting to the right in much of the world, including in developing countries. In other words, as we learn more about the importance of environmental services, people everywhere arguably tend to value such services more highly than was the case in the past. Also, as our technical knowledge of the nature of environmental degradation improves, there is a shift to the right in the supply curve for environmental protection. Basically, advancing technology often makes it less expensive to protect or to clean-up the environment than was the case in the past. This should not be taken as an argument for continually postponing environmental protection or clean-up, unless one is willing to assume that such an approach is fair to future generations who would have to bear such costs.

The foregoing statements do not necessarily mean that most governments are now truly serious about greatly reducing pollution and rectifying past environmental degradation. It simply means that, in general, it appears that people around the world are now becoming more aware of the dangers of environmental degradation and of the short-term and long-term benefits of a cleaner environment. And there seems to be an increasing acceptance that additional investments in a cleaner environment are necessary and appropriate, even for places with relatively low or moderate income. If the above statements are valid, then what constituted an equilibrium quantity for environmental protection in the past is not necessarily the equilibrium today, or the most appropriate one for the future. Chapter 3 extends this review of basic supply and demand relationships to explore more fully their important implications for environmental management.

NOTES

1. Utility theory is an important construct because it establishes the theoretical foundation for an individual's demand. Although utility cannot be directly observed, an individual's behavior and preferences can be empirically determined. Later in this text we will consider how such behavior and preferences for environmental quality may be

evaluated.

2. In arithmetic notation price elasticity of demand is:

$$P_\varepsilon = [(Q_1 - Q_2) / (1/2(Q_1 + Q_2))] / [(P_1 - P_2) / (1/2 (P_1 + P_2))]$$

Which, despite the number of terms, is computationally quite simple. For example, if a 10% increase in price leads to a 30% reduction in quantity demanded, the elasticity is 3. Since price and demand are normally inversely related (higher prices bring about lower demand and lower prices lead to higher demand), the elasticity is actually -3.

3. For this balance to take place, a number of conditions must be met to enable a perfectly functioning market. Among these are: a large number of consumers and producers, no one of which is large enough to affect price; perfect mobility of all factors of production; and all consumers and producers have complete information. We are assuming that price is free to adjust to find the equilibrium. Thus, if there is excess production, competition will allow price to adjust downward, and if there are shortages, prices are free to move upward, thus providing incentives to producers to eliminate the shortage.

3

Assessing Economic Efficiency: Comparing Values at the Margin

While economics is concerned about maximizing total welfare, its focus of analysis is typically on incremental choices. In this method of analysis a decision is broken down into a series of incremental choices, and the benefits and costs compared at each step. So long as the additional benefits of a step are greater than the additional costs associated with it, we increase our net welfare by taking that step; we then move on to evaluate the next increment of choice. When taking another step would impose additional costs that are greater than the additional benefits, we stop.

In economics, the common term for the incremental or extra unit in a decision situation is the *marginal* unit. In more theoretical treatments the term marginal tends to be used in the narrow sense of a very small unit of choice. Here, however, we use the term in a broader meaning—of the next increment or extra full unit—because in the real world, choices often consist of rather large units.

Economic decisions, whether made by individual consumers, firms, or society at large, typically are made at the margin. For an individual, the decision may be whether or not to buy a car; then, if one decides to buy the car, whether to purchase the basic model or one with additional features, such as a compact disk player or eye-catching leather seats. Each unit of choice is made on the basis of the added net benefit, and the effect each benefit would have on the consumer's total well-being, or, in economic terms, his or her total utility. The individual adds specific items (CD player, leather seats, etc.) so long as it stays within his or her budget and so long as each particular additional purchase is worth more to the buyer than it costs. Overall, the buyer maximizes his or her utility by purchasing the model that includes the particular features most highly valued while staying within budget.

In deciding whether, and if so, by how much, to expand environmental monitoring, a local pollution control board may want to equate the marginal value of information gathered from water quality sampling stations against the marginal costs of collecting the information. For one particular additional monitoring station located near a pollution source, the benefits might be substantial and far exceed the costs. For another possible site in a cleaner area, the costs might be the same but the benefits much less. However, the board might feel that the value of the additional information is worth the cost. For a third possibility, such as providing additional data from a remote corner of a water body that is already monitored, the value of the additional information, while positive, may not be worth the additional cost.

Producers also compare values at the margin. A farmer will hire an additional laborer on the basis of the added contribution the worker is expected to make to total farm production compared to the cost of hiring him. The manager of a pulp and paper plant will compare the marginal costs of pollution control with what he sees as the marginal benefits of pollution abatement.

MARGINAL ANALYSIS

Marginal analysis is fundamental to the study of environmental economics. We now take a closer look and extend the principles sketched out in the previous chapter. We begin by revisiting the model of a perfectly competitive market introduced in Chapter 2.

In a perfectly competitive market, individual consumers and producers attempt to maximize their own self-interest. However, because there are so many producers and consumers, no one of them is able to affect prices by changing the amount of the good or service he demands or supplies. Monetary prices in this model are assumed to represent the full value of a good's or service's benefits and costs. While this is an idealistic model, and not representative of the real world, it provides useful insights into the nature of decisionmaking and welfare maximization. Later in this chapter, we will consider how the relationships outlined under perfect competition may change in other types of settings. Here and in subsequent chapters we refer to the behavioral tendencies suggested by the perfect competition model and consider in which ways, and to what extent, they may help in assessing environmental decisions in the real world.

When decisions are made at the margin in a perfectly competitive market, net social benefits are maximized. The individual actions of consumers and producers maximizing their own self-interest results in the market producing what society wants at the lowest cost. We begin our discussion with marginal analysis in consumption, followed by marginal analysis of production. We then tie these together and discuss the concept of economic efficiency in a competitive market. This is followed by a brief discussion of one type of imperfect competition: monopoly. In later chapters, we apply these principles to situations in which prices do not reflect full value. It is such situations, of course, that constitute the major concern of environmental economics.

Marginal Analysis and Consumption

Utility theory is an important concept in economics because it establishes the theoretical foundation for individual demand. Although utility cannot be directly measured, an individual's behavior and preferences can be empirically calculated.   This is important because it provides the theoretical base for estimating value, as measured by willingness to pay, for certain environmental goods in which market prices are poor indicators of value or for which market prices simply do not exist. Recall that the demand curve discussed in the previous chapter represents marginal willingness to pay (marginal benefits), and the area under the demand curve represents total willingness to pay (total benefits), which is the amount paid plus the consumer surplus.

The basic premise of utility theory is that the individual consumer attempts to maximize his own welfare or utility.   An individual employs available resources in order to increase consumption of some good or service, up to the point at which the marginal utility derived from that added consumption is equal to its price or its opportunity cost.[1] If the individual stops before reaching this point he would be keeping money, or some other resource, which he values less than the value of the additional things that he could be obtained by spending it. If the individual goes past the point where the marginal benefits equal marginal costs, he would be obtaining additional benefit, but it would be of less value than the resources spent to obtain it. This would lower his overall utility.

More generally, with a given income and a fixed set of prices, utility is maximized when the marginal utility of the last unit of income spent on each good and service is equal to the marginal utility of the last unit of income spent on all other goods and services. That is, each good or service should yield the same marginal utility per unit of income spent. If this were not true, then it would be possible to increase consumption of one good while decreasing consumption of another, and thereby to increase utility at the same level of expenditure.

Let us consider how we might measure willingness to pay. The left-hand part of Figure 3.1 shows a market demand and supply curve with an equilibrium price (P_1) and quantity (Q_1). The demand curve indicates that some consumers are willing to pay higher prices, but since only P_1 is paid, in effect they experience a surplus, because they value the purchase more than they had to spend to obtain it. Over the entire range of demand, the total surplus for all consumers is equal to the triangular area P_1AB. Total economic benefits are equal to what is actually paid ($OP_1B\,Q_1$) plus the consumer surplus (P_1AB). Obviously, if we were interested in estimating total benefits, we would have to know quite a bit about demand.

Figure 3.1

Change in Price and Quantity with Shift in the Supply Curve

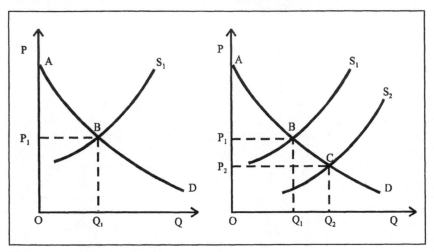

Note:
S1 is the original supply curve.
S2 is the new supply curve.
D is the demand curve.

Let us consider a situation in which the supply curve shifts outward, as shown in the right-hand part of Figure 3.1. This effectively increases output from Q_1 to Q_2 and reduces price to P_2. In this case, total consumer surplus will increase from P_1AB to P_2AC.

Now, instead of considering the question of measuring willingness to pay, let us say we are interested in estimating the change in benefits resulting from the increase in output due to undertaking some project. Do we need to know the exact shape and position of the whole demand curve? The answer is no. We need only look at the change in the consumer surplus between Q_1 and Q_2. The change in total benefits is equal to the new price (P_2) times the change in quantity ($Q_2^* - Q_1^*$) plus the change in consumer surplus ($2(P_2 - P_1)(Q_2 - Q_1)$). The important point here is that when we are interested in the economic benefits associated with some specific change (e.g., implementation of a project), we need only be concerned with marginal changes and these will often be much easier to estimate.[2]

Marginal Analysis and Production

A Firm's Decision on Inputs. In seeking to maximize profits, producers typically face two decisions. First, they must determine what and how much to produce; second, they must determine how to produce this output at the lowest cost. The costs of production are the sum of the costs of each individual factor of production, for example land, equipment, buildings, labor, fuel, materials and other resources, and other expenses, such as taxes. Within certain limits, usually defined by technology, factors in a production process may be substituted for one another.

For example, a farmer could substitute labor used in weeding for materials, such as herbicides. Likewise, a construction firm can employ men with shovels and wheelbarrows to dig a foundation, or it can use a backhoe tractor with a single operator. The construction firm also has a choice of buying the backhoe and employing the operator, or leasing the backhoe and contracting the operator, which would save capital. An electric utility might consider purchasing a highly energy efficient steam boiler or it might buy a less efficient, less expensive boiler that requires more fuel to operate. If fuel is inexpensive, then in a strictly financial sense it may be appropriate to purchase the inexpensive boiler. If the local pollution control board has set emission standards with appropriate penalties, then the electric utility will take these into account by installing emissions reduction equipment or by purchasing a more efficient boiler, or both.

A basic assumption of economic analysis is that firms examine factor substitution possibilities, such as energy for labor or capital for consumable materials, continuously and carefully. And when conditions permit, the firm will always chose the least-cost combination of factor inputs to produce its goods or services. In other words, the firm chooses its combination of factor inputs so that for any possible level of output its total costs of production are as low as possible.

How can the firm determine if it would be cheaper to use more capital and less labor, or more of chemical X and less of chemical Y? The combined costs of the factors of production are lowest when the additional contribution to total output per unit of expenditure is equal for all factors of production. If an additional dollar spent on capital can save the firm two dollars in labor, without changing the level of output, the producer should begin reducing labor and increasing capital. However, this cannot go on for long, because at some point the only remaining substitution possibilities would require very sophisticated and expensive machines to do jobs that labor can do easily. Eventually, investing more money in equipment and using less labor will increase costs. When the marginal product of an additional dollar spent on capital and labor are approximately equal, the firm has reached the least-cost combination of these factor inputs. The real world decision would probably be less precise than suggested here but the basic tendencies would almost certainly apply.

The approach of determining the least-cost combination of the factors of production by equating the marginal products applies not just to the production of goods and services, but also to achieving least-cost pollution control. A government mandate for all polluters to employ a specific technology would result in a more uniform and rigid combination of factor inputs. Yet the mandated technology might not be every firm's least-cost method for achieving a reduction in pollutant emissions. Further, the combination that is least-cost today might not be the least-cost one next year, or the year after that. For this reason, in most situations economists are strongly against pollution regulations that mandate the use of a specific technology. For any given level of pollution reduction, the financial impact on the industry is least when the industry can achieve that pollution emission reduction at the lowest possible cost. Hence, economists generally prefer that, whenever feasible, the government should set limits on allowable emission levels but then allow individual firms to decide how to meet such target levels. These points are elaborated in Chapter 10.

Related to this idea is the fact that the least-cost combination of inputs tends to vary along with changes in the cost of input factors and available technology. For example, the least-cost combination of capital and energy was clearly different when oil was about U.S. $40 per barrel in 1980 compared with the price of about $20 per barrel in the 1990s. At low oil prices, investments in energy efficient equipment are less attractive to firms than when oil is much more expensive. Likewise, the least-cost method of pollution control changes when the production process changes. Hence, the most economically appropriate approach to pollution control (i.e., the least-cost approach) will change when energy or offer factors of production become relatively more or less expensive.

A Firm's Output Decision. Let us now consider a firm's output decision. We saw from the previous chapter that the equilibrium market price is the one, and only one, at which quantity supplied is equal to quantity demanded. At any other price, the quantity supplied is either greater or less than the quantity demanded. One of the conditions of perfect competition is that there are many suppliers in the market and no single supplier can set the market price. The individual producer must then accept the market price; he is a price-taker. In other words, he will accept (take) the market price, rather than being able to influence it like a monopolist, who is a price-setter.

In the perfect competition model, the demand curve faced by the individual producer is thus perfectly elastic. The producer can sell as little or as much as he wants at that prevailing price. Total revenue is the quantity of good or service produced multiplied by the market price. If price were to change because of shifts in market demand or overall supply conditions, the slope of the firm's total revenue curve will change accordingly. This does not, however, tell us how much of the good the producer will put on the market. For this we need to know something about the producer's cost of production.

The producer in a perfectly competitive market will attempt to maximize profits by selling the quantity that maximizes the difference between his total revenue and total cost. The idea of consumer surplus has a counterpart on the production side. Even in conditions of perfect competition, not all firms face exactly the same costs of production. Some will have advantages of location or specific expertise, or other advantages that allow them to produce a good or service at a cost lower than their competitors. However, because of the single prevailing market price, these lower cost (*inframarginal*) firms enjoy a surplus similar to that enjoyed by consumers who would be willing to pay a higher price than is required by the market. The inframarginal firms could sell at a price lower than the prevailing market price and hence when they are able to sell at that market price they enjoy a producer's surplus.

In the previous chapter, we briefly mentioned that the producers' costs include a normal profit. *Normal profit* is the economic return a producer could earn if he were to invest in some other activity. Normal profits are considered part of costs, because they represent the opportunity cost of alternative investments and hence must be accounted for. Remember that in perfect competition prices reflect all values and costs reflect all foregone opportunities. The presence of profits above and beyond the normal profit—described as a situation of abnormal profits—implies the existence of returns in excess of what is required to keep firms in production. The presence of abnormal profits would cause new firms to enter the market under conditions of free entry and free flow of information. The added production from these new producers would shift the supply curve outward to the right. With a demand curve remaining unchanged, the market price will tend to fall to a new equilibrium, eliminating the abnormal profits.

Economists sometimes prefer to look at decisions on a per unit basis, as opposed to a total quantity basis. Average revenue is simply the total revenue divided by output, and since total revenue is price multiplied by quantity, dividing by quantity gives us price. The producer can sell all he wants at that price.

Marginal revenue is defined in a similar way as marginal cost. It is the change in revenue attributable to a change in output. Mathematically, marginal revenue is the slope of the total revenue curve and is equal to the selling price. Under perfect competition, price is equal to average revenue and average revenue is equal to marginal revenue. Figure 3.2 shows the profit maximizing level of output for a producer in a perfectly competitive market. A firm achieves maximum profit when the marginal revenue (price) is equal to the additional cost of producing that unit (marginal cost). In Figure 3.2, we show our short-run situation of abnormal profits. Here, with price at P_s (short-term price), the firm produces Q_S (short-term quantity supplied) units of output and earns an abnormal profit equal to the shaded area. Over the long-term, other firms enter the market. This leads to a shift in the market supply curve outward, and results in a lower equilibrium market price. In the long-run, under perfect competition, the profit maximizing output level corresponds to Q_L (long-term quantity supplied) with a price of P_L (long-term price).

Economic Efficiency and Perfect Competition

The individual actions of consumers maximizing their utility and producers maximizing their profits, if conducted without hindrance and on the basis of complete, accurate information, would result in a perfectly competitive market.

Figure 3.2
Marginal Cost and Profit

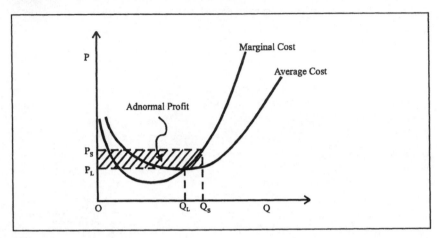

Note:
P_S is the short-term price.
P_L is the long-term price.
Q_S is the short-term quantity.
Q_L is the long-term quantity.

Figure 3.3
Consumer and Producer Surplus

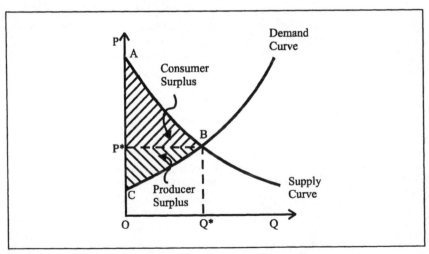

Note:
P* is equilibrium price.
Q* is equilibrium quantity.

Such a market would produce exactly what society wants, at the lowest possible cost. In this situation, the market is efficient, and it is not possible to reallocate consumption or production in any way to make society better off.[3]

The market demand curve shows the marginal benefits received by all individuals in the market consuming the particular good or service. Similarly, the market supply curve is the summation of the marginal costs (opportunity costs) of all producers supplying this market. The demand curve expresses all benefits or value on the part of consumers, and the supply curve reflects all foregone opportunities.

The maximum net benefits to society occur when marginal benefits equal marginal costs, or, in other words, at the intersection of demand and supply. Figure 3.3 summarizes these relationships. Net benefits represent the increase in supplier profit and buyer utility attained by producing and consuming a certain quantity of this good, minus the opportunity costs required to obtain it. In other words the net benefits to society are the sum of the producer and consumer surplus.

We can use the basic demand and supply framework to assess how net economic benefits might change as a result of changes in demand and supply conditions. Consider the left-hand part of Figure 3.4. If price is artificially decreased from the equilibrium price P^* to P_G, (for government set price), then consumer surplus increases by the amount consumers gain at the expense of the producers (the area denoted by P^*DCP_G minus the area of ABD). Note, however, that while consumers gain, the total area of the combined consumer and producer surpluses is less after the lower price is imposed. In other words, the consumers' gain is less than the producers' loss. The overall net benefits to society are decreased by the area ABC due to the reduction in quantity supplied. Furthermore, because consumers want more of this good or service at this reduced price (Q_d for quality demanded) than producers are willing to supply (Q_s for quality supplied), some form of rationing must take place. This is what some analysts believe happened in the United States in the 1970s with price controls on oil. A portion of the producers' surplus was, in effect, transferred to consumers, and the unmet demand was indicated by long lines of drivers waiting to purchase gasoline.

The demand and supply framework also can be used to examine a situation in which price is artificially high, perhaps due to the presence of a few suppliers who control the market, or again because of government involvement. As shown in the right-hand part of Figure 3.4 at the artificially high price of P_M (for monopoly price), output falls from Q^* to Q_d. Producer surplus increases by the difference between the area bordered by P_MADP^* (a wealth transfer from consumers to producers) minus the area DBC. However, as in the previous case, the gain by producers is less than the loss by consumers with the net social loss again being equal to the area ABC. If the artificially high price is set by government, this may result in unsold production which the government must purchase. This was a common situation in various parts of the world when governments set artificially high agricultural prices to assist farmers.

Figure 3.4
Impact of Supply and Demand of Non-Equilibrium Price

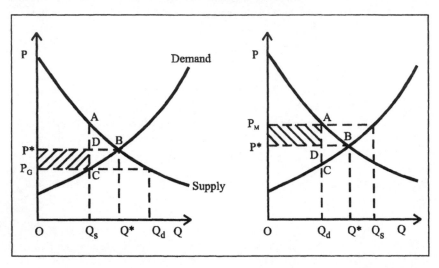

To sum up, society is better off at P* than at P_G or P_M because net benefits (consumer plus producer surplus) are maximized.

Failure of the Perfectly Competitive Market

Of course, we know that there are very few situations, if any, in which all the conditions of the perfectly competitive market are met. Markets fail for any number of reasons and these fall into three broad categories:

♦ The presence of imperfect competition

♦ External effects (externalities)

♦ Public goods

The presence of any one of these factors leads to malfunctioning markets. The obvious question is, if perfectly functioning markets rarely exist, then why should they be studied? We study the perfect market model because we can determine how specific forms of divergence from this model affect market outcomes. This information provides insights into how some actual markets are working more or less properly, and how others are not, and it can illustrate how we might attempt to correct some cases of market failures. We will now look at one form of imperfect competition: the monopoly.

Imperfect Competition: The Monopoly

The presence of imperfect competition changes the efficiency condition of profit maximization. Under monopoly markets, prices are set by the producer, and are no longer equal to marginal costs. In its purest form, monopoly is defined as a situation where one producer supplies all of a product for which there are no close substitutes. In the real world, there are also situations in which a limited number of producers may work together to set prices and control production levels. Such an *oligopoly*, in effect, is able to function much like a monopoly. A monopoly may arise where a limited number of producers control resources or where a single producer has a patent for a particular process or product. The key to the success of monopolies is their ability to control access to the market so as to prevent competition. Monopolies also exist where there is a high degree of public interest in having only one supplier, as is often in the case of the provision of electric power and water. In the latter cases, the electric or water utility is usually regulated to prevent the taking of excessive profits by suppliers.

Since the monopolist is the only producer in the market, the demand curve facing the monopolist is the full market demand curve. It is downward sloping and usually somewhat inelastic (recall that one tenet of monopoly is that there are no close substitutes for the good). This is in contrast to the situation where each of the many producers in the competitive market encounters a perfectly elastic demand curve. If the monopolist decides to increase output, then he will have to lower the price. Total costs for the monopolist, and hence his marginal cost, are the same as that under the perfectly competitive market.

Let us next examine the monopolist's behavior from the perspective of a marginal analysis. We found that a perfectly competitive producer maximizes profits by equating price and marginal cost. The perfectly competitive producer can sell all of his good or service at the market price. This means that the marginal revenue received for the last unit produced is simply the price. For the monopolist, who faces a downward-sloping demand curve, different output levels mean different prices. If a monopolist wants to increase output, price must go down.

The monopolist will try to price discriminate among his customers. If possible, he will seek to charge higher prices to those customers he believes are willing to pay more and offer lower prices to those who he believes are willing to pay less. In other words, the monopolist will try, if at all possible, to acquire the whole of the consumer surplus for himself. One example of this is some developing countries, policies of charging foreigners more for state-run services, such as airlines, trains, and hotels, than is charged to national citizens for the same service. Another example is airline fares for the same origin-destination round trip, which often differ depending on how many days the traveler spends in the destination city. Such fare schedules may be viewed as an attempt by the airlines to separate out business travelers (who presumably wish to avoid weekends within their trip and who would be willing to spend more money for the trip) from leisure travelers (who presumably would seek to include weekends within their trip period and whose travel decisions tend to be more price sensitive). There are a number of other features of monopoly behavior which are interesting and by extension are of relevance to some environmental management situations. However, in the interest of moving on to economic theory as it focuses primarily on the environment, we will end this discussion of monopoly on the few points briefly outlined here.

CONCLUSION

The conditions of a competitive market require that individual consumers and producers behave rationally and maximize their own self-interest, called utility for consumers and profits for producers. Under competitive markets, when all individual decisionmakers act to maximize their own self-interest, society's welfare is also maximized. The goods and services demanded are supplied at the lowest costs in just the right quantity.

Before we conclude this chapter, several additional points should be made. First, marginal analysis is not about sunk costs, which are costs that have already been incurred. Previously incurred costs are, for all intents and purposes, irrelevant to economic decisions. Marginal costs include only variable costs. Fixed costs and previously incurred costs do not matter in decisions at the margin. Suppose you purchased a home computer last year. A few months later you find out that there are some new computers on the market that run much faster than your computer and cost half as much as you paid. You would like to have the new computer because it would save time and be able to run some sophisticated software. However, you decide not to purchase the new computer because you feel you have already invested enough money in your current computer. Is this the correct way to approach this decision? The answer is no, assuming that you could afford to buy another computer. The correct approach is that you should not buy the new computer if its value above that of your existing one is less than its cost. If its addition value is greater than its cost, you should buy it even though that may mean letting your original computer sit idle or be scrapped. This matter of sunk costs is considered further with regard to project appraisal in Chapter 6, in part because projects for which additional environmental costs are discovered late in the assessment process may be difficult to stop due to the feeling that we have already gone too far to back out now.

Another point is that marginal analysis is about all values and not just monetized value. The problem for environmental economists is that market prices often do not reflect all values. That is, even competitive markets tend to systematically exclude some important values (e.g., environmental services) because they are external to the market. Environmental economists consider ways in which prices can be adjusted to reflect full value. We can think of three ways in which market prices do not reflect value (in order of increasing divergence):

1. Inappropriate prices. We may use certain goods or factors of production that generate pollution, without incorporating such consequences into the prices paid. For example, the external effects or damages of the nitrogen oxide and sulfur dioxide emissions that result from burning coal may not be fully reflected in electricity rates.

2. Situations where market prices do not exist, but where it is possible to measure or at least impute economic values. An example of this is the fee charged to enter a national park which may be much less than the value consumers place on the park, what they would be willing to pay to visit it, or what they would be willing to pay to ensure that the park is preserved for future generations. Hence, it would be wrong to use the entrance fee paid as the basis for estimating the value that park users place on the park.

3. Situations in which it is very difficult to develop a reliable technique for estimating value. For example, the value of some amenity resource, such as the view from the rim of the Grand Canyon, or the preservation of an endangered species, are clearly quite important and yet difficult to price.

In subsequent chapters, our discussion of environmental economics will largely be confined to situations where prices do not capture all values. However, we hope that the reader will appreciate how the lessons learned from situations in which markets are assumed to adequately reflect value help in illuminating some of the important underlying relationships we expect to find in situations where this is not the case.

NOTES

1. In most examples in this text we describe situations in which at one increment of choice marginal benefits are greater than marginal costs and at the next step are less than marginal costs. This reflects the fact that in the real world choices tend to be discrete rather than perfectly continuous. However, under the assumption of perfectly continuous choices, it is mathematically convenient to determine the point at which marginal benefits equal marginal costs. Since this step is neutral in value terms compared to the one before it (i.e., net benefits are the same), it is typically used as the shorthand rule for optimization.

2. A problem with this method of measuring consumer surplus is that a fall or rise in price changes the value of income. Hence, a change in demand might reflect the change in that purchasing power, as well as a change in the value the consumer places on the good. Although the problem can be circumvented by looking at what economists refer to as the income compensated demand curve, the above approach serves as a reasonable approximation provided the change in price is relatively small.

3. The basis for the principle of economic efficiency comes from Vilfredo Pareto, who first proposed it. Allocations are deemed "Pareto efficient" if there exists no reallocation of the market system that could make some people better off without resulting in a worse situation for others.

4

Externalities and Property Rights

What distinguishes environmental economics from standard market economics is the stress that the former places on externalities. Although externalities may be positive or negative, the negative ones are of primary concern to environmental management. Externalities are unintended side effects of an activity in which two conditions hold. First, the full impact of the side effect is not experienced by the person responsible for it. Second, no compensation is provided to those who endure the side effects. Since the person causing the side effect does not fully experience its impact, the perpetrator tends to ignore all or part of the consequences, and treats such impacts as external to his assessment of the benefits and costs associated with his activities.

Some externalities are important because when they are not included in the decision-making process, society is in a worse position than it would be if the consequences of these side effects were taken into account. This loss in welfare occurs when a negative externality can be prevented at a cost lower than the value of the foregone benefits or avoided loss. Likewise, a positive externality results in a loss in potential social welfare when the side effect could have been increased at a cost lower than the value of the additional benefits.

Basically, the loss in welfare stems from the fact that when side effects are treated as external, their value, in the eyes of the person causing them, is implicitly zero. Hence, if there is any cost to the perpetrator of changing his behavior, then he sees a negative payback from doing so.

For example, when the owner of a motor vehicle determines the frequency and level of engine maintenance, he probably weighs the benefits, such as improved engine performance, against the costs in money and time. In the absence of regulations for polluting vehicle emissions, the owner may leave the effect of auto maintenance on local air pollution and its impacts on human health out of his benefit-cost assessment. Likewise, when a consumer purchases a camera battery, he might view the potential environmental damages associated with its eventual disposal as beyond his control or responsibility, and hence external to his decision about the type of battery to purchase. Yet the soil contamination from the battery's decomposition in a landfill, or the release of toxic gases during its incineration are relevant, and therefore should be internal, to the well-being of society as a whole.

If the consumer of the batteries and the vehicle owner were to incorporate the environmental impacts (or even the risk of such effects) into their calculation of benefits and costs, then the level of such activities might be different. In other words, the demand for particular types of batteries and decisions about how to dispose of them would probably change, as would the decisions of motor vehicle owners about the appropriate level of engine maintenance.

As our knowledge of the natural world increases, it has become increasingly evident that many forms of environmental change previously thought to be of little relation to society's welfare are actually of considerable importance. The accumulation of heavy metals in harbor sediments, pesticide residues in birds, the effects of lead in paint and in gasoline, biodiversity loss, deforestation, and wetlands destruction are only a few examples which come readily to mind. Indeed, we are coming to recognize that important environmental externalities exist where we previously had been largely unaware of them. Some specific examples of these relatively recently discovered externalities include the destruction of stratospheric ozone by chlorofluorocarbons (CFCs) used as coolants in air conditioners and refrigerators, and the creation of acid rain as a result of long distance transport of sulfur dioxide.

While we all may want a better environment, questions of how much to pay and how the burden should be shared are more contentious. As a society attempts to mitigate environmental damages, in many cases it is requiring people to pay (directly or indirectly) to prevent impacts that previously were considered to be acceptable.[1] Even when society as a whole experiences a net gain from restricting previously tolerated environmentally damaging activities, there are often shifts in the incidence of costs borne by different groups, and no one likes to see his own burden go up disproportionately.

In addition, it is also important to remember that in many cases of improved environmental management, people are paying more in terms of explicit costs, such as behavior restrictions or taxes, while gaining benefits that may not be immediately visible, and indeed, may mostly benefit future generations. People's willingness to exchange their own concrete, short-term assets for more distant, long-term social gains is understandably limited. It is the task of environmental specialists to make the benefits of such tradeoffs clear to the average consumer and taxpayer, and to work toward an economic system that incorporates long-term environmental considerations at a fundamental level through the process of internalizing externalities.

POSITIVE EXTERNALITIES

While environmental management is primarily concerned with negative externalities, it also encompasses positive externalities, which result in the under-production of desirable side effects. This type of situation is likely when people capable of creating beneficial side effects cannot obtain payment from the beneficiaries. The aesthetic benefit to people living near beautiful private land is a commonly cited example. If people creating or preserving such beauty could collect a fee from those who enjoy the view, it is likely that there would be more of such attractive landscapes. Another example is the potential for positive externalities from replacing annual crops with a long rotation tree plantation on marginal lands. Here, some of the benefits are in the form of side effects associated with reduced water and soil runoff and downstream siltation of a reservoir. Yet, if the owner of the land does not receive compensation for these effects, he is likely to consider them as external to the benefit-cost assessment with respect to putting the land to a less intensive use.

DISTINGUISHING PECUNIARY FROM REAL EXTERNALITIES

Unintended, unpriced external effects are common, and part of the ordinary functioning of the market economy. For example, consider a beer bottler using a certain type of easily recyclable glass container. Let us say that a major soft drink bottler decides to use the same type of container, and that when the soft drink bottler enters the market for that type of container, total demand goes up substantially. Let us say that as a consequence of this higher demand, the container manufacturer decides to raise his price.[2] Hence, the cost of the containers to both beer and soft drink bottlers goes up.

The impact of higher costs imposed on the beer bottler is unintended, and external to the soft drink bottler's benefit-cost assessment in choosing its type of container. Additionally, in a case like this, the soft drink bottler typically would not be expected to compensate the beer bottler. From the perspective of economic efficiency, the question is, are the damages suffered by the beer bottler a matter of concern to society as a whole?

Before addressing this question, let us consider another situation. Assume now that a single corporate entity owns both companies, and thus is responsible for choosing beer and soft drink containers. Under this circumstance, the single owner would probably recognize that when his soft drink bottler enters the market for the easily recyclable container, both companies may face higher container costs than the soft drink company faced when it alone was the consumer. In order to maximize his profits, the single owner would attempt to determine how the benefits of using the new containers for both operations compares with the costs. If the benefits (added profit) to his soft drink branch are greater than the costs (reduction in profit) to his beer branch, he would use the easily recyclable containers in both his businesses. In this case, the external effect was a *pecuniary externality*. Pecuniary externalities are communicated through the normal functioning of a competitive market. In contrast, real (or technological) externalities represent a market failure.

In the two related examples above, when the external effect (as seen by the independent soft drink bottler) is internalized within the joint ownership of the beer and soft drink bottling companies, the single owner did not change his decision about his soft drink bottler switching to that container. Referring back to the theoretical framework outlined in Chapter 2, we may view the unintended side effect as a consequence of the movement *along* the supply curve for the easily recyclable containers, due to a *shift in* the demand curve.   These relationships are illustrated in Figure 4.1.

In contrast to that situation, those externalities of concern to social welfare represent a shift in the "true" supply curve away from the "apparent" supply curve, as illustrated in Figure 4.2. In this case, the market price fails to provide the correct signal to consumers and suppliers. Hence, we are dealing with what are termed *real* or *technological* externalities.   These affect not only the allocation of benefits and costs among various members of society, but also the total welfare of society. The likelihood of a loss in social welfare stems from the fact that those persons making decisions about the real externality-causing activity do so on the basis of misleading cost information.

When a real externality exists, and if subsequently the external costs or benefits are borne by the perpetrator, the result would be a change in behavior.

Figure 4.1
The Case of a Pecuniary Externality

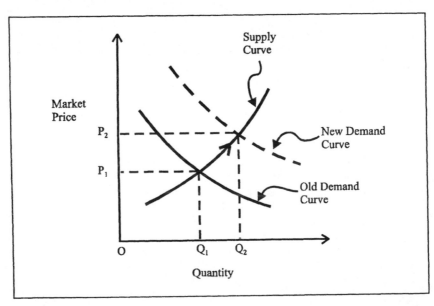

This change is reflected in Figure 4.2 as a fall in the level of activity, from Q_1 to Q_2, when the full costs are felt (i.e., internalized). One example of this type of situation is cigarette smoking, which has decreased in popularity as its true costs to human health have become known. This change in behavior, as a result of internalizing an external cost, is key to the distinction between real externalities, which are of concern from an economic efficiency standpoint, and pecuniary ones, which are not.

The Case of the Smoking Wok

Let us consider another example. Assume you have just moved to a new apartment. You enjoy cooking, and often make stir-fried vegetables in a wok. The kitchen of your new apartment is poorly ventilated, and thus using the wok has the effect of filling the apartment with smoke. This smoke has no direct and immediate cost in money terms, but it is nonetheless a very real problem. Do you ignore the smoke? Probably not, because your health and that of your family is affected. And besides, the kitchen walls are getting greasy!

Let us assume you now install an exhaust fan and send the smoke and grease out the window, thereby externalizing the problem. Normally we might assume that the smoke is sufficiently diluted by the time it affects others, but let us say that your apartment is in a crowded urban area where the next apartment building is only a short distance away. Part of your smoke is now blowing into

Figure 4.2
The Case of a Real Externality

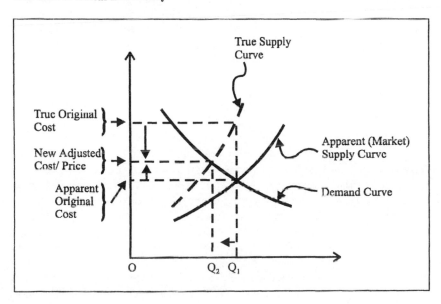

the bedroom window of another apartment. Does your neighbor have the right to stop you from sending smoke into her bedroom? Do you have the right to continue emitting smoke?

The answer depends on how the environmental property rights are assigned. How can you and your neighbor come to an understanding? Perhaps your neighbor would be willing to help pay for a different type of exhaust system which would emit the smoke at the roof-top level. While you and your neighbor could make this decision as individuals, your ability to negotiate successfully depends in part on the availability of social conditions or institutional arrangements to facilitate such private dealmaking.

Let us assume, initially, that the implicit property right in this case lies with the person doing the cooking. In other words, the user of the wok has the right to emit an unwanted by-product (greasy smoke) into the environment, even if this causes some nuisance to other people. Let us further assume that the complexities of working out a negotiated settlement with your neighbor are too great for this to be a practical alternative (economists would refer to this as a problem of the transaction costs being prohibitive). With this as the context, let us consider the situation from the standpoint of internal and external costs.

From the polluter's perspective, yours in this case, the smoke was an internal cost prior to installation of the exhaust fan. So you externalized the problem by emitting the smoke into the environment. Your neighbor's discomfort is an externality to you, if her loss in well-being is not part of your benefit-cost assessment when deciding what to do about the smoke.

But your neighbor is worse off. Perhaps, she works a late-night shift and is trying to sleep while you are cooking and blowing greasy smoke into her bedroom. You might say, "I regret this, but I must get rid of the smoke. And isn't this like the beer bottler who saw the prices of recyclable bottles go up because the demand increased from another user of that product?"

Well, perhaps it is. But remember, in that example, when one firm bottled both the beer and soft drinks, the owner did not change his decision about the type of bottle used by his soft drink operation, despite its negative impacts on his own beer bottler. The reason, of course, was that the single owner found the additional benefits to his soft drink bottler more than enough to fully offset (compensate for) losses suffered by his beer bottling company. That situation involved a pecuniary externality, not a real one, and the decision remained the same even after internalizing the externality. The total welfare of society was not reduced by the externality. Hence, internalizing it made no difference in terms of the decisions regarding the use of recyclable containers.

Now, how can this be applied to the case of the smoking wok? Consider a change in the situation. Instead of the occupant of the nearby apartment being a stranger, let us assume that your parents are moving in. From the perspective of the extended family, the smoke you emit from your kitchen is now no longer an external cost. When your parents become the recipients, it is internalized (assuming, of course, that you treat your parents as part of your family). Now, would you deal with this new situation in the same manner as you would if the recipient of the smoke were a stranger? If you act differently when the effect of the smoke is on members of your family, rather than others, then your smoke is probably a real externality. From the viewpoint of the overall welfare of society, you were probably producing too much smoke.[3]

From this point on, we will discuss only real externalities. When you see the word *externalities* in this text and in others, you should generally assume (unless explicitly stated otherwise) that the discussion is about real externalities, rather than pecuniary externalities.

ENVIRONMENTAL DEGRADATION AS AN EXTERNALITY

The natural environment provides a wide range of essential and convenient services to us all. A moment's reflection suggests so many examples that listing them is perhaps unnecessary. Yet, often such services are taken for granted, not just by individuals, but also collectively as a society and a global community.

One particularly unfortunate example of this is that, under the standard national income accounting, a country receives no explicit recognition for the value of maintaining forests in a fragile watershed. Protecting these forests may yield many economic benefits, such as soil stabilization and the accompanying decrease in flood damage downstream. Yet, if these same forests are cut down and the wood sold, the national income accounting would credit the country's agricultural-forestry sector with an increase in income. And it would do this despite the added risk of flooding, which is likely to result in significant priced losses later. The costs would eventually show up, of course, but their cause might be obscured. In any case, as noted in Chapter 8, the present value of the postponed negative consequences would be discounted.

In the same vein, pollution and other forms of environmental degradation diminish the environmental services we receive, in terms of human health and productive ecosystems. Yet still we tend to treat such losses as externalities.[4] Unfortunately, the loss of environmental services has very real consequences on our well-being, regardless of whether our accounting conventions and perceptions reflect those consequences.

Environmental degradation is an unintended and unpriced side effect of many economic and social activities. For example, all motor vehicles directly or indirectly pollute the air.[5] Chemicals commonly used to make refrigerants find their way to the upper atmosphere where they destroy ozone. The draining of marshes destroys breeding grounds for marine and terrestrial flora and fauna; and siting a golf course in a previously undeveloped natural area may (among other impacts, such as those from the heavy use of pesticides) diminish the quality of scenic vistas in the area. Such examples illustrate the breadth and depth of environmental services undermined by daily activities. These environmental services provide benefits of all sorts: breathing clean air is valuable to human health (i.e., in avoiding some illnesses); stratospheric ozone screens out harmful ultraviolet rays; a well-functioning estuary supports commercial fish stocks; and natural areas, if preserved, are of significant aesthetic and genetic value. As you might expect, what is typically of concern to economists is *not* the fact that natural systems have been disturbed, but rather that such disturbances tend to reduce the ability of environmental systems to provide services that are highly valued by people. Further, economists focus on the reasons why such impacts are treated as external to our benefit-cost calculations, even though they do affect overall welfare.

Disturbances to the environment, and the resulting loss of environmental services, are common to all societies, regardless of the type of social organization, level of income, or technological sophistication. Unfortunately, it is also true that damages from environmental externalities have been growing in recent decades as a result of increasing population pressure and changing lifestyles around the world.

In the past it was often argued that most forms of environmental degradation represented tolerable nuisances. Even when an environmental impact was acknowledged as significant, it was often argued that the value to society of the activities causing pollution exceeded the value of the damages done to the environment. According to this logic, even if we were to consider such impacts as internal costs, we would not change our behavior. It is sometimes argued today that developing countries should tolerate environmental degradation for now in order to keep the short-term monetized costs of production low and hence maximize their economic development potential. Once these countries are more developed (and richer), it is argued, they will be in a better position to move toward a less environmentally damaging economy.

The thrust of such arguments is that even when we recognize the unpriced costs associated with environmental degradation, these should be considered as acceptable losses relative to the benefits resulting from the externality-generating activity. While this argument may be valid in particular cases, several developments have added weight to the counter argument for the need to reduce many environmental externalities in developing economies as well as in higher income economies.

First, we have learned that negative consequences of known forms of environmental degradation are often higher than we believed them to be in the past. Second, we are learning more about previously unknown aspects of environmental degradation, such as regional and global effects. And third, as discussed in Chapter 3, we have realized that it is essential to consider not only the options of complete elimination of environmental damage or inaction, but also to compare the benefits and costs of different levels of damage avoidance. When we use more comprehensive measures of the value of environmental services and pay greater attention to comparing the marginal benefits and costs of environmental controls, we conclude that we should reduce (but not necessarily completely eliminate) many previously tolerated environmental externalities.

Let us consider a few examples. In the past, when many people used coal for heating, we thought the negative health effects from the coal smoke could be largely externalized by emitting the smoke from our houses. However, we came to realize that much of this smoke remained in the vicinity and caused harm to people, as well as to buildings and ecology. Most people would probably conclude that the residents of London, for example, are better off as a result of being forced by regulations to move away from a reliance on coal, and to find alternative heating sources. In the future, this will likely be said of now coal-dependent nations such as China, India, and parts of Eastern Europe.

In recent years, we have learned that even when we are able to dilute pollutants in the atmosphere or oceans, contamination results in previously unanticipated regional and global changes. For example, the construction of tall smoke stacks for large coal-burning power plants is one way for plant operators and regulators to send sulfur emissions to the high winds, thereby treating that part of the pollution as an external cost of coal combustion. Yet these same high-altitude emissions may cause problems hundreds or thousands of kilometers away. From the perspective of the region or the planet, such emissions have negative impacts that are in fact an internal cost. Ignoring such impacts leads to misinformed decisions about what type of power plant to build and what level of emission control to impose. In turn, to the extent that electricity tariffs reflect costs faced by the utility, consumers tend to see artificially low costs for electricity in situations where utilities rely on tall stacks, since the costs of preventing long distance environmental damages are not fully reflected in the price of electricity.

And just as environmental property rights are an issue when it comes to the actions of individuals, so are they included in the rights and obligations of nations and other political entities to each other. Faced with the task of producing enough electricity to meet demand, does one nation have the right to emit substances directly responsible for the acid rain that kills forests across its border? Does one metropolitan area have the right to make the air unhealthy for a city downwind? Perhaps not surprisingly, the evolution of systems for determining the appropriate assignment of environmental property rights among political entities has lagged behind the machinery for assigning rights at the individual level. However, given the growing importance of transboundary environmental damage, this will inevitably be a major area of development.

It should be noted that the points raised in Chapter 3 regarding the need to carefully compare benefits and costs at the margin are directly relevant here. While zero pollution is likely to be very expensive in most cases, the cost of the first increments of pollutant reduction may be comparatively low. In many cases, the marginal cost curve for pollutant reduction only begins to rise steeply for relatively stringent levels of control, especially when attempting to remove the last few percent concentration of a pollutant. In a more or less complementary fashion, living organisms and natural environments have a tolerance for relatively low levels of many types of pollution, even when the pollutants represent a chronic problem and occasionally reach acute levels. Problems occur when pollutant concentrations exceed such tolerances. Hence, the benefits of pushing pollutant levels below such thresholds may be quite high, while the additional (marginal) benefits from further reductions in pollutants may be relatively moderate, though still positive.

Where these conditions hold, it is likely that the optimal level of an externality causing environmental degradation is somewhere between the upper limit of human and ecosystem tolerance and zero pollution. Yet even this broad statement is only useful for policy purposes, if we are willing to define such tolerances in rather specific ways. For example, should the limits be set considering what the average person could tolerate or what particularly sensitive populations might require?

REDUCING ENVIRONMENTAL EXTERNALITIES

Appropriate Level of Reduction

Not all real negative externalities should be completely eliminated. It is necessary to compare the benefits of doing so against the costs. In the examples given earlier in this chapter, we noted that an important test of whether an externality is of concern to society is the matter of whether the perpetrator would change his behavior if he himself felt the full impact of the side effects generated by his actions. Such a change in behavior might mean modifying his actions so as to lessen but not necessarily completely eliminate the side effects.

For example, if a household were charged fees that fully covered the cost of the safe and effective disposal of household solid waste, that household would probably reduce its amount of solid wastes. That said, it is unlikely that the household would find it economically rational to completely eliminate the trash it produces (even in the unlikely event that it could physically do so).

As illustrated in Figure 4.3, in many situations one way to determine the appropriate level to which negative environmental externalities should be reduced is to separate the choice into a series of discrete steps, with each step involving (in sequence) an additional increment of impact reduction.[6] We would then compare the benefits and costs for the first step. If the benefits of attaining that reduction in the negative externality are greater than the costs, then we should go at least that far. Next, we consider the second step, and so on, using the same decision rule of undertaking a step only where the additional benefits of doing so are at least equal to the additional costs of doing so.

Figure 4.3 shows four discrete levels of environmental impact reduction (25%, 50%, 75%, and 100%). For the first step, the benefits substantially outweigh the costs. Hence, society experiences a net gain if it takes this step. Raising the level of impact reduction from 25% to 50% has an incremental benefit that is still higher than the incremental cost, although the gap between incremental benefits and costs is narrowing. If we go from 50% to 75%, the additional benefits are still somewhat higher than the additional costs. Still, since there is some net gain by going from the second to third stage,   we should

Figure 4.3
Comparison of Incremental Benefits and Costs

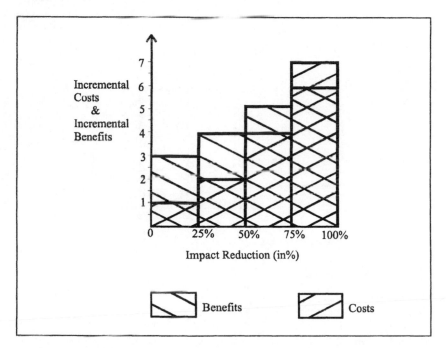

raise the level of impact reduction to 75%. However, if we were to raise the level of impact reduction from 75% to 100%, the additional benefits of taking this final step are outweighed by the additional costs and so this step represents a net loss to society.

Using the same data as in Figure 4.3, Figure 4.4 shows the total benefits and costs for each stage. Notice that at 100% reduction of the externality, total benefits still exceed total costs in this example. Yet the optimal level nonetheless remains 75% reduction rather than 100%. This is because the net benefits to society from 75% reduction are greater than they are from its complete elimination. As noted in Chapters 2 and 3, a basic rule for attaining economic efficiency is to seek solutions which involve the greatest *net* benefit, rather than simply to maximize total benefits where these are greater than total costs.

Putting the Burden of the Side Effects on their Perpetrators

When environmental quality is threatened by human activity, we have two basic choices: to focus on controlling the impacts themselves, or to change the activity ultimately responsible for the impacts. Preventing damages in the first place through changes in the underlying activity is often the least expensive and the most effective way to protect the environment.

Figure 4.4
Cumulative Net Benefits

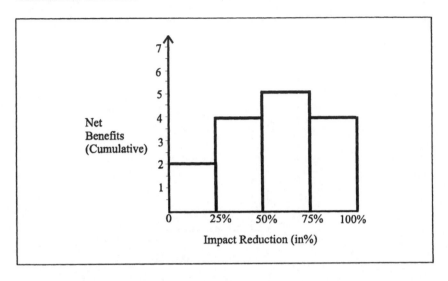

Reductions in environmentally damaging side effects may be brought about directly, through restrictions or behavioral requirements (such as installing filters), or indirectly, though such things as pollution taxes or voluntary controls. To the extent that an environmental management measure imposes a real cost (including non-monetized costs such as inconvenience), we may think of that measure as not only reducing environmental externalities, but also at least partly or indirectly as internalizing them. Of course, what the person generating the externality now sees is not the actual cost of the negative side effects he creates. Instead, he sees a *surrogate cost* associated with the need to comply with the environmental control measure. And such costs may be influenced by many factors, including administrative convenience or political acceptability, as well as the value of the damage being caused. Nonetheless, it is useful to think of the ultimate aim of environmental management as not only to reduce externalities directly, but also to induce long-term changes in behavior by at least partly internalizing those externalities. While the necessity of this process is becoming increasingly recognized, we should acknowledge that putting this idea into practice may be difficult.

Consider a simple example. Let us assume that a brick kiln in a remote village is producing bricks for the local construction market. The kiln's energy comes from high-sulfur, high-ash coal. Let us further assume that we are the people in this village and we have the choice of buying the bricks from the kiln or using local stone for construction. The manufacture of bricks results in visible local air pollution. But unknown to us villagers living a relatively isolated existence, this smoke also damages our lungs. While stone is also available as a building material, it is more costly and considered inferior to bricks.

Let us also say that we are not particularly aware of environmental matters, and base our decisions about quantities of brick purchases solely on the monetary costs. Assuming that the apparent supply curve and the demand curve for bricks have the normal shapes, the situation probably would look something like that in Figure 4.5.

Now, let us say that a visiting doctor comes to our village, and finds that many of us suffer from reduced breathing capacity. After considering a range of possible causes, such as burning wood and using tobacco, the doctor concludes that our respiratory problems are a result of breathing particulates and noxious gases from the kiln's coal smoke. We had recognized that the kiln's smoke was unpleasant, but we considered it only a nuisance, an acceptable cost of producing superior and inexpensive building materials. Since the visiting doctor knows something about economics, she explains things to us that "the actual cost of producing the bricks is much higher than you think. You would not buy so many bricks if you considered the full costs, which include unpriced side-effects in the form of damage to your health."

How might we represent this in our graph? As we did for Figure 4.1 let us add a dashed line to suggest the *true* supply curve for the bricks, after incorporating health damages. Of course, the vertical axis in this particular example, as illustrated in Figure 4.6, probably can no longer be strictly in money terms. But let us assume, for the moment, that we can combine the money and health impacts into a single measure of cost.

Figure 4.5
Village Market for Bricks

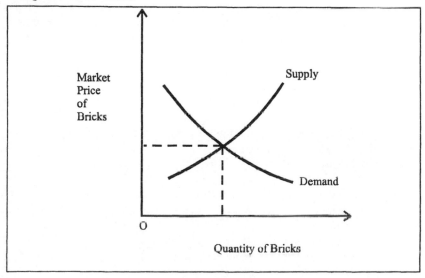

Figure 4.6
**Apparent (i.e., market) and True (i.e., including environmental costs) Supply
  Curve for Bricks**

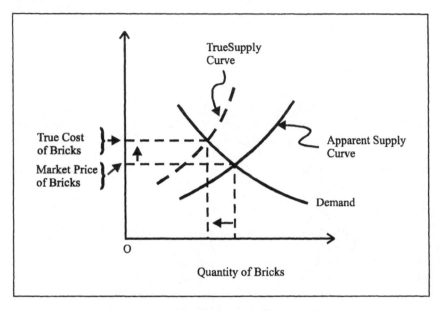

If we are dealing with a case of a real externality, once we have internalized the previously unattributed health effects of coal use, we would buy fewer bricks.[7] Notice that brick production (and its associated health impacts) in Figure 4.6 do not fall to zero. It may be reasonable for our village to accept some level of smoke-induced health problems in order to obtain the benefits of continuing to use bricks, but only for their most highly valued uses. Before the doctor arrived, we failed to see the full cost of brick supply. So we demanded more bricks than was optimal or efficient, from the standpoint of our overall well-being. Thus, we induced an over-production of an activity with an environmentally damaging externality.

Drawing on the village brick kiln example, one might ask, why not simply internalize the externalities as suggested earlier? Unfortunately, the matter is not necessarily straightforward. If we attempt to determine, explicitly and objectively, the extent to which we should internalize a particular type of environmental externality, we need to be able to compare directly the benefits with the costs of doing so.

In order to determine the optimal level of environmental quality, we need to be able to compare the marginal benefits of different levels of quality with the costs of attaining each level. Yet, in the real world, to actually do so typically would be rather complex. For example, the environmental damage caused by two sources of the same type of pollution may be quite different depending on the location. Likewise, the two sources of the same type of pollution may have very different costs for emission control, if one uses a different process than the other. Ideally, the marginal benefits and marginal costs should be compared individually for every case of environmental impact.

In many cases, the costs of reducing a negative environmental externality are rather straightforward, for instance in the case of determining the capital and operating costs for an emission control technology. Indeed, often it is possible to develop a rather complete supply curve (or at least a step function) for reducing a certain type of pollutant. In contrast, achieving agreement among many different people about the appropriate amount of money chosen to represent the value of reducing a health or an ecosystem-damaging externality is much more problematic.

In the absence of a market where individual preferences can be exercised, how do we estimate the demand curve for an improvement in the environment or human health? To what extent are people willing to even consider certain types of environmental or health values in monetary terms? What is the monetary equivalent of feeling healthy? How can we express the psychic value of wilderness in dollars, or the price of leaving a degraded environment to later generations? And in cases involving uncertainty about the nature of environmental impacts, even if we are able to agree on a monetary value for known impacts, how do we assess society's collective acceptance level of risk for uncertain ones?

A number of methods are available for assigning a monetary equivalent to various aspects of environmental impacts. Likewise, there are a variety of approaches that may be used in dealing with risk. Chapters 7 and 9 outline techniques for monetization and risk assessment respectively, noting their potential usefulness and limitations.

What is important to note here is that, despite their usefulness, such methods have important limitations. In the end, an important part of the process of valuing the environment remains subjective and beyond the scope of formal determinations of what is optimal.[8]

This does not mean that we should simply give up the idea of internalizing externalities. Rather, it is to underscore the point that we need to be realistic in our expectations. Even when we cannot precisely quantify the monetary value of various environmental impacts, the basic logic of attempting to internalize externalities still holds. We may not be able to say exactly how much pollution is appropriate, but often we can agree that the present level is too high. In the end, the decision is often based on implicit minimum or maximum valuation rather than on explicit precise valuation.

In other words, the decision comes down to a determination of whether society values a specific environmental improvement at least enough to be willing to spend the money it takes to attain it. For example, are we willing to spend 10% more for bus transport (e.g., for improved engine designs and stricter emissions testing) so as to help keep average daily particulate levels within an ambient standard of 80 micrograms per cubic meter?

If we assume that people can agree on the need for specific environmental improvements, how might we determine appropriate means for obtaining those improvements? There exists a wide range of control options, including direct controls—such as mandates for effluent clean-up, requirements for input substitution (e.g., switching to cleaner fuels), process modification, new zoning to force activity relocation, or the outright banning of certain types of products or activities. Alternatively, environmental improvement may be attained through market-based measures, such as taxes on pollution or the selling of permits for limited amounts of pollutant emission. We might also try community education and explore the possibilities of voluntary measures.

Some environmental control measures are more cost effective and robust than others. Economists are particularly concerned about the efficiency implications of one method of control versus another. The advantages and limitations of mandates, market-based measures, voluntary measures, and other environmental policy instruments are examined in Chapter 10.

Regardless of the type of control measure, the additional costs of reducing environmental externalities ultimately are borne by someone. When all or some of the additional costs are imposed directly on those who produce externalities (in a competitive market, this would mean imposing the costs of externality-generating production on the consumers of the resultant goods), then producers' and consumers' decisions would change to reflect what is actually the true cost of production. As noted earlier in this chapter and elaborated in Chapter 10, incentives to change the level or nature of activities with environmentally-damaging externalities is often the most effective approach to environmental improvement. This incentive, perhaps even more than appeals to equity and distributive justice, provides a strong argument for what is known as the *polluter pays principle*, also discussed in Chapter 10.

For better or worse, the political process often serves as the nearest approximation we have to a market for the collective offering and purchasing of various forms of environmental quality. One consequence of this is that environmental management is often linked to other components of the political agenda, such as issues of equity. In light of this, and considering the data limitations and differences with regard to how people value specific aspects of environmental quality, we should consider the process of internalizing externalities as a worthy goal, but one whose attainment will often be limited to crude approximations. How the burden of the newly internalized costs is split between producers and consumers depends on market conditions and, in practice, on how the property rights are assigned.

ENVIRONMENTAL PROPERTY RIGHTS

The term *environmental property rights*, as used in economics, refers to the bundle of entitlements (and restrictions) that accompany use of a resource. Such entitlements may be a matter of law or custom. The idea of property rights applies not only to things such as real estate, the ownership of physical items, and intellectual property, but also to the right to create and to be protected from environmental externalities.

The process of attempting to internalize environmental externalities may be viewed as a shift in the balance away from the right to pollute or otherwise degrade the environment and toward the right to be protected from such impacts. For example, in the past, the bundle of entitlements attendant to having a home in a cold region with abundant but dirty coal, or operating a chemical factory on a riverbank, included the right to emit virtually any type or level of by-product (coal smoke or toxic liquid wastes, respectively) into the environment. In much of the world today, either through law or custom, such entitlements are now severely restricted. We may think of the basic rationale for restricting the right to emit pollutants as putting a greater emphasis on defending the rights of those affected.[9] In other words, the bundle of entitlements associated with the reliance on environmental services in much of the world is now taken to include such things as access to air and water in which the level of man-made contamination is strictly limited.

Going back to the case of the smoking wok, remember the issue of whether you and your neighbor might be able to negotiate a settlement. If you could negotiate, you might be able to come to an agreement that would leave both of you better off. For example, if you have the property right to emit the smoke, your neighbor might be willing to buy the exhaust fan for you. She avoids the smoke and you get a free fan. Likewise, if the property right lay with your neighbor and you could not afford the fan yourself, you might get her to agree to let you use your wok on special occasions (perhaps you could give her a bottle of wine as a token of your appreciation for her cooperation). The point is that if the value of the damage is higher than the costs incurred to avoid it, then there is a potential gain. That gain can be split, evenly or otherwise, between the parties. Of course, the level of benefit accruing to each party of the negotiation depends largely on how the environmental property rights are assigned and their skills as negotiators. The bottom line is that each party is likely to be at least as well off after the negotiation as before it, and perhaps both will be better off.

There is a subtle but important aspect to this negotiation. What is going on in the process is the weighing of marginal costs and benefits associated with various alternative solutions (e.g., full use of the wok without a fan, restricted use without the fan, installing the fan). Let us say that the solution that would provide the greatest net gain would be restricted use of the wok without the fan. Perhaps you could agree to use the wok only on special occasions (e.g., holiday periods), so long as your freedom to emit smoke during these selected periods is explicitly acknowledged by the other party. Likewise, your neighbor who does not want to be bothered by the smoke might be willing to accept some smoke if it is only an occasional occurrence, and one which is limited to times when she is not trying to sleep.

One interesting aspect of this situation is highlighted by Ronald Coase in his seminal work "The Problem of Social Cost" (1960). If the parties to an externality are fully able to negotiate, Coase shows how they tend to arrive at the same solution, regardless of how the environmental property rights are assigned. Of course, the environmental property rights determine whether you provide compensation to your neighbor or she to you, but the solution that results in the greatest potential net gain would be the same in either case. Hence, in principle, the level of environmental damage is not dependent on how environmental property rights are assigned.

Yet, as Coase himself pointed out in his initial work and reaffirmed with greater emphasis several decades later, the existence of imperfect institutional arrangements and transaction costs often effectively precludes attainment of the type of mutually beneficial results he describes. In "Notes on the Problem of Social Costs" Coase states: "The reason why economists went wrong was that their theoretical model did not take into account a factor which is essential if one wishes to analyze the effect of a change in the law on the allocation of resources. This missing factor is the existence of transaction costs" (1990).

We may think of this problem, that transaction costs limit the ability of those affected by environmental damage to negotiate effectively with those who cause it, as an argument for government intervention.[10] One example of a government-enforced shift in the assignment of environmental property rights in recent years regards regulations on cigarette smoking. As Figure 4.7 suggests, in the past the balance was rather heavily in favor of the right to smoke. Today, in much of the world, the right to be protected from the effects of passive smoking (involuntary exposure to others' smoke) is much more heavily favored. Now supported by government regulations, non-smokers who previously endured smoky restaurants and offices have greater leverage when arguing their case against those who assert their right to smoke.

Many people concerned about the state of the environment assume as a matter of course that there should be no "right to pollute." Nonetheless, on reflection, it becomes clear that, historically, the right to pollute has been and continues to be freely claimed, not only by industry but by all members of society. We all pollute, each and every time we ride in a motor vehicle, cook, heat our homes, or flush the toilet. Each of our daily actions is based on an implicit assumption of our right (specifically, our property right) to use the physical environment as a sink for unwanted, and of course unintended, side effects. In the modern world such side effects inevitably result from desires for such basic comforts as long-distance or rapid transport, a wide variety of available food, a pleasant indoor climate, and convenient disposal of bodily wastes. Perhaps many of us would willingly shift to less damaging, though perhaps more expensive or less convenient, alternatives. Yet, no matter how environmentally conscious we may be, our lifestyles still generate a significant amount of pollution, and people assume that the right to discharge an amount of necessary pollution is fundamental to our existence on the earth.

Figure 4.7
Relative Balance of Property Rights With Regard to Cigarette Smoke

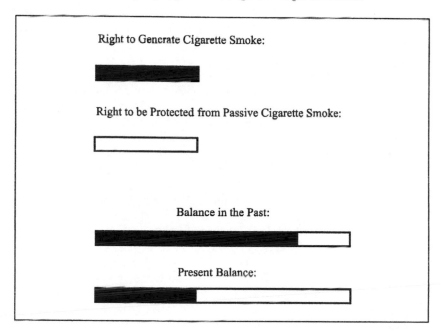

Our basic approach to the assignment of environmental property rights reflects society's rough estimate of the level of the benefits and costs of controlling such effects. When the assimilative capacity of the natural environment appears to be high compared to man-made demands on it, property rights tend naturally to be assigned in the form of the right to pollute. Yet, when the externalities of our actions begin causing serious and clear harm to society, property rights tend to be reassigned. These may take the form of enforcing the use of one particular type of heating fuel during winter months so as to protect air quality, or forbidding the collection of plants and animals from protected areas, or even the right to burn dead leaves or trash. However, in the absence of clear and present danger, the attitude toward pollution in most societies has evolved from a default assumption that the right to create environmental externalities lies with each of us. This assumption is gradually changing around the world, but it is important to recognize that such developments are still relatively new.

While personal attitudes toward the environment may slowly be changing, what about those of industry? It may surprise many people to learn that disputes over the environmental impacts of industry have featured prominently in legal traditions for a long time, particularly during the expansion of the industrial revolution in the nineteenth century. Perhaps less surprising is that the courts often sided with industry on the right to emit new types or much greater levels of pollutants into the air, water, and land. Based on the more limited environmental knowledge of the time, and the prevailing attitude that economic growth and technological development were of paramount importance to the progress of society, the legal and political systems in North America, Europe, and other industrializing areas tended to give industry pre-eminent property rights. The environment was seen as a necessary dumping ground for unwanted by-products. The benefits to society through lower costs and hence more competitive industry were viewed as outweighing the negative value of the environmental degradation.

Yet, since at least the mid-twentieth century, societies around the world have been implicitly or explicitly re-assigning property rights with regard to creating and being protected from environmental externalities. One increasingly widely embraced concept is the polluter pays principle. As elaborated in Chapter 10, the polluter pays principle, in effect, seeks to internalize externalities under three assumptions: first, that the property rights to use the environment lie with society as a whole; second, that it is in society's interest to reduce environmental damages; and third, that the best way to do this is to price products and services so as to reflect either a penalty for the value of their associated environmental damage, or the cost of mitigating the damage.

The validity of the polluter pays principle notwithstanding, we should recognize that much of our existing industry and infrastructure were built during times when very different assumptions prevailed about the assignment of environmental property rights. Few societies have the resources or the will to conform rapidly to the new, more environmentally conscious ethic, particularly with regard to cleaning up past damages. When it comes to the question of who should pay and how much should be paid for reducing environmental damages, three points bear taking into account:

1. The proper assignment of property rights, with regard to use of the environment, may be less straightforward than what many of us tend to assume. As explained above, in the past, such rights were often automatically assigned to the polluters, and questions of equity may arise when it comes to a drastic, rapid re-assignment of such rights.

2. The process of internalizing externalities is necessary, but may often be quite complex.

3. Even if we are successful in internalizing externalities, as illustrated by the example of the village brick kiln, the appropriate level of pollution is not necessarily zero.

A BRIEF NOTE ON PUBLIC GOODS

In concluding this chapter, it is useful to withdraw for a moment from concerns about specific forms of pollution and environmental degradation, and instead to think more generally about environmental quality. Some of the most important aspects of environmental quality involve benefits that are, or ideally could be, available to everyone. Further, very often the environment's capacity to provide important, often essential, services to one person or group does not seriously diminish its provision of similar services to other groups or individuals. For these reasons we may think of basic elements of life like clean air and a diverse, well-functioning ecology as public goods.[11]

Public goods are those that, at least in principle, can be provided at the same cost to many people as they are to one person. Further, one person's enjoyment of a public good does not significantly lessen the ability of other persons to benefit from it. And once this good is provided, selected individuals or groups, even those who do not pay for the good, cannot be excluded from enjoying the benefits.

Until the 1970s, the most often cited public good was national defense. Now we might more readily identify a clean environment as an example of a public good. One important feature of public goods is that because potential beneficiaries cannot be excluded from enjoying the benefits, regardless of whether they help pay to meet the cost of providing them, markets tend to under-provide public goods. This is termed the *free rider problem*: those providing a public good are providing something that is valued, but which is enjoyed without dues by some consumers, who are thus getting a "free ride."

Returning to a previous example, a farmer upstream from a reservoir who replaces his annual crops with orchards and natural woodlands may provide important benefits, such as reduced siltation, to the users of the reservoir. Yet the upstream farmer may be unable to collect payment from these beneficiaries. The inability to exclude non-payers limits the market's ability to allow the private providers of such public goods to recover their costs, and hence they tend to provide less.[12] This results in a problem of economic efficiency, because an opportunity for a net increase in welfare is foregone due to the problem of collecting adequate compensation from the beneficiaries.

This type of situation is often used to defend the need for a governmental role in the provision of important public goods, in order to ensure that the costs of providing them are met with user fees or general revenues. Indeed, as many forms of environmental quality are in the nature of public goods, there is a strong case for public intervention to protect the environment. Even when environmental quality issues are not in the public domain, the limitations posed by transaction costs to developing private solutions further add to the argument for government intervention. Chapter 5 deals with one particularly important aspect of the role of government: the management regime for common property resources.

NOTES

1. As noted in Chapter 1, costs and benefits are not always defined in terms of money. In some cases, the costs of environmental management may be in the form of

restrictions on (or requirements for) certain behavior, such as a municipality's requirement for households to separate solid wastes to facilitate recycling. Likewise, industry generally faces tighter controls, including increased reporting requirements, on its disposal of hazardous chemical wastes so as to reduce problems with contaminated sites. Again, as used in this text, cost in the broadest sense simply means something of negative value.

2. Depending on cost structure, the container maker who perhaps has at least a temporary monopoly (e.g., due to holding a patent) may find it more profitable to raise prices than to expand output rapidly, particularly if he wants to wait to ensure that the higher demand level is a long-term phenomenon.

3. The use of the qualifier "probably" here relates to the possibility that you, your parents, and your neighbor might place different values on the nuisance caused by the smoke. However, to the extent that each puts a higher value on the impact of the smoke than on the cost of dealing with it then the qualifier is unnecessary.

4. For example, our accounting systems would show the net profit of an industrial activity as being higher if pollution control costs were kept to a minimum. As for the possible health or nuisance effects of the pollution, these would only be reflected to the extent that people spent money to deal with them. Since the accounting system does not distinguish between expenditures for things desired and defensive expenditures to compensate in part for the lost unpriced environmental services, the more people spend to protect themselves from the effects of environmental degradation, the better it looks on the balance sheet.

5. The use of electric vehicles results in emissions from the power plants providing their electricity; hydroelectric and nuclear power, while less damaging in some respects compared to fossil fuel fired plants, have other negative impacts.

6. This approach is valid where the costs and benefits of each stage increase with each level of impact abatement, and where it is meaningful to assess the incremental benefits and costs of going from one stage to the next stage. Clearly, such conditions characterize many, but by no means all, environmental management situations.

7. We might do this directly, for example through a collective decision to buy fewer bricks, or more likely indirectly, through requirements for emission controls, or by relocating the kiln. Especially as a substitute building material is available, to the extent that the emission controls or kiln relocation increased the selling price of the bricks, we would buy fewer bricks.

8. Baumol and Oates (1988), for example, recommend that economists accept the practical limitations on our ability to determine what the economically optimal level of environmental quality should be, and instead focus on the efficient attainment of whatever general level of environmental quality society is able to agree on. They refer to this as "efficiency without optimality."

9. Such rights might relate to individuals or to all members of society. By extension, such rights may apply to future generations and to the natural environment to the extent that society today is able and willing to pay the cost of protecting natural systems for their own sake or to provide future generations with a greater environmental legacy.

10. Another argument is that some types of environmental quality are in the form of public goods. This is considered later in this chapter.

11. Some public goods are undesirable. These might be termed negative public goods, or even "public bads." As with positive and negative externalities, the definition of public good remains the same whether it is positive or negative.

12. Presumably if all boaters had to pay to use the reservoir, those who really enjoyed it and could afford it, would pay. If enough boaters valued the experience highly enough, the up-stream farmer could be adequately compensated. and he might be induced to take further actions to reduce run-off.

5

Overuse of Common Property Resources

Common property resources are those with open access. Ownership of these resources is either not defined or, by common practice, is not exercised; hence, individuals are free to use a common property resource as they wish. Common property resources are not to be confused with public resources which, though also held by society-at-large, are managed by the government or some designated body. For example, a national forest may permit logging only by those holding licenses. Under common property regimes, the resource is public in the sense that it is owned by the community, but no agent, government or otherwise, exercises control over its use.

Common property resources exist in all societies. A river may be one example; likewise, the air circulating through the atmosphere and transport on the high seas are treated as common property. In the past, a wider range of resources, including high mountain pastures, open-range lands, and many forests were treated as common property. Also subject to no restrictions were such basic resources as the atmosphere, which was regarded as a sink of infinite capacity for by-products of industrial combustion. Waterways often served as the ultimate repository for a host of biological and chemical wastes, no matter how toxic. Today, the number and types of such resources are far more restricted.

Two conditions typically hold when resources are treated as common property. First, a resource is treated common property when its absorptive or productive capacity is not considered to be scarce relative to expected demand levels; this is particularly so for renewable resources. The second condition is that restricting access to or use of the resource is difficult or costly. In such cases, legal systems may simply fail to deal with the matter of how these resources may be used. In the absence of legal restrictions, social conventions become the only form of control. Social conventions may be effective in controlling resource use, particularly in close-knit and stable societies. Yet, when the condition of the resource or of society itself changes, for example as a result of population pressures, technological developments, or other forms of social evolution, prevailing social conventions may become ineffective in controlling destructive changes in uses of the resource.

In order to address the over-exploitation of a common property resource, societies often find it necessary to replace common property regimes with some form of management, including restrictions on access to and use of the resource. For example, in much of the developing world today, it is illegal for people in certain overpopulated or environmentally sensitive areas to take live trees or branches for use as cooking or heating fuel. Hunting wild animals, once a common practice among lower income groups in rural areas, is now strictly limited or forbidden in much of the world, whether rich or poor. Settlers of European ancestry, who moved from the Eastern United States to the North American West in the 1800s, found that the legal arrangement for water rights in use in the East (one based on European water laws) was not appropriate for the West, where water was in much shorter supply. They responded to the scarcity of what they had previously regarded a common resource by establishing a new management regime, based on appropriation rather than riparian rights. In many urban areas of the United States, the traditional practice of burning autumn leaves is now restricted. Throughout much of the world, restrictions on waste disposal in waterways have increased as the intensity and extent of waste dumping has exceeded the ability of these systems to cleanse themselves. Indeed, the history of common property regimes is one of a generally shrinking set of resources to which they are applied.

When exploitation of a resource threatens to exceed its ability to renew itself, government typically steps in as manager of the resource on the basis of its powers of eminent domain or other presumptive rights to prescribe limits for individual action. Still, as one would expect, government often encounters strong resistance to the prospect of formerly unmanaged, open-access regimes becoming subject to controls. The most widespread and problematic common property resources today are fisheries; as fish stocks around the world decline drastically, the need for a new management regime is clearly evident. As such a management system is the only way to guard fisheries' stocks against massive depletion, it is clearly in the best interest of those whose livelihood hinges on whether or not those fisheries will thrive or fail. Yet, often, it is the fishermen themselves, accustomed to free use of the resource, who lead the opposition to imposing new restrictions.

THE FISHERY: THE CLASSIC TRAGEDY OF THE COMMONS

In his 1968 article, "The Tragedy of the Commons," Garrett Hardin outlined how market forces result in the over-exploitation of open-access renewable resources, sometimes to the point of extinction. Here we examine the fishery as a classic illustration of what happens to a resource that everyone wants to protect, and yet for which it is difficult for a government or any other body to take effective management responsibility.

We begin by outlining a general economic model of the fishery, in which benefits and costs are functions of the level of effort invested in fishing. We define *total benefits* here as the price per ton of fish multiplied by the weight of fish caught. If we assume that the price per unit of fish is constant, then the total benefit (TB) curve has the same shape as the total catch function. Indeed if our fishery is one of many supplying the market, it is not too unrealistic to assume that the wholesale price of fish is unaffected by changes in output of this one fishery. To simplify the presentation, let us assume that total cost (TC) increases linearly with the level of fishing effort. In other words, each unit of fishing effort is assumed to cost the same (i.e., marginal costs (MC) are constant). *Effort* is defined as the combination of people, equipment, and time devoted to finding and catching fish. For the purposes of illustration we define a unit of effort as a "man-day," representing a particular combination of labor, equipment, and time.

The primary concern for renewable resources is, of course, long-term production. In the short-term, anyone harvesting a renewable resource can increase total yield by also harvesting the breeding stock, whether this be seeds, saplings farm animals, or fish. However, when there is excess removal of breeding stock, then total yield over the longer period tends to decline. To reflect such population dynamics, we refine the definition of total catch to be the average annual catch over some period of time (e.g., five years). Likewise, let us redefine total cost as the average annual total cost over the same period. Figure 5.1 illustrates what may be viewed as typical longer-term Total Benefit and Total Cost curves, as functions of the average annual effort in catching fish over a period of several years.

In Figure 5.1, the total benefits curve initially is a positive function of the level of effort. However, because it is possible to over-exploit a stock of fish, if the level of effort increases too much, longer-term average catches actually decrease. This is the heart of the problem. With renewable resources there typically are negative returns to effort after some threshold level of use.

As noted in Chapter 3, the most economically efficient level of effort is where marginal costs (MC) equals marginal benefits (MB); in other words, where the slopes of the TC and TB curves are equal.[1] We designate this as level E (for economic efficiency). Let us consider the possibility that for some reason the fishermen ignore the MC = MB rule of profit maximization and increase their combined level of effort past point E. Now, one might expect them to increase their effort only up to the level corresponding to the maximum sustainable yield (MSY), designated here as level of effort M (for maximum output).[2] Surprisingly, and quite tragically, the actual level of fishing effort in many fisheries throughout the world is well past that of MSY. Indeed, without controls, the level of fishing effort is likely to increase all the way to the point where total benefits and total costs are equal (here designated as level B, for breaking even). At level B, all potential extra profits (in economic terms,

Figure 5.1
Long-Term Fishery Yield as a Function of Effort

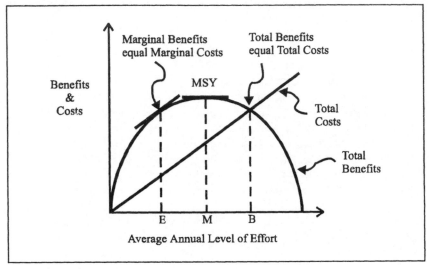

Note:
E is the economically efficient level of effect.
M is the level of effort associated with maximum sustainable yield.
B is the break even level of effort.

economic rents) are dissipated and the fishermen are just breaking even.

The wastefulness of maintaining the level of effort at B is immediately evident in Figure 5.1. We can see that the same long-term catch provided at level of effort B could be provided at far less effort (graphically in this example, at some point close to the level of effort E). Further, the yield is even lower and costs higher than at the level of effort M. Why would such obvious waste become so widespread? The explanation lies with the nature of open access resources.

To illustrate the incentives to over-exploit open-access renewable resources, we begin with a numerical example. Let us go back to the relationships presented in Figure 5.1 and examine them more closely by employing hypothetical values. Let us say the price of fish is $1,000/metric tonne ($1/kilogram) and that this price is constant regardless of the level of effort. Hence, if average annual catch is 2,500 metric tonnes, then the total benefit is $2.5 million. If longer-term average annual catch increases to 3,000 tonnes, then total benefit is $3.0 million a year.

As more fish are caught, those that remain become more widely dispersed, and harder to catch. Eventually, investing an additional man-day of fishing effort this year will increase this year's catch, but removes too many potential breeders and thus weakens the ability of the fish population to reproduce. In other words, we have passed the point of MSY.

Employing the same assumptions as in Figure 5.1, Figure 5.2 shows the monetized costs and benefits as functions of specific levels of effort, in average annual man-days. The point at which net returns are greatest (i.e., where MB = MC) is about 420 man-days. This provides a total (annual average) benefit each year of about $160,000 at an average total cost of about $60,000 per year, leaving an annual average *net* benefit of $100,000. MSY is reached at about 170 tonnes of fish annually. At the point of MSY the catch requires an average of about 660 man-days of effort per year. Total benefits at MSY are about $175,000, while total costs are about $95,000, leaving net benefit at about $80,000. If the average annual fishing effort each year increases beyond the 660 man-day level, the longer-term sustainable catch declines. At 1,000 man-days of effort, for example, the average annual catch is only about the same as that for 340 man-days! If we go much beyond 1,000 man-days, net returns are negative and the fishery will go out of business unless it is subsidized.

As we asked earlier, why would anyone set a level of effort past the point of maximum net benefits, and even more incredibly past the point of MSY? Clearly, a single owner of a fishery would not. The reason why so many fisheries around the world are over-exploited lies in the fact that they are not generally under the control of a single owner or manager. Instead, they are common property resources, in which access and use are open to all.[3]

A single operator of a fishery would presumably attempt to maximize his long-term net benefits, and act in the best interests of protecting fish stocks. But suppose that the fishery in Figure 5.2 is fished by a group of five fishermen who form a club in order to set a limit for total fishing at 420 man-days a year, and divide the surplus among themselves. Let us assume that this club is not legally binding, and a sixth and seventh fisherman decide to enter the fishery without abiding by the club's limit on total fishing effort.[4] Let us say that the newcomers raise the total number of man-days from 420 to 660. Longer-term net financial benefits are now reduced to $80,000 and this smaller profit is split among seven fishermen, rather than five. Also, the fishery has now reached its maximum sustainable yield.

Remember that although the net benefits available to the *group* of fishermen decrease, the newcomers as *individuals* profit by entering the fishery, as they now share a portion of the $80,000 in profits. The fact that net benefits have actually fallen and that this smaller amount is now split among more participants hurts the original participants, but this may mean nothing to the newcomers, who see only their own personal gain.

How might the original cartel members respond to the actions of the two newcomers? If, as noted in Chapter 4, transaction costs are high, then the scope for negotiation may be inadequate. Disregarding, for the purposes of this example, the possibility of negotiation, and having previously discarded the option of excluding the newcomers, the attitude of the original five cartel members might well become like that of the newcomers: "every fisherman for himself."

Figure 5.2
Illustrative Fishery Economic Model

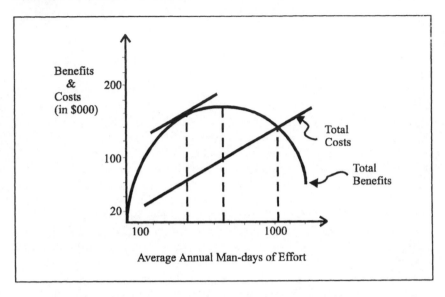

Perhaps each fisherman knows that the point of MSY has been reached, but without the functioning cartel, no one feels he can trust his neighbor to limit his catch.   The effect of this situation is a fundamental and highly damaging shift in the time frame for viewing benefits and costs, from one of longer to shorter-term yields.   Why?   Because the longer-term benefits of managing the renewable resource to ensure its efficient operation and sustainability accrue to *all* participants, regardless of whether each individual plays by the rules.   Even more important is the fact that a fish not taken this year by a fisherman purposely limiting his catch may be taken this year by someone else. So, even the conscientious fisherman will be tempted to over-fish, if he expects the same of others in terms of failing to exercise restraint. When such thinking becomes widespread, each fisherman continues to fish each year so long as his personal, short-term marginal benefit from an extra unit of fishing is greater than his personal, short-term marginal cost. When all the fishermen are of the same mind, the number of extra man-days of effort continues to increase, even though each may know that such actions are damaging long-term productivity.

A Doomsday Scenario

As some readers may suspect, common property resources contain a built-in tendency toward over-exploitation and eventual resource extinction. Consider the consequences of continuing improvements in fishing technology. Figures 5.1 and 5.2 reflected changes in effort and yield subject to the assumption of constant technology. What is the effect of relaxing this assumption?

Figure 5.3 shows our fishery model with several levels of technology for each man-day of effort. We now have three total cost curves, rather than one; total cost curve two (TC_2) and three (TC_3) represent progressively greater enhanced fishing power for each man-day. Graphically, for each level of effort on the abscissa (x axis) there is now a lower total cost on the ordinate (y axis) and lower marginal costs for each unit of fishing effort. As we can see, the effect of increasing technology is to drive the level of effort ever higher since net profits are greater at each level of effort. Hence, the point at which net benefits are fully dissipated moves further and further to the right. With sufficiently advanced technology the resource may be pushed out of existence.

MANAGING RENEWABLE RESOURCES

Earlier, we described the fishing cartel losing its self-proclaimed property right over the fishery. We also said that things got much worse after this event, until eventually every fisherman suffered a loss. A new student of economics might point out that this is simply the natural functioning of a competitive market! Shouldn't anyone who wants to fish be allowed to? Besides, don't cartels constitute oligopolistic restrictions which limit production and artificially raise prices to consumers? Why should we lament the dismantling of a cartel?

Figure 5.3
Effects of Technological Improvements

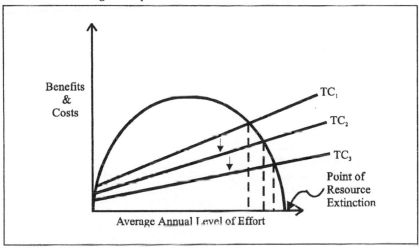

Note:
TC_1 is the total cost under technology level 1.
TC_2 is the total cost under technology level 2 (improved).
TC_3 is the total cost under technology level 3 (further improved).

Consider the following distinction between renewable common property resources and typical production systems. In a manufacturing or other normal production situation, producers bid for use of the various factors of production. With the exception of non-renewable resources, the owners of those factors presumably charge prices at least equal to the minimum requirements necessary for their sustained availability. But in the case of fisheries, as with other open-access renewable resources, a major and necessary component of the production process, in this case the fish, is not owned by anyone. (And while one factor of production, namely labor, can object to its over-exploitation, fish capable of future breeding can only try to escape.)   In this case, those consuming this crucial factor of future production (i.e., potential breeding stock) simply take the resource before others are able to, and no one can impose limits to ensure sustainability.

A first step toward preventing the over-exploitation of an open-access resource is to grant ownership or management of the resource to a single, accountable individual or group. The owner/manager might then limit access to the resource. Some economists would argue that once ownership has been established, the best way to manage the fishery is simply to limit the number of fishermen and then, as far as possible, refrain from interfering further in the fishing market. Although generally much less efficient, another alternative is to limit the other factors of production, such as time allotted for fishing or capital invested.

Over the past half century or so, governments have taken an increasingly active role as the owner/manager of over-exploited fisheries. The decision in the 1960s and 1970s of most coastal nations to extend their areas of control out to 200 miles is indicative of this trend. However, while willing to take the first step of imposing themselves as the fishery owner/manager, governments typically have proven much less effective in managing it. Some countries now limit certain fisheries to domestic users; in these cases, foreigners are either excluded or charged substantial fees. Generally, however, governments have been reluctant to severely limit the number of domestic fishermen, and have set the basic management goal in terms of limiting catch to MSY, rather than limiting effort so as to maximize net benefits. Why?

One explanation, if not necessarily a justification, is cultural values. People tend to resist having previously existing rights limited or taken away. Likewise, we tend to resent barriers to freedom of action. Fishing is often seen as an activity for independent people who make a living from the sea and demand little from society but the freedom to exercise their own initiative. Even where the reality of these situations is quite different, the persuasive power of such images may still hold.

Under a rational fisheries management program, including a limit on the number of participants, prospective entrants would have to bid for available licenses and such licenses presumably would be sold on the open market to the highest bidder.[5] Hence, a newcomer would have to make a large investment up front, in addition to substantial capital requirements for his boat and equipment, simply to obtain the right to fish.

Some governments attempt to lessen opposition to licensing by offering to existing fishermen free licenses, valid for their own use and eventually for sale.[6] Surprisingly, this is often not enough to ensure support of the affected fishermen, since if technology continues to improve, the number of licenses would need to be gradually reduced (see Figure 5.3). Fishermen may see the likelihood of this as being the end to their way of life as the fishing occupation passes into the hands of a few corporate, license holders. Like the family farmer, the independent fisherman holds a special place in the hearts of many, and we are often reluctant to see this way of life pass, even at the cost of losses in efficiency.

If governments are reluctant to limit the number of participants in a fishery, they may try to handicap the effectiveness of each participant. Restrictions on equipment or the length of the fishing season are common. Yet when one component of the fishing effort is limited, fishermen naturally attempt to substitute others for it. If the time for the fishing season is limited, then each fisherman may invest in better equipment or a larger boat during the open fishing season. As with other such interference in the production process, shortened fishing seasons, gear, and other restrictions raise the unit cost of production. In one extreme example, some fisheries in the Chesapeake Bay of the United States were limited to using sail power part of the time as a means of handicapping effectiveness. While the result may be picturesque, and may temporarily have the desired effect of reducing total catch by pushing the total cost curves upward to the right, the approach is clearly inefficient, since net benefits continue to be dissipated.

Even when there is little effective opposition from fishermen or others to limiting access to a fishery, the capacity for its rational management may be severely constrained. So far we have presented the fishery model as one involving known relationships among effort, costs, and catch. In practice, we often know rather little about the exact nature of the catch function. Even the approximate level of the point of MSY may be a matter of considerable controversy. Fisheries operate in a complex web of ecological relationships. Species may be subject to poorly understood cycles of expansion and contraction based on climatic variation, predator-prey relationships, and competition among different species for food. Activities to control the exploitation of one species may have unintended impacts on others.

The existence of such substantial problems does not mean that we should abandon rational fisheries management. Rational management is a worthy, if somewhat elusive, goal. However, we should be careful to recognize the information limitations and the socio-economic constraints within which we propose to impose management regimes on formerly common property resources. With this noted, it is important to recognize the undeniable evidence that global fisheries have been severely over-exploited; the effects of this include unnecessarily high costs, low production, severe disturbance to many ecosystems, and the likely extinction of commercially important species. While even markedly sub-optimal management regimes represent a substantial improvement over conditions prevailing under unmanaged open access regimes, the record overall is not encouraging, and fisheries today arguably represent one of the major environmental management failures of all time.

Before concluding this chapter, we should perhaps note that alternatives exist to government ownership/management of fishery resources.   One alternative is for the government to sell or lease ownership/management rights to private entities, for instance to a firm offering the highest bid, or perhaps under concessionary terms to the current fishermen with the understanding that they will form a legal cartel to limit future access. A middle approach might be for the government to assign some types of rights to private individuals and retain others. For example, a limited number of fishermen might be given ownership of the fishery (i.e., have the right to fish and to keep others out or to charge others a fee), but the government might set the allowable number of fish taken each year.

The next three chapters outline benefit-cost analysis and consider how we may incorporate environmental factors in the assessment of management options for renewable resources, such as our threatened fisheries and other environmental concerns.

Articles in daily newspapers often describe the on-going continuing tragedy of the commons for one or another of the world's fisheries. These articles make for instructive reading, particularly with regard to what is suggested in the article as the cause of the problem and proposed solutions to it.

NOTES

1. As you remember, marginal benefit is the slope of the total benefit curve; we can show the level of marginal benefit at any point by drawing a tangent to the total benefit curve. Where this tangent is parallel to the total cost curve, the slopes of the TB and TC curves are equal, and hence MB and MC are equal.

2. The concept of sustainability is being raised in more and more situations. People now often talk about sustainable agricultural practices and about sustainable development. At the heart of the matter is how to meet near-term needs without lowering our ability to meet longer-term ones. In the case of natural systems this means ensuring that we do not exploit them past the point at which they can continuously renew themselves into the distant future.

3. In some cases there may be restrictions imposed on certain participants, such as foreigners. However, so long as the number of potentially qualified participants is large relative to the level of effort that the fishery can sustain, then it retains the essential features of a common property resource.

4. Of course, if the newcomers had agreed to abide by the club's limit on total effort, the only way they could participate would be if the original five members agreed to give or sell part of their share of permitted man-days of fishing to the newcomers.

5. In a free market the selling price of the license would more or less come to equal the discounted present value of the net benefits which the license holder could expect to acquire during the term of the license. This is similar to the situation which occurs when taxicab licenses are restricted.

6. Of course, one might argue that this is inappropriate, since it transfers the rent from the fishery from society as a whole to existing fishermen. At a minimum, the need for such a grant should be discussed and debated.

6

Benefit-Cost Analysis for Environmental Management

Benefit-cost analysis (BCA)[1] is an important and widely used tool in making environmental management decisions. It is a method for evaluating proposed projects, programs, or plans through the systematic comparison of the value of the inputs with that of the expected outcomes. Conceptually, the incorporation of environmental impacts into the benefit and cost streams of BCA is possible; however, in practice, there are difficulties. Many environmental impacts do not have explicit prices, and we may be unable or unwilling to develop monetary equivalent values for them. Techniques for developing monetary equivalent measures of value and their limitations are reviewed in Chapter 7. Another difficulty lies in applying time-dependent discounting procedures by placing a present value on certain types of future environmental impacts, especially those that are permanent and irreversible. Issues and options associated with time-dependent valuation are reviewed in Chapter 8. Here we describe the basic features of standard benefit-cost analysis (SBCA), as well as several variations designed to address some of its limitations. Techniques of valuation and discounting are noted briefly, with more detailed descriptions and elaboration of problems left to Chapters 7 and 8.

THE KEY ROLE OF PROJECTS

In a basic planning hierarchy, broad goals are set out in policies or strategies; in turn these policies are carried out through plans or programs, each of which involve one or more very specific and clearly defined projects. While policies are broadly defined, and plans and programs more specifically focused, specifications for implementation of measures to meet the aims of policies and plans are usually defined in terms of projects. Although it is arguably useful to examine the benefits and costs of a plan or program, or even for a policy, in practice most applications of BCA occur at the project level. Indeed, this connection is so common that the terms *benefit-cost analysis* and *project evaluation* tend to be closely linked.

The decision-making process is improved when the comparison of benefits and costs is as systematic, rigorous, and explicit as possible. BCA is typically applied at the project level because the measurable inputs and outputs associated with a particular project are easier to identify than are those for broader programs or plans. In general, projects have an explicit statement of planned actions, a specified budget and indications of other required resources, and a finite period over which benefits and costs are considered (known as the *planning horizon* or *project evaluation period*).

As noted in Chapter 1, in this text we define the desirable impacts of proposed projects as *benefits*, and label those that are undesired *costs*, regardless of whether those impacts are expressed in money terms or whether they are inputs or outputs of some activity. Effects to which the project evaluation is indifferent are left out of the analysis (i.e., they are external to it). The issue of how to measure the value of different types of impacts is considered later in this chapter and in the following two chapters. Here, for introductory purposes, we note that the evaluation process is simplified when a money value is assigned to as many inputs and outputs as possible.   With money as the *common unit of value*, it becomes possible to compare different types of inputs and outputs, such as apples and oranges, or time and energy, which we might not otherwise be able to compare so readily.

One potential problem for a BCA is that some existing prices reflect a tax or subsidy, or the monopolistic pricing power of a producer or consumer. In such cases the existing prices may be so distorted that some form of alternative price should be used to more accurately reflect true value. Another problem is that, as noted in Chapter 4, many environmental impacts have historically been treated as externalities, despite the fact that they clearly affect the overall welfare of society and should be internalized into project economic assessments. It is difficult to include impacts in a BCA when they have not been assigned a price. For example, the unregulated market price for a wetland generally would not fully reflect the value of the environmental services it provides, many of which are unpriced; and the costs of operating a bus may not include consideration of the damages its fumes inflict on people's health.

Often, at least a portion of the unpriced impacts may be assigned a monetary equivalent value or *shadow price*. These are artificially constructed prices, developed for the purposes of analysis, to show what we think prices would be if they existed under competitive market conditions.[2] A simple shadow price may consist of the nominal price for an item minus the tax on it. Likewise, the monetary equivalent value for a wetland might be the market price of the area if it were to remain a wetland, plus an estimate of the value of the environmental services (indirect use value) the wetland provides. Similarly, the monetary equivalent cost of a bus ride might be the fare plus the value of the health damages its exhaust cause.

It is important to note that in practice the monetary equivalent measure for most environmental impacts is likely to be more narrowly defined than is implied by the general statements above. In the case of the loss of a wetland, the readily monetizable impacts might be limited to the income lost by an offshore fishery as a result of decreased fish catches in the future. As regards the polluting diesel bus, the only available course of action might be to set an emissions standard and then consider the costs to the vehicle owner of employing emissions controls to meet that standard.

Unfortunately, the limitation on our ability to develop money measures for important values is even more fundamental. Certain types of values simply cannot be reflected adequately in money terms. In some cases the intrinsically non-monetary values may be quantifiable, but involve great uncertainty. In other cases they may simply be intangible. Examples of environmental damages that may be quite difficult to quantify and monetize include the impact of biodiversity loss on further breakthroughs in medicine, or the psychic value of wilderness. In such cases we may be limited to attempting to determine what people would be willing to pay to avoid a damage to the environment or human health. Methods of assessing willingness to pay include conducting public opinion surveys or debating the issue within the political process; due to the ambiguous nature of both of these routes, the valuation estimates are likely to be at least somewhat inconclusive.

An additional factor for consideration is intergenerational costs, which are not easily dealt with by standard BCA. Because project evaluation is typically conducted within a specific planning horizon of well under fifty years, and, as noted later in this chapter, because of the need to discount future benefits and costs, impacts on future generations will be systematically undervalued and essentially excluded. Chapter 8 considers these issues further.

BCA—GETTING STARTED

Before we determine whether a particular project is worth undertaking we must take several steps:

1. Identify the activities associated with the project, and their expected impacts.

2. Select the inputs and outputs that are relevant (i.e., internal) to our analysis. We must then label each internal impact as either a benefit or as a cost.

3. Determine the appropriate value for each benefit and cost. Questions to consider here include the following: Do market prices accurately reflect value? Can the resources required by this project provide a greater yield in some other use (i.e., what are the opportunity costs)?

4.   Weigh the benefits against the costs. If the benefits are greater, then the project is potentially a good one.

Potential impacts are identified through the *with and without test,* which can be summed up by the following question: What are the expected differences between present and future conditions when we have implemented the project (with), compared with those if we do not (without)? Some readers may wonder whether it is worth mentioning such an obvious rule. The problem is that without such an explicit statement, some analyses may include in a project's projected benefit or cost stream impacts that will occur even if the project is not undertaken. For example, we might view some type of infrastructure development, such as upgraded rail service, as a beneficial outcome of constructing a large housing project in a previously sparsely populated area. Yet, it may be that the decision on the rail service is independent of our project; perhaps ours is only one of several development activities, any one of which would be sufficient to justify the rail service improvement. By making explicit the specific future conditions that are to be considered a result of the project and those that are expected to occur in any case, the with and without test may help avoid this type of error.

One useful approach to putting a value on inputs and outputs is to place each internal benefit or cost into one of three categories:

1.   Those inputs and outputs with readily identifiable (and not obviously distorted) market determined money values (prices) ($).

2.   Those impacts for which it is possible to develop credible monetary equivalent values (shadow prices) ("$").

3.   Those impacts for which the values are in whole or in significant part considered to be intrinsically non-monetary in nature (/$\).[3] This might include, if only temporarily, those values for which we presently lack sufficient information to develop monetary equivalent prices.

STANDARD BENEFIT-COST ANALYSIS

When all significant internal project impacts can be assigned monetary values with reasonable confidence, we may carry out a standard BCA (SBCA). The first step of the SBCA is to put all impacts in present value terms by systematically *discounting* future values. We then sum up the benefit and cost streams, and compare the sum of the discounted benefits with the sum of the discounted costs. The calculation procedures for discounting are outlined below. Readers should be aware that while such calculation procedures are widely used in practice, they are not without controversy. For the sake of exposition we touch only briefly on these issues in this chapter and deal with them more fully in Chapter 8.

A Brief Review of Standard Discounting Procedures

A basic consideration in economic analysis is how to treat benefits and costs that are expected to occur in the future. The question goes beyond that of uncertainty and its associated risk. Even if we are certain that some benefit or cost will occur, we still have to find a way to compare the value of a benefit or a cost which occurs today with one occurring one, five, or fifty years in the future.

Economists attempt to put near-term and long-term benefits and costs on an equivalent basis by calculating their present value (PV). The intent of employing a PV is to develop a systematic and consistent framework by which a benefit or cost occurring in the future can be given a revised, lesser value compared to that of the same benefit or cost occurring today. If it were possible to do this accurately, then decisionmakers would be indifferent to the distinction between x worth of benefits or costs today and $x + y$ worth of benefits or costs in the future year.

Standard practice is to devalue, or discount, the nominal value of all future benefits and costs using a single annual rate for the discount factor. The value of the discount factor increases exponentially on a year-by-year basis; hence, the PV of a future benefit or cost declines exponentially as it occurs farther and farther into the future. The PV calculation of any future cost or benefit is:

$$PV_t = (B_t \text{ or } C_t) / (1 + i)^t$$

Where,

B_t is the nominal value of a benefit which occurs "t" number of years in the future.

C_t is the nominal value of a cost which occurs "t" years in the future, $t_0 =$ the present year, $t_1 =$ next year, $t_2 =$ two years into the future, etc.; and $t = 0, 1, 2, 3, ...$ T, ("T" being the final year for which the benefits and costs are counted, i.e., if a benefit or cost occurs in year T+1, we ignore it for project evaluation purposes).[4]

i is the interest or discount rate shown as a fraction of 1 (e.g., an 8% discount rate is 0.08)

The usual way to deal with monetized benefit and cost streams over time is to summarize them into a net present value (NPV) through a formula like the one below or another that is mathematically equivalent.[5]

$$NPV = \sum_{t=0}^{T} (B_t - C_t) / (1 + i)^t$$

i.e., $[(B_0 - C_0) / (1 + i)^0] + [(B_1 - C_1) / (1 + i)^1] + ... + [(B_T - C_T) / (1 + i)^T]$

A few examples should serve to make the calculation procedures clear. If our base year (i.e., the year defined as present for purposes of analysis of this project) is taken as 2000 and a project has an expected cost of $20 million in the year 2004, what is the PV of this cost at a 10% discount rate? In this case, year 2000 = t_o and 2004 = t_4, and the PV = $20 million divided by 1 + discount rate raised to the 4th power, i.e., PV = $20/(1.1)^4$; PV = $20/(1.4641)$; PV = $13.66 million. If we expect a benefit in the year 2004 with a future value of $30 million and the same cost as above, then the NPV = $ 30/(1.4641) - $ 13.66; NPV = $ 20.49 - $13.66; NPV = $ 6.83 million.

In practice, the project evaluation period typically covers a period of fewer than 50 years. While calculation of the NPV for a 30-year project would require more calculations than the simple example above, it would still be computationally similar. Calculating a NPV may be tedious without a computer spreadsheet or programmable calculator, but the process itself is conceptually quite simple.

Clearly, discounting is a mechanistic, and sometimes overly simplistic method of converting future values into the terms of such value as seen from the present. Yet it remains a basic element of SBCA. We can sometimes sidestep issues of discounting, as noted in the following, but such possibilities remain the exception rather than the rule.

Real Versus Nominal Money Values

When considering a discount rate or an interest rate, it is essential to distinguish between nominal and real rates. This distinction is required because of general price inflation. If, for example, the cost of living is increasing at an overall rate of 5% per year, it would on average cost you $105 to purchase today what you could have purchased for $100 last year. If this rate of inflation continues into next year, then your expenditure requirement for the same goods and services would be $110.25 [$100 x $(1.05)^2$]. If your salary is increasing at 5% a year, then your nominal salary is increasing, but not your real income, since your income is only sufficient to purchase the same amount as before. If you deposit money in a savings account with 8% interest, then your real return after inflation adjustment is 2.875% (1.08/1.05).

What if a particular cost or benefit is given in nominal dollars (including the effects of general price inflation) for some future year? In this case you should determine the expected rate of inflation during that period, and eliminate its effects before discounting.[6]

For example, suppose the Finance Ministry expects that the wage bill for a project will be $300 million in 2004. The ministry bases this figure on an expected annual increase in the price index of 8.5% between the base year (2000) and the year for which the bill is projected (2004). What is the real (or constant) PV of this future wage cost in year 2000 dollar values if the project is evaluated at a discount rate of 10%? First we convert the nominal wage bill into real (constant) year 2000 dollar values by dividing the year 2004 nominal wage bill by the projected total cumulative general price increase for the next 4 years: $300 million/$(1.085)^4$ = $216.47 million. Now, we take the real (in terms of constant 2000 dollars) wage bill and discount it to determine the present value: $216.47 million/$(1.1)^4$ = $147.85 million.

Commercial interest rates (those quoted to consumers) are always stated in nominal terms. This must be so, since no one can determine in advance the exact rate of inflation for this year or next, or the year after that. However, the nominal interest rate is based on some real rate of interest, influenced by many factors including the availability of funds to lend, plus the bankers' expectations about general price inflation over the period of the loan.

Choice of Discount Rate

The choice of the discount rate depends largely on three factors: first, the degree of time preference; second, the opportunity cost of investment funds; and third, the perceived riskiness of the project. These matters are elaborated in Chapter 8. For now, we simply note that pure rates of society's time preference are generally assumed to be a few percentage points, for public sector investments. In many private decisions, much higher rates of time preference may be appropriate. As for the opportunity costs of funds invested in the project, these typically range from about 2% to 6% in mature economies, to perhaps 10% to 15% and occasionally even higher in a rapidly growing economy or economic sector. Finally, there is considerable controversy about the inclusion of a risk premium on the discount rate. Markets clearly do add a risk premium on the rates charged for investment funds. However, there are arguments for not doing so with public sector investments. In addition, there are arguments about whether it is acceptable to add a risk premium to the discount rate, rather than using risk to lower the expected value of the return and then discounting that value at a riskless discount rate. These and other issues are considered in Chapter 8. For the present we simply note that the real discount rate for most projects ranges from about 2% to 6% for mature economies, and up to about 15% in rapidly growing economies.

Measures of Project Worth

Net Present Value. The most commonly used summary measure of project worth is the NPV. The NPV is simply the sum of discounted benefits minus the sum of discounted costs. Only projects with a positive NPV should be considered for possible implementation. The higher the NPV, the better the project; hence, projects can be preference-ranked on the basis of their NPVs.

The main limitation on ranking projects by their NPVs is that we cannot immediately determine the investment requirements. When faced with budget constraints, projects with the highest NPV may simply require a greater level of investment funds than are available. Hence, in addition to ranking possible projects by their NPV, we need to know whether the investment costs are within our budget. When we face a budget constraint, but can potentially fund several projects, ranking the potential projects on the basis of the ratio of their benefits to costs and then investing up to the level allowed by our budget enables the investing agency to maximize the total returns from the sum of affordable projects.

Benefit to Cost Ratio. The benefit-cost ratio (B/C) is the sum of discounted benefits divided by the sum of discounted costs.

$$B/C = \sum_{t=0}^{T} [\, B_t \, / \, (1+i)^t \,] \, / \, \sum_{t=0}^{T} [\, C_t \, / \, (1+i)^t \,]$$

Any project with a B/C greater than 1 is potentially acceptable, and the higher the ratio, the better. The advantage of the B/C is that it shows the relative scale of benefits over costs for each dollar invested. Its main limitation is that it tells us nothing about the absolute level of total benefits over total costs or the investment requirement. That is why it is often used in combination with the NPV.

Internal Rate of Return. The internal rate of return (IRR) is the discount rate that would make the discounted sum of benefits equal to the discounted sum of costs. In other words, the IRR is the discount rate that would make the NPV = 0. If a project's IRR is higher than the discount rate used for project evaluation, then the project is potentially acceptable. As in the case of NPV, the higher the IRR, the better the project; however, some analysts consider the IRR inferior to the NPV.

Its weaknesses include the possibility that a project might have more than one discount rate for which NPV = 0; and the fact that the IRR ranking of various projects may not always fully agree with an NPV ranking. However, the IRR is widely used by economic bodies such as the World Bank because it provides an indication of the profitability of the project in percentage terms. Such an indication is not immediately evident in the NPV measure.

Payback Period. The payback period is the number of years required for the undiscounted sum of benefits to equal the undiscounted sum of costs. In other words, how many years must pass for the investor to receive sufficient benefits to cover the costs of his investment? To the extent that the investment context is considered highly unstable, the longer the payback the greater is the level of fundamental risk (i.e., where the entire investment or a large portion of it might be lost). The benefits and costs might be discounted to provide a discounted payback period.

The payback period is a measure of project worth that theoreticians love to hate. It is very crude and, as it tells us nothing about longer-term net benefits, it is potentially misleading. However, its merit is in its simplicity, and it is still commonly employed for one major reason. It provides useful information to potential investors for projects being undertaken under very unstable conditions. For example, if our project might be favored by the present administration but likely would to be discontinued should another government take power, the payback period tells us how long conditions must remain relatively stable in order, at least, to recover the funds invested.

In practice, no competent investor or analyst would use the payback period or discounted payback period as the sole basis for accepting one project over another. However, many businesses continue to use it as an additional indicator of project vulnerability during unstable times. Some businesses use guidelines involving maximum permissible payback periods as a preliminary qualification screen for a potential project. In this situation, only those potential investments that have payback periods beneath some threshold, for instance three to five years, go on to be compared and ranked on the basis of their NPV, B/C, or IRR. Such a two-stage evaluation process is potentially quite useful in cases of highly risky projects, or where the context for investment might change fundamentally within a relatively short period of time.

CONSTRAINED BENEFIT-COST ANALYSIS

Environmental economists have focused a great deal of their attention on the matter of developing monetary equivalent measures of all important values, with the aim of enabling the direct incorporation of environmental considerations in an SBCA. As elaborated in Chapter 7, such efforts have resulted in a number of interesting approaches, but to date significant limitations still apply.

For example, our best monetary equivalent estimates of the value of health damages expressed in terms of the cost of lost productivity and medical expenses tend to leave out the potentially important psychic value of feeling well compared to feeling ill.[7] Likewise, in calculating an NPV for a project that is likely to result in substantial soil erosion, we may be able to identify the expected crop loss and put a monetary value on this loss in agricultural productivity. Yet we may be uncomfortable with the idea of discounting the value of such soil loss when the impacts extend to future generations.[8]

Finally, some important impacts fall into our third category of value: the intrinsically non-monetary. These may include impacts that are measurable in physical terms, but for which we are reluctant to assign a money value. Other impacts, measured in aesthetic or psychic terms, may themselves be unquantifiable. In still other cases, the specific dimensions or even existence of an impact is conjectural and yet we may be concerned about the very possibility of its occurrence. Concern that a particular project might destroy the last habitat of a certain species is one example of the last situation; the fear that bio-engineering might result in the spread of new dangerous pests is another.

Some economists believe that any type of impact can and should be given a shadow price, based on people's willingness to pay for its avoidance. Yet in practice our ability to develop sufficiently credible monetary equivalent measures of value is often quite limited. Almost inevitably there will remain significant values for which no convincing monetized measure is available.

Whenever important project impacts fall into the category of intrinsically non-monetary values, we cannot simply subsume them into the measures of the PV of benefits minus costs. Hence, they do not fit into an SBCA. One way to deal with intrinsically nonmonetary impacts is to carry out a constrained benefit-cost analysis (CBCA). For example, we may simply decide that the health impacts of some projected level of air pollution or the expected rates of soil erosion associated with some project are unacceptable, even though we are reluctant to assign them a dollar value. We might attempt to set ambient or emissions standards to keep these impacts within levels deemed acceptable by the decisionmaker. Only projects that are capable of meeting these standards are considered for assessment. Hence, the BCA is carried out subject to the constraint that projects evaluated must be designed with explicit environmental damage mitigation measures.

In enabling a project to meet the imposed constraint, a competent project designer attempts to determine the most cost-effective method for dealing with the constraint. When we use cost-effectiveness analysis (CEA), we are in effect making something other than maximization of net monetized benefits the objective. Once the alternative objective—for example, improving air quality to meet a basic standard, or keeping soil erosion to some maximum level—is set, we then systematically examine the benefit and cost implications of alternative means of achieving that objective. We would then proceed to evaluate the project with the design feature selected through the cost-effectiveness assessment as a required component of project design.

Sometimes CEA is employed much more broadly. When specific types of environmental improvement are taken to be of overriding importance, we then evaluate a range of possible projects specifically designed to attain these goals. For example, in order to attain a given level of ambient air quality we may wish to determine the most cost-effective combination of cross-sectoral actions to be undertaken in transport, industry, and electric power. Likewise, to meet the explicit goal of limiting soil erosion in a mountainous area, we might attempt to determine the most cost-effective combination of a number of options, including such measures as banning commercial logging, limiting local villagers' consumption of wood for fuel, planting additional trees, and terracing steep slopes. Readers may recognize this approach as the one described in Chapter 4 and put forward by Baumol and Oates (1988) as "efficiency without optimality." While it may be efficient to determine the cost effective means of meeting some environmental goal, CEA does not enable a systematic determination of whether the standard itself is set at an optimal level—one, as explained in Chapter 3, where marginal benefits equal marginal costs.

CBCA and CEA allow us to employ the standard benefit-cost analytic procedures, including discounting, for most project impacts. One advantage of these alternative techniques over SBCA is that, in addition to enabling consideration of non-monetary impacts, they also allow us to remove certain types of impacts from discounting (i.e., in such cases the objective or constraint is not defined in present value terms).

It is important to recognize that using CBCA and CEA for assessing activities to meet environmental goals has its own drawbacks. If we set a great number of environmental objectives or constraints, then we probably will be unable or unwilling to meet them all. And since these approaches put some aspect of environmental quality above the standard economic considerations, inherent in them is the lack of a systematic value-ranking process for such different goods as human health and species protection, or the protection of one natural environment versus another. We may thus find it difficult to select the most important objectives, and work to achieve those first. Remember the concept of opportunity costs. We simply cannot do everything, and when we chose to do one thing, we forgo the opportunity to put our resources toward another use. We must use environmentally constrained BCA and CEA sparingly.

TRADEOFF ASSESSMENT (IMPLICIT VALUATION)

As noted in Chapter 1, assessments are facilitated when as many factors as possible are quantified in a common unit of measure. Economics is about value, and when as many elements in the decision may be assigned acceptable money measures of value, then the assessment process is rendered that much more straightforward. However, as also noted, often it is not possible to monetize all considerations. In economic analyses of the environment we often must engage in multi-objective decisionmaking, in which the pursuit of one objective is tempered by the need to avoid unacceptable costs in terms of losses to other objectives.

One approach to multi-objective, or multi-criteria, decisionmaking using BCA is to carry out a tradeoff assessment, which places an implicit minimum/maximum monetary valuation on the non-monetized impacts. Here, the SBCA is used for those project effects that have prices or have been assigned monetary equivalent values. In this case the SBCA is treated as a first stage of project evaluation; any project with a positive NPV (or acceptable B/C or IRR, etc.), is now subject to a second stage of evaluation.

After the analyst has identified as clearly as possible the project's non-monetary impacts, a decision must be made about whether such non-monetized effects represent an acceptable tradeoff in order to obtain the projects' monetized net benefits. This is not a job for the technical analyst; instead, this value judgment is passed to a decisionmaker, typically a representative of the agency sponsoring the analysis or a government body. The use of tradeoff assessment requires that the decisionmaker be willing to make an implicit minimum or maximum valuation of the non-monetary impacts.

For example, the decisionmaker must be willing to make a statement such as: "the project's expected monetary benefits, of x dollars outweigh (or do not outweigh) the value we place on the loss of y hectares of marshlands which would be filled in as a result of this project." It is important to note here that the decisionmaker does not need to assign an explicit value to the lost marshland in this example, but simply states that the value of these environmental losses is less than (or more than) the x dollars of net present value that is expected from the project. In effect, the decisionmaker is expressing his assessment of society's maximum or minimum willingness to pay for some aspect of environmental quality.

As some readers may have realized, such a tradeoff is always a conscious or unconscious part of almost any decision. Every project approved without this tradeoff assessment carries with it the de facto declaration that the value of the residual non-monetized impacts associated with the final project design, after incorporating any particular environmental mitigation measures, is less than the project's monetized net benefits. Our point here is simply that the decision-making process is improved when this second stage of project evaluation is an open and explicit one.

This process of assessing tradeoffs could, and typically should, be an iterative one. If the first version of the project design is unacceptable on the basis of the residual non-monetized costs, then a revised version of the project with reduced residuals might be developed. This process can be repeated until the residuals are acceptably small, or until the added monetized costs associated with environmental impact reduction results in an unacceptable NPV. In the former case the project could be accepted and in the latter it should be rejected.

Alternatively, in the first instance the project might be developed with a number of alternative designs, each with its own NPV estimate and list of non-monetized residual costs. The cost in monetary terms of reducing the non-monetized impacts would be clear, and the decisionmaker could decide on the appropriate tradeoff between the two.

Clearly, it is possible that the set of non-monetized impacts might include things both of negative and of positive value. Also, while we may not be able to put a precise present value on non-monetized impacts occurring in the future, we still need to consider how to compare present and future values. In practice each of us faces these types of questions every day. Yet what may be common sense decisionmaking at the individual level may be quite difficult to act on at the collective level because of differences in value judgments. In practice it will be the decisionmaker who, hopefully acting as a responsible leader, decides according to the best information available and his or her best judgment of what the common good requires.

For negative non-monetized impacts, we may summarize the tradeoff assessment process as follows:

Step 1:   Carry out a SBCA;

If the NPV > 0 proceed to step 2

Step 2: Decide if the NPV is greater than or less than the value we place on the net non-monetized costs (i.e., is NPV [$ + "$"] > or < the value we place on /$\?)

Where $ = priced values,
         "$" = money equivalent or shadow price values, and
         /$\ = the non-monetized values.

SBCA, CBCA, AND IMPLICIT VALUATION: SOME COMMON FEATURES

The techniques just described share certain features. In each case we must:

1. Identify all project inputs and outputs

2. Decide which ones are relevant (i.e., internal) to the assessment.

3. For relevant inputs and outputs, determine which ones have reliable prices or may be assigned plausible monetary equivalent prices.

4. Select the discount rate for calculating the present value of all monetized values relevant to the assessment.

5. Decide how to deal with non-monetized impacts (e.g., through a CBCA, in a tradeoff assessment) or by simply ignoring them (i.e., by doing only step 1 in an SBCA).

The advantages and disadvantages of each of these analytic procedures are summarized in Appendix 6.A. When using these techniques to look at benefits and costs to society as a whole, we may tend to overlook politically crucial issues about the incidence of benefits and costs among specific groups, including that between present and future generations. Such concerns might be addressed by carrying out group-specific BCA, so as to help in deciding whether compensation to those who lose most heavily is warranted and feasible. It is also a matter related to the distinction between an economic analysis and a financial analysis.

ECONOMIC AND FINANCIAL ANALYSIS

When evaluating a particular project or policy, the first question is from whose perspective should the analysis be carried out? Should it be done from the standpoint of the beneficiaries or from the standpoint of the funding agency? Perhaps it should be done from the standpoint of those who will bear the heaviest costs. The question of which project impacts are relevant to the benefit-cost analysis and which ones are left out depends largely on the perspective of the evaluator.

A basic distinction is between a financial analysis, usually undertaken from the perspective of those implementing the project, their financiers, or those most directly affected; and an economic analysis, which is undertaken from the perspective of society as a whole.   A financial analysis is more narrowly defined than an economic analysis.   It may be made strictly from the perspective of the organization that actually undertakes the investment, or the organization that is most directly affected by a proposed project.   This organization might be a private company, such as a cement factory evaluating a new smoke control system, or a public organization, such as a municipal water authority evaluating a sewage treatment plant.   An economic analysis is usually undertaken by a public agency with broad responsibility for public welfare.

The major specific differences between an economic and a financial analysis are:

1.   Some things considered external to a financial analysis are likely to be considered internal to an economic analysis.   These may include environmental impacts that are not subject to specific legal controls, such as exhaust gases in amounts less than the emissions standards but which are still considered to be potentially harmful.

2.   Market prices are always used in a financial analysis when they exist, but in an economic analysis, sometimes shadow prices and monetary equivalent prices are used to reflect subsidies, taxes, or market imperfections.

3.   In a financial analysis, taxes are treated as a cost and subsidies are treated as benefits (or avoided costs).   In an economic analysis, taxes and subsidies are considered to be merely transfer payments among members of society, which do not add or subtract wealth from society as a whole.   Thus, from the standpoint of overall social welfare, they should not be included in the measurement of benefits and costs.

For example, if a price for a certain good, such as the rental price of an apartment in a government-owned housing block, is subsidized, the level of subsidy should be estimated and eliminated from the calculations in an economic analysis.   The occupant of a government housing development might pay $300 a month in rent.   Yet, if someone living in the same type of apartment in a privately-owned building is paying $800, then the true cost to society for that government apartment is $300 plus the $500 government subsidy.   Even if the apartment does not cost the government anything, there is likely to be an opportunity cost, since the government could presumably set its rates based on market conditions and collect the full market value, which then could be used to support other activities.   However, if we were considering housing costs in a financial analysis, from the perspective of the renter or the government, we would take the rental value to be $300.

Consider another example.   Let us say that a privately-owned electric utility is evaluating a project to control fly ash.   This electric utility undertakes a financial analysis and the government's Environmental Management Board undertakes an economic analysis of the same proposed project for controlling the ash. How might the financial and the economic analyses employ different prices and include different factors?

To the electric utility, the long-term and off-site environmental impacts of disposing the ash in a landfill might be considered external to the financial analysis. In other words, the electric utility might have to dispose of its fly ash in a specific manner and pay a disposal fee, but certain types of impacts, such as leaching contaminates to nearby fisheries, might not be an object of financial concern to the utility if it has no liability in this regard. But in the economic analysis of the Environmental Management Board, such impacts hopefully would be considered relevant, as they affect society as a whole.

Let us say that part of the labor for building temporary storage ash containment ponds is provided by public works' employees who were hired for another purpose but are temporarily under-employed. For the Environmental Management Board's economic analysis, a low or even zero shadow price for labor might be used to reflect its low opportunity cost. In other words, these workers must be paid whether they work or not. The alternative to putting them to work in this situation is to let them sit idle. Thus, the added cost to the government of them working on the pond is zero. However, in the utility's financial analysis the cost of this labor is whatever the government charges for it.

If the power plant burns coal, which is taxed, and the cost of equipment for pollution control is subsidized by the government, in the electric utility's financial analysis the tax on coal is simply part of its cost and the subsidy on pollution control equipment is likewise part of its benefits (in this case, a lower cost). But to the Environmental Management Board's economic analysis, the true cost of coal is calculated by subtracting out the tax. This is done because the tax is a transfer payment from one part of society to another. Likewise, the cost of pollution control equipment in the economic analysis should be calculated by adding in the value of the subsidy.

The aim of the economic analysis is to obtain a true set of values by avoiding the use of prices distorted by taxes and subsidies. It also aims to incorporate certain types of important impacts into the analysis rather than to treat them as externalities. In contrast, the aim of the financial analysis is to determine how the project affects the financial position of the organization undertaking the analysis. Environmental impacts would tend to matter in a financial analysis only to the extent that such impacts are regulated.[9]

Both economic and financial analysis are important and the latter is typically carried out for a given project evaluation in a public sector project in order to determine the project's implications for the government's budget. While we might expect that for public sector projects the economic analysis would be the deciding one, in practice, it may not be so straightforward. While a public sector project with a negative value for its economic analysis and a positive value for its financial analysis would normally be rejected, a project with a positive economic value and a negative financial one might simply be postponed indefinitely due to budget constraints.

There is another important distinction between financial and economic analysis. A financial analysis focuses on income distribution impacts of the project. Often, an economic analysis will not be directly concerned with income distribution so long as the overall welfare of society is advanced, and hence the winners could potentially compensate the losers as called for in Pareto optimality. In other words, equity considerations may be separated from efficiency considerations.

Let us consider an example. A society has a total wealth of 100 units of value, and this society is divided into 3 groups—peasants, warlords, and merchants. It might have the following initial income distribution, where units of value indicate wealth:

> Peasants   :   20 units of value
> Warlords :   50   "   "   "
> Merchants :   30   "   "   "

Now, if this society undertakes an investment project adding another 10 units of value and the new income distribution becomes:

> Peasants   :   22 units of value
> Warlords :   55   "   "   "
> Merchants :   33   "   "   "

In this case the income distribution is unchanged by the project, and the total income increases. Presumably there is no problem here. However, what if after the project, society as a whole still has 10 additional units of wealth, but the income now looks like this:

> Peasants   :   17 units of value
> Warlords :   58   "   "   "
> Merchants :   35   "   "   "

Here one group loses (no surprises about which group), and the other groups gain. Is the investment project a good one? (Remember that society as a whole gained 10 units!) A financial analysis carried out by the warlords or by the merchants would view the investment as a good one; a financial analysis carried out by the peasants would not view it as a good one. In contrast, an economic analysis focuses on the question, does the project make society as a whole better off? If so, by how much? From an economic perspective, the project is a good one because the benefits to the winners more than outweigh the loss to the losers. The winners (in this case, warlords and merchants) could compensate the losers (peasants) with some of the value of their profits and they would still have more wealth than before the project.

Table 6.1
Income (in millions of dollars)

	Without Project	With Project A	With Project B
Group 1	1,000	1,030	1,000
Group 2	3,000	2,950	2,950
Group 3	1,500	1,550	1,560

To return to environmental concerns, consider the following comparison of the net present value of two projects. The goal is to replace an old, unsafe landfill, and the alternatives are a new, state of the art recycling/ and landfill facility (Project A) or a modern waste to energy incinerator (Project B).

Project A NPV = $80 million
Project B NPV = $60 million

The economic analysis would simply take the above information and, if only one of these projects can be undertaken because the projects are mutually exclusive or the budget would allow for only one or the other, it would identify Project A as superior. But let us look at how the benefits might be distributed as shown in Table 6.1.

Group 2 loses if either Project A or B is undertaken. One might point out that under either Project A or B, the net benefits are more than adequate for the gainers to compensate the losers. In other words the government could tax a portion of the profits to Groups 1 and 3 and rebate this to Group 2. Let us say that Group 2 is composed of businesses located in the area of the projected facility site. Group 2's financial analysis would indicate that regardless of whether the facility chosen is a new landfill or a new incinerator the quality of Group 2's work environment, and subsequently its ability to attract customers, decreases. In Group 2's financial analysis, both Projects A and B have a negative value! Of course, if they were confident that the government would in fact compensate them for their loss, then they might drop their objections. Yet in the real world, when the need for compensation is acknowledged or even promised, it is not always forthcoming.

Often in environmental management some groups will support or oppose any particular project on the basis of their own estimate of how it will affect them; if they are likely to be losers, their decision will incorporate the likelihood of actual compensation for their loss. Indeed, in much of the developing world, one of the environmental planner's major tasks is to work out ways in which groups living within or near protected natural areas can benefit from projects designed to maintain the ecological integrity of those areas.

SOME ADDITIONAL FACTORS IN PROJECT EVALUATION

Sunk Costs

Sunk costs are amounts spent prior to the project evaluation period. The important point to remember is that such costs are not relevant for the analysis of future expenditures. For example, the government may have made an initial outlay to build a water pipeline several years ago, but ceased construction when it found that the area was geologically unsuitable. When the government considers the benefits and costs of a new pipeline route today, the money spent on the first pipeline should not be regarded as part of the benefits or costs of the new one. This is, of course, simply common sense. Unfortunately, sometimes a political authority may wish to undertake a project because, "we have already invested too much money in it to back out now."

Consider, another example, a plan to flood a river valley. Let us say that the plan was approved under an assumption of rapid growth in demand for electric power. By the time the dam was partly constructed, revised demand projections made the generating capacity of the dam unnecessary for at least the next decade. Should construction be stopped? The basis for the decision should be the answer to the following question: Are the full benefits of completing this project greater than the additional costs (excluding the sunk costs) of completing it? If so, then the project should go ahead. If not, then it should be rejected, no matter how embarrassing it might be to those who authorized the project in the first place.

Salvage Values

Salvage values are the values of things sellable at the end of a project. Such values should be estimated and appropriately discounted.

Replacement Costs

If some capital items are expected to require replacement during the project evaluation period, then these should be included in the analysis. They should be discounted for the year in which these costs are expected to occur.

CONCLUSION

Benefit-cost analysis provides a framework for the systematic comparison of desired and undesired impacts of our actions. It is an essential part of project evaluation and environmental assessment. Monetizing the value of as many environmental impacts as possible, improves the assessment process. However, important aspects of environmental value often are not adequately reflected in even our best estimates of monetary equivalent value. Hence, approaches such as carrying out a tradeoff assessment of the monetized net values versus the non-monetized residual values as the second stage of the BCA, or conducting the BCA with stringent constraints (i.e., a CBCA), would normally be part of the evaluations for projects in which environmental protection is taken seriously.

A number of important valuation issues associated with BCA are only briefly touched on in this chapter. Chapters 7 and 8 discuss monetization and time-dependent valuation in greater detail. Appendix 6.A summarizes the potentials and limitations of the various approaches and techniques for BCA. Appendix 6.B presents two illustrative examples of how BCA and its variations might be applied. Some readers may find this useful in making the information provided in this chapter more concrete. Appendix 6.C outlines the basic features and uses of Life Cycle Analysis, a framework for evaluating the environmental effects or consequences of a product or process across its entire life-cycle (also referred to as a cradle-to-grave analysis).

APPENDIX 6.A

BENEFIT COST ANALYSIS TECHNIQUES: MAJOR ADVANTAGES AND DISADVANTAGES

Standard Benefit Cost Analysis (SBCA or simply BCA)

Definition: Each relevant (internal) effect is labeled as a benefit or a cost and assigned a monetary value; values of future effects are discounted, and the net benefits calculated.

Advantages: It is precise, explicit, and the decision rules are well established.

Disadvantages: An SBCA excludes non-monetized impacts, and some of the monetary equivalent values it includes may be questionable. The treatment of time values and uncertainty in SBCA may not be acceptable to some groups and may be challenged as insufficiently comprehensive or unfair in terms of intergenerational equity.

Constrained Benefit/Cost Analysis (CBCA)

Definition: The objective is to maximize monetized net values, but to do so in a way that does not violate stated environmental quality constraints.

Advantages: It sets limits on selected non-monetized impacts without making these the primary objective. Like a cost-effectiveness analysis, it may allow us to sidestep the rigid discounting of selected future impacts.

Disadvantages: It creates the problem of how to select and rank possible constraints from a potentially infeasibly large list.

Cost-Effectiveness Analysis (CEA)

Definition: The objective is to minimize the cost of reaching some predetermined goal.

Advantages: Like CBCA, it allows us to deal with goals other than those fully valued in monetary terms. It can help sidestep rigid discounting of the time values associated with the goal.

Disadvantages: Again like CBCA, CEA raises the question of how the non-monetary goals are to be selected and ranked in the first place.

Tradeoff Assessment (Implicit Minimum/Maximum Valuation)

Definition: Certain important impacts are left in non-monetary terms and the question becomes one of whether the net non-monetized costs are valued by the decisionmaker sufficiently highly to forgo the project's net monetized benefits.

Advantages: It incorporates non-monetary impacts directly into the evaluation process, requiring the decisionmaker to implicitly assign minimum or maximum values for these.

Disadvantages: It may be too flexible, leaving the decisionmaker with too much room to impose his or her own preferences or presenting an insufficiently structured evaluation context; in some cases the decisionmaker may not wish to have the trade-offs between dollars and the environment made so explicit.

APPENDIX 6.B

SIMPLE ILLUSTRATIVE EXAMPLES OF BENEFIT COST ANALYSIS AND COST EFFECTIVENESS ANALYSIS

A Dredging Project

Let us begin with a relatively simple example. Assume that a project to make a deep water port by dredging a shallow inlet has the annual money benefits and costs as shown in Table 6B.1. The direct costs are mostly for the dredging work and the benefits, such as port fees or increased economic activity, are in money terms and indirect money terms. Assume all costs and benefits are in real 2000 dollars.

Table 6B.1
Project Returns

Year (t=)	Cost Million $	Benefits Million $
2000 (0)	50	0
2001 (1)	100	0
2002 (3)	80	10
2003 (4)	0	20
2004 (5)	0	40
2005 (6)	0	40
2006 (7)	0	40
2007 (8)	0	40
2008 (9)	15	20
2009 (10)	0	40
2010 (11)	0	40
2011 (12)	0	40
2012 (13)	0	40
2013 (14)	0	40
2014 (15)	0	40
2015 (16)	0	40
2016 (17)	0	40
2017 (18)	0	40
2018 (19)	15	20

- What is the PV in the year 2000 of the cost stream discounted at 10%? It is $50 + [$100 / (1.1)] + [$80 / (1.1)^2] + [$15 / (1.1)^9] + [$15 / (1.1)^{19}] = $215.84 million.

- What is the PV of the benefits at a 10% discount rate? It is $246.65.

- What is the NPV for this project? PV of Benefits minus PV of Costs = $246.65 - $215.84 = $30.81 million.

- What is the B/C for this project? It is $246.65 / $215.84 = 1.14.

- What is the IRR for this project? You might try to calculate this yourself, but clearly it is more than 10%. (why?)

- What is the payback period? It is 8 years.

From an environmental management point of view, what is left out of the above analysis and how might we incorporate it into our assessment? The environmental impacts of the project are not considered. These might include: ecological effects of the dredging itself, combustion products of the energy used to power the equipment, and the danger of oil spills and other emissions by the ships using the new port. These might be handled through a tradeoff assessment or a CBCA.

SO_2 Emissions Control Project

Let us assume that a political decision has been made to attain a certain ambient air quality standard. Here, the analytic problem is finding the least cost method of attaining the standard. Consider two basic approaches to reduce sulfur dioxide emissions from industry, and two possible implementation levels for each approach.

Project Option # 1: Require Use of Low Sulfur Fuel

Implementation Level:

a) switch from 2.5% sulfur to 1.0% sulfur fuel
   PV Costs : $550 million
   Benefits : Lower SO_2 emissions by 60%

b) switch from 2.5% to 0.5% sulfur fuel
   PV Costs : $800 million
   Benefits : Lower SO_2 emissions by 80%

Project Option # 2: Flue Gas Desulfurization (FGD)

Implementation Level:

a)   mandate FGD use by largest 20% of all industrial firms
     PV Costs : $200 million
     Benefits : Lower SO_2 emissions by 40%

b)   mandate FGD use by largest 60% of industrial firms
     PV Costs : $ 800 million
     Benefits : lower SO_2 emissions by 70%

We can see that Project Option # 1(b) is clearly more cost effective than project Option # 2(b), since, for the same cost, Option 1(b) reduces sulfur dioxide by 80% compared to the 70% for option 2(b). Hence, option 2(b) may be dropped from further consideration, as it is, at least in one respect, inferior to 1(b) and in no respect is superior to it. (In the terms of decision theory option 2(b) is *dominated by* option 1(b).)

We can also see that for each 10% reduction in total SO_2 levels, the costs for the options would be ranked as follows:

Option 2(a) $50 million
Option 1(a) $92 million
Option 1(b) $100 million

However, we should be careful here, because option 2(a) only gives us a 40% emission reduction while the others give us 60% or 80% reduction. If the government were to decide that sulfur levels must be reduced by at least 50%, then Option 2(a) is unacceptable and Option 1(a) meets this goal at a lower cost than Option 1(b).

APPENDIX 6.C

LIFE CYCLE ANALYSIS

The purpose of this short appendix is to introduce and briefly describe in rather broad terms life-cycle analysis (LCA). LCA is a procedure used in the field of industrial ecology to evaluate systematically the environmental implications and impacts of a material, product, or process across its entire life-cycle (i.e., cradle-to-grave analysis) (EPA, 1993; Graedel and Allenby, 1995). LCA is most often used in material selection and product evaluation, and to make comparisons among alternatives based on such environmental impact measures as: resources depleted, environmental wastes generated (air emissions, water effluents, solid wastes), embodied energy, recycling and waste management practices, energy used during service life, indoor air quality, and others. As customarily defined, LCA involves four distinct and related steps: goal setting and definition of scope, inventory analysis, impact assessment, and improvement analysis.

The first step, goal setting and definition of scope, is primarily concerned with identifying the purpose of the LCA and the drawing of study boundaries (i.e., determining what environmental impacts will be assessed and to what degree). It involves decisions about what factors will be evaluated and what, if any, indirect environmental effects are to be included (e.g., including fuel used in mining equipment but excluding the energy embodied in the equipment itself). This step also entails assumptions about geographic/location specificity and assumptions about how generic to make the LCA. This is important in the assessment stage as many impacts on ecological systems and human health and safety are very site and location specific. For example, soil erosion will produce greater environmental impacts when resource extraction is done on steep sloped sites as opposed to relatively flat sites.

The second step is to identify and quantify energy and raw material inputs at each life cycle stage as well as the environmental outputs—land disturbances, solid wastes, water effluents, and air emissions at each life-cycle stage. The significance of resource and energy use and resulting environmental effects and associated impacts will vary considerably by life-cycle stage. The inventory analysis step attempts to quantify as best as possible and within system boundaries these life-cycle inputs and outputs. This step may be streamlined by using qualitative data for some environmental outputs when quantitative data are too costly to collect or simply unavailable or inappropriate given the boundaries placed on the LCA.

The third step is the most difficult and contentious. It involves translating the resource and energy inputs and environmental outputs or effects (e.g., amounts and types of solid wastes, water effluents, air emissions) into ecological, human health and safety, resource depletion, other impacts. For example, the inventory analysis might quantify the amount of land disturbed from the logging of old-growth forests. This disturbance, measured in kilogram of soil eroded, would then be translated in the impact assessment step into increased sedimentation and, perhaps, harm to aquatic life. Typically impact assessment involves two stages—classification and characterization. Classification is the grouping of all environmental outputs that give rise to a given environmental impact, such as emissions of CO_2, CH_4, and other gases from fuel use during resource extraction and product transport, and from manufacturing processes that give rise to global warming. Characterization is the definition of impacts (e.g., global warming) and the development of appropriate indicators to characterize the impact, e.g., a global warming equivalency index.

Impact assessment is relatively straightforward when dealing with impacts of a global or even regional nature, such as global warming and acidification. However, a difficulty arises when environmental outputs can only be assessed with reference to specific sites and have relatively localized consequences and cannot be easily aggregated across life-cycle stages. Some examples include impacts associated with resource extraction and land disturbance, impacts from water effluents, and impacts from solid waste generation. The last step,

Improvement analysis, is designed to identify systematically opportunities to reduce or prevent environmental impacts associated with resource and energy input use throughout the life-cycle of the material, product, or process.

As practiced, LCA has been subject to substantial criticism on the grounds that it is too data intensive and, generally, too expensive and time consuming to undertake detailed life cycle inventories let alone translating these inventories into impacts and recommendations for product improvements. Because of the cost of conducting detailed LCAs and the difficulty in quantifying certain types of impacts, reduced form or abridged approaches to LCA are now being advanced Graedel et al. (1995)

NOTES

1. Some texts use the term Cost-Benefit Analysis (CBA). CBA and BCA represent the same process, with a different nominal emphasis.

2. In this text, when dealing with efforts to internalize externalities we use the term monetary equivalent values, regardless of whether such accounting prices are adjusted market prices or come from use of approaches to monetize unpriced values. In both cases, the purpose is to assign an appropriate price to something that has either an incorrect money price or no money price at all.

3. The symbols "$" and /$\ for monetary equivalent and non-monetized values, respectively, are used throughout this text. Other texts may use different notation.

4. Some texts use the convention of the current year as "t_1". When this convention is used, then the present value formula becomes: $PV_t = (B_t$ or $C_t) / (1 + i)^{t-1}$.

5. Recall that any value raised to the zero power equals 1.

6. When a report does not state the expected rate of inflation, it is usually an indication that the future values included in it are in real (constant) dollar terms (in terms of the purchasing power for some base year).

7. Some people presumably would be willing to assign a specific monetary value to the difference in comfort. Methods to elicit such values are described in Chapter 7. We note here however, that many people might prefer to leave the valuation of such feelings in non-monetary terms until forced to evaluate a very specific situation, such as in a trade-off assessment (outlined later in this chapter).

8. As described more fully in Chapter 8, at any positive discount rate, an impact occurring more than about 50 years into the future is going to have a relatively low present value. Thus, it will not have much of an effect with respect the NPV.

9. Of course, some types of environmental impacts may not be strictly against the law, but could result in negative publicity for those responsible. To the extent that this is true, environmental degradation might represent a relevant cost and hence become part of the financial analysis.

7

Monetary Valuation Techniques:
Potentials and Limitations

VALUING BENEFITS AND COSTS

Economic assessments of environmental issues are more precise when as many inputs and outcomes as possible are measured in a common unit of value, such as money. We begin our discussion of monetary valuation by reviewing several important points about the economist's perspective on the environment:

1. Values tend to be variable rather than fixed; they change in response to circumstances.

2. In order to maximize net benefits, we should find the level of action where the incremental (marginal) costs are equal to the incremental (marginal) benefits. (This rule applies to situations in which benefits and costs continue to rise with increasing levels of an activity.)

3. As a result of externalities, we tend to over-produce and under-price certain activities, including the generation of pollution and other forms of environmental degradation.

These insights, while rather intuitive on reflection, are sometimes overlooked in environmental assessments. Even when such rules are recognized and appreciated, they are sometimes hard to act on, since many important environmental values are not expressed in money terms. For example, decisionmakers might be convinced that people benefit from improved air quality, yet we typically find it difficult to measure this benefit with much precision.

What does this mean for environmental management? First, it often leaves the economist arguing for the acceptance of certain general principles, such as declining marginal utility, and for the application of particular analytic approaches, such as willingness to pay, rather than arguing for a particular decision.   Second, it may translate into the placing of constraints on the quantitative component of economic assessments, as only indirect information may be available for some environmental impacts. We should keep in mind that, in the final analysis, the economist's estimates of value often is as much, or more, a matter of judgment and rough approximation than of scientific rigor and hard evidence. The economist working on environmental management problems is often unable to give planners firm, completely objective answers. Instead, the more appropriate role is to guide the overall assessment process, and to provide partial measurements for the reasonably quantifiable aspects of the benefit and cost streams. Before we consider techniques for monetary valuation, let us first consider the limitations on determining how people value public goods.

A BRIEF LOOK AT PUBLIC GOODS AND VALUATION

Public goods are goods and services for which one person's consumption has virtually no impact on another's ability to enjoy it as well. It is usually difficult to exclude non-paying consumers of a public good; in other words, even if the good or service is "owned" by someone, the owner cannot successfully impose a fee on those who enjoy that good or service. Consider someone who builds a beautiful building. The public good is expressed in people's enjoyment of the view, which is equally available to all and in unlimited supply. One person's enjoyment does not limit that of others, and the building's owner would be hard pressed to develop a way to charge people for the view. Air is another example of a public good. One person's breathing has little effect on another's ability to breathe. Likewise, a building owner cannot charge for the air his occupants breathe, though he might charge for cleaning the air brought in from outside.

For such reasons, public goods are often unpriced, or their cost of provision is divided equally among all potential users, in the form of a general tax. Thus, when a society sees the need to fund a library or school, to provide for national defense, to maintain a police force, or to protect a watershed, the government may impose a tax on all members of the society.

The implications of public goods for environmental management are many. Much of the natural environment is by its nature a public good: one person's use of environmental services such as clean air does not significantly diminish others' use, and it is often difficult to exclude non-payers from enjoyment of environmental goods and services. Additionally, public goods typically are not incorporated into market mechanisms. The resulting lack of systematic pricing creates a greater need for public sector intervention. The government then is prompted to take the place of a market allocation process for providing environmental goods and services, or to ration access to them.

Public goods often present difficulties for economic analyses because they are unpriced and because it is difficult to determine just how much people really are willing to pay in order to continue to enjoy them. We may readily measure the value of private goods by noting their market price, which is a reflection of willingness to pay. We are offered no similar indication of how much people value features of environmental quality, and further, of how much people are willing to pay, in terms of taxes or higher product prices, to preserve that quality.

By now you are familiar with the economists' argument that people's willingness to pay for a cleaner environment depends on two factors. First, it depends on the value people place on each additional increment of improvement in quality. This in turn depends in part on the state of the environment, and how much improvement in it is perceived to be necessary. Second, willingness to pay depends on the cost of each increment of improvement. It all begins with society's environmental values.

A Taxonomy of Environmental Values

The natural environment provides a variety of essential services, some of which are indirectly reflected in economic transactions, and others which, though unpriced, are of sufficient value that people clearly would be willing to pay for them if required. Regardless of how such values are categorized, it is vital that the taxonomy be comprehensive so as to include all important types of value. Figure 7.1 illustrates one possible taxonomy of environmental values.

One useful distinction is between values for short- and long-term environmental services. Within the category of near- to mid-term services, one may distinguish between direct uses and *indirect uses* (as well as existence values). For example, ground water systems (aquifers) provide immediate and near-term benefits such as clean drinking water. If necessary, these systems could be replaced by man-made ones, such as surface reservoirs with filtration facilities, but this cost would need only be incurred if the natural systems fail to function. Likewise, the existence of a diverse ecosystem in a protected area may have indirect uses, such as providing a natural reservoir of genetic information. This information can be called on at any time, and could become of direct use in the event that, for example, a particular crop proves vulnerable to a new breed of pest, and new genetic crop varieties are called for. It also may be that even where some feature of the environment, such as one particular species, provides no apparent economic service, its existence still might be valued.

Near-term direct and indirect uses and existence values have counterparts in the longer-term. We may wish to preserve some feature of the existing environment so that there will be the option of exploiting it later. Option values often include an element of risk aversion, in which the mere existence of a wider set of options for future action to meet unanticipated conditions is

Figure 7.1
Taxonomy of Environmental Values

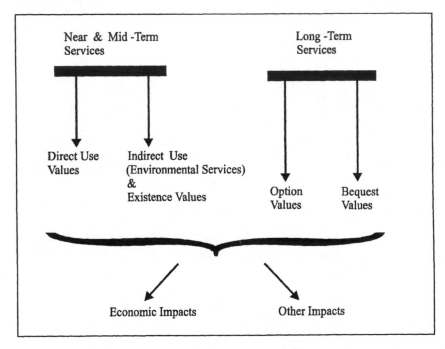

considered beneficial. For example, we may not know the specific economic or existence values preserved along with an ecologically diverse area, but we may value the presumed reduction in the risk of losing potentially highly desired genetic information. Also, we may wish to pass some features of the natural environment on to future generations. Each type of value may be reflected in market transactions, as a price for goods and services bought and sold in the market (e.g., the sale of ecologically friendly merchandise). It also may have a non-market impact, which could be illustrated by a change in personal behavior, such as a commitment to personally refrain from purchasing certain types of products whose production harms threatened species.

Clearly, the taxonomy laid out in Figure 7.1 represents a highly heterogeneous set of values, some of which have potential for overlap. In some instances particular types of value might be easy to identify in principle, but difficult to measure. What is important is that decisionmakers consider the range of potentially relevant values. Failure to do so increases the risk that some important aspect of environmental values may be left out of the assessment process. We will return to this point when considering ways to impute a monetary equivalent measure of value for unpriced environmental impacts. Let us now look at some of the standard techniques for monetizing the value of those environmental impacts that, according to economists, can reasonably be represented in monetary terms.

MONETARY VALUATION TECHNIQUES

It is important to attempt to monetize that which is potentially monetizable. A number of classification schemes may be used. For our purposes we group the most common approaches to monetary evaluation of environmental impacts into several broad categories: direct cost (defensive expenditure) estimates; hedonic pricing; and contingent valuation. Each of these is considered below.

Direct Cost Techniques

Direct cost estimates are based on the idea that if people spend money to protect themselves, others, or their property from environmental damage, then the value they place on avoiding such impacts is at least as great as the level of such defensive expenditures. In addition, if they incur penalties such as lost work time or schooling from poor environmental conditions, then the value of such losses should be included in the minimum value estimate of the direct benefit losses.

For example, suppose that high levels of industrial SO_2 are causing upper respiratory problems in the local population. Near-term direct costs (defensive expenditures) might include additional doctor consultations and related expenses, such as the purchase of medicine. Near-term direct costs also might include greater use of air-conditioning in the hopes of filtering out some of the pollution. In addition, the value of lost work time or reduced productivity due to SO_2-related illness should be considered as a direct cost. The money value of lost work time would generally be equivalent to the value of lost productivity, whether this was absorbed by the employee in the form of lost wages or by the employer in the form of reduced output or the cost of replacement labor. Since SO_2 corrodes metallic surfaces, persons with property in areas of high SO_2 concentrations would likely incur added near-term and mid-term direct costs in the form of more frequent maintenance or replacement for vulnerable materials.

From a longer-term perspective, we might estimate the (discounted) economic value of the effects of lower school performance for children and the additional health care for those suffering the cumulative effects of chronic exposure to lung-damaging pollutants. In the case of lost schooling, this might conceivably be estimated in terms of lower educational attainment and the associated long-term change in earning potential. If we are in a position to develop reasonable estimates of such near- and longer-term direct costs, then we may say these likely represent a lower bound on the value people place on avoiding such impacts.

In a similar way, the dredging of an estuary may eliminate a spawning ground for a commercial offshore fishery. One might measure a portion of the direct environmental costs of the dredging in terms of the near- and longer-term economic losses to that fishery. Likewise, the money value of part of the environmental damage caused by a project which results in increased soil erosion in an agricultural area can be represented by the discounted lost income associated with the reduced crop yields over time.[1] Such monetizable losses represent a potentially important cost that should be reflected in the measures of project worth (as outlined in Chapter 6) for the dredging project.

Another common form of direct cost estimation is to consider the value of travel cost. This technique attempts to measure the amount of money people spend in order to attain some unpriced good such as an environmental amenity. For example, if a family of four travels 100 kilometers to a scenic area and spends $40 for transport, $30 for food, $5 for maps, and a $5 admission fee, then clearly they value that trip at least as much as the $80 out-of-pocket expenses. Through a survey of users to the scenic area, it may be possible to estimate how much those persons from various distances spend in travel costs. If we assume that direct substitution between travel costs and possible higher admission fees to the scenic area is possible, then we could construct a demand curve for use of the area, with those persons travelling the greatest distance effectively paying more than those who travel a shorter distance. With such a demand curve one could then calculate the estimated consumer surplus (see Chapters 2 and 3) and use this as an indication of the value people place on having that environmental amenity.

Some of the various types of costs in the category of direct cost estimates are relatively easy to measure, while others are more difficult. In addition, the use of each of these approaches typically involves assumptions about the comparability of different costs. A more basic question is whether individual preferences, as reflected in direct cost expenditures, accurately reflect the values of society as a whole, particularly where some of the impacts may be long-term and extend to future generations.

With these limitations noted, we emphasize that among the broad categories of valuation techniques available, direct cost estimates are, in general, the most reliable and easiest to calculate. They are however, also the most limited in scope. In all cases, direct cost estimates represent a *minimum monetized representation of value* for the unpriced impacts of concern.

One example of the direct costs of air pollution came out of a series of respiratory health surveys in Hong Kong in the late 1980s and early 1990s. It was found that school children living in an industrial part of the territory had approximately a 3% higher likelihood of visiting a doctor for such symptoms as chronic cough, sore throat, and nasal problems, compared to a control group in an area with much cleaner air. After a ban on high sulfur fuel oil by industry greatly lowered ambient sulphur dioxide and particulate levels in the industrial area, the excess risk of visiting a doctor for these symptoms disappeared (Ong et al. 1991; Tam et al., 1994). Hence, one direct cost borne by people in the industrial area was more doctor visits for their children. This cost could be easily monetized and scaled to the relevant school age population. In an economic analysis such a cost could then be directly subtracted from the costs to industry of the mandated switching to higher quality fuel.

In a review of direct costs of corrosion due to air pollution, particularly sulfur dioxide, one study found a range of damages valued at between about $3 and $28 per person per year in Europe and the United States (OECD, 1989). (These prices date from the early to mid-1980s and would need to be scaled appropriately for current dollar values).

As for travel costs estimates, a set of studies carried out for public lands in the upper northeast of New South Wales, Australia estimated the market value of recreation and tourism at 437 million Australian dollars (A$) and an overall economic value, including estimated user (consumer) surplus, of A$1.1 billion (RCAC, 1996). Beaches accounted for over one half of the values cited. At about 2.2 million visitors per year, the average value of a recreation visit is about A$500 (in 1995 A$ values). These estimates of value illustrate that it is often feasible to develop such estimates either as part of an assessment process for decisionmaking purposes or as part of an *expost facto* assessment of a policy implemented earlier.

Hedonic Pricing Techniques

Hedonic pricing approaches estimate the value people place on some apparently unpriced good or service, by attempting to separate that component from a larger expenditure decision. The most common application of this is in property values. For example, if two otherwise identical houses are in areas with much different air quality, and there is a significant difference in the market value of these two houses, it might be attributable at least in part to the value people place on living in a cleaner airshed.

Another application of this approach is wage differentials between two otherwise comparable jobs with clearly different risks in terms of occupational health or safety. Lower wage levels in the less risky occupation may indicate the willingness of workers in the less risky job to give up some potential income in order to work in a safer environment; the reverse would be true for those working in the more risky environment.

Hedonic pricing techniques are similar to direct cost estimates in that they take actual expenditures (or foregone income) as an indication of monetary equivalent value of otherwise unpriced values. In this sense both hedonic pricing and direct cost techniques are market-oriented approaches to valuation.

One obvious problem with the use of hedonic pricing techniques is how to ensure that other factors are held constant so as to enable accurate measurement of the causal factor in question. In many cases it may be virtually impossible to identify two properties that are alike in all important respects, except for the environmental quality of the area in which they are located. The market prices for similar properties in different locations might vary due to differences in the distance to major employment or commercial centers, prestige, crime rates, and so on. In the case of wage differentials, we may face the problem of imperfect local labor markets. If unemployment is significant, workers in the riskier industry may not be able to command higher wages even though they are aware of the health risk, and prefer to be compensated for it.

In practice, the problems noted above are addressed by basing estimates on rather extensive data sets from numerous locations or situations in which the effects of a wide range of different factors might be accessed as part of the analysis (e.g., through the statistical technique of multiple regression). Yet, beyond the question of model specification, another issue is that the data available to the analysts often are not sufficiently detailed to clearly separate the environmental or health/safety values from others. Finally, the estimates obtained from hedonic pricing studies are greatly influenced by the context in which they are measured. It may be highly questionable to apply findings from one area, such as California, and attempt to draw implications for an up-coming environmental management decision in Illinois, let alone in Kyushu, Japan or Shanghai. But because hedonic pricing studies, like other approaches to monetization, are often expensive and difficult to do in a credible way, very often the only data available to suggest even a preliminary range of monetized values is from a study done some time ago for some place far away. Our point here is that such data from elsewhere should be considered if it is the only data available, and that at most it should be treated as suggestive of the broad range of values that might be applicable in the case at hand, rather than as in any way definitive.

With these limitations noted, we stress that where data availability and analytic resources permit, hedonic pricing techniques may be quite helpful. One review of attempts to measure the effects of pollution on property values shows estimates of the percentage fall in property values compared to the percentage increase in pollution ranging 0.01% to 0.50% (OECD, 1989). In other words, if pollution were to increase by 10% in a particular area, property prices would tend to fall by 0.1% to 5.0%. Housing prices in this study were most sensitive to particulates and sulfation. While the ranges cited here are obviously very wide, they nonetheless suggest a reasonable bound for this one aspect of how the market values environmental impacts. Put simply, environmental quality is not likely to be a dominant factor in housing prices, but it is not likely to be entirely left out either.

In a review of the data on the effect of ambient noise levels above the baseline of 55 db on property values in the United Kingdom (U.K.), one study estimated property value loss at 32.8 billion pounds (1993 prices) which was shared among some 13.4 million households (Maddison et al., 1996). The average loss was roughly £5,000 per household in areas with noise levels from 65 to 70 db and over £9,000 for those households situated in areas where levels were 75db and above. Here again, economic valuation assessments are useful for the ranges of relevant values they suggest. Housing prices in Jakarta, Sao Paulo or New Orleans may be more or less responsive than those in the U.K. study but in the absence of local information the U.K. data may serve as a useful first approximation of what the range of local responses elsewhere might be .

Contingent Valuation Techniques

Contingent valuation (CV) uses questionnaire surveys in an attempt to measure how much people would be willing to pay to protect the environment and to avoid environmental risk, or how much they would be willing to accept as compensation for the loss of some environmental service or amenity. The basic difference between contingent valuation techniques and direct cost estimates and hedonic pricing is that whereas the latter two attempt to observe preferences and values as exhibited in actual market transactions, contingent valuation approaches attempt to elicit information on preferences in hypothetical situations.

Within the general class of CV approaches it is useful to distinguish between those surveys that assess willingness to pay or to accept compensation through direct questions, from those that attempt to indirectly indicate revealed preferences. The direct questions might ask respondents to make budgeting decisions, to assess tradeoffs among conflicting goals, or to bid for various choices. The revealed preference questions might involve choosing from among alternative combinations of environmental and other goods (with or without explicit prices), and then using the ranking to reveal preferences for specific items within the combinations.

The advantage of contingent valuation techniques is that in principle they are capable of including the full range of environmental values and of reflecting the full value the respondent places on something. This is in contrast to information on direct costs and hedonic prices revealed in market transactions which indicate only minimum value or partial values.[2] This is because in addition to estimates of direct or indirect use value as reflected in the market situations, estimates of option, existence, or bequest values also might be obtained through contingent valuation surveys.

Despite the advantages in terms of its potential breadth of coverage, in general, contingent valuation techniques are the least certain and reliable of the broad classes of monetary valuation techniques considered here. The basic problems are those of honesty in response, due to an intentional or unintentional bias, and accuracy of the judgment of respondents.

With regard to honesty and accuracy, answers may be biased by the respondents' desire to see the survey arrive at a particular finding. For example, if people are questioned about the value of improving air quality, those whose jobs might be adversely affected, such as employees of a polluting factory, might consciously understate the value they place on improved air quality. More generally, when the respondent is asked about a hypothetical situation, then she or he may feel that no personal gain or loss is involved, and so may not carefully evaluate the alternatives outlined in the survey.

Beyond the obvious problem of the respondents' lack of sufficient information about the specific issue being raised, the presumption of who will be expected to pay for an environmental goal is also a major factor. For example, if asked about willingness to pay to clean-up a toxic dump, the answer might well depend on whether the respondent assumes that the cost will be borne by the polluter or by society at large. This is the free rider problem in which someone tends to support something if he or she presumes that others will pay for it.

To continue on this point of who will pay, it is useful to note the distinction between willingness to pay (WTP) in order to secure some environmental benefit and willingness to accept compensation (WTA) for some environmental loss. While in concept there presumably would be a symmetry between these two (e.g., the level of WTP to acquire some benefit should be in the same general range as the WTA compensation to accept this loss), in practice they may differ significantly. Why might this be so? An important factor may be how the respondent to the CV survey views the assignment of environmental property rights (as discussed in Chapter 4). If the respondent feels that some environmental amenity is his (or mankind's) *by right*, then he or she may demand more in compensation for its loss than he or she would be willing to pay if he or she had to. Such distinctions need to be kept in mind when designing CV questionnaires and in assessing their findings.

As with the other valuation techniques, we urge readers to keep in mind the limitations of contingency valuation. However, we also hope readers will come to appreciate that in certain situations, where the issues are clear and the surveys well designed and carried out, contingency valuation may provide useful insights into a wider range of environmental values than it is possible to assess in other ways.

The potential application of CV is quite wide. We present here a few brief examples to suggest something of this range. One study by Hall et al. (1992) showed WTP by respondents in California for avoiding such symptoms as cough, headache, eye and throat irritation, and congestion due to ozone and particulates exposure ranging from about $0.50 to $7.25 per symptom episode (in 1990 U.S. dollar values). When combined with their estimates of exposure, the analysts estimated the value of avoiding exceedances of the air quality standards within a specific air basin. Another study from California by Richer (1995) estimated the willingness of state residents to pay for desert protection to be between $177 to $448 million per year. He feels this information is useful in assessing the *California Desert Protection Bill of 1993*. In another ecological protection case, Gonzales-Caben and Loomis (1997) estimate the local WTP of preserving from reservoir development a set of stream systems in Puerto Rico at about $27 per household. They recommend that the total monetary values that come out of this estimation ($11 million for one river and $13 million for another) be compared to the cost of alternative sources of water supply; namely, repairing leaking water supply pipes and in-home water conservation measures.

General Comments on Monetary Valuation

The three general categories of monetary valuation outlined here (direct cost estimates, hedonic pricing, contingent valuation) are broad classes of techniques that include more types of tools than have been illustrated here. For example, when an area is classified as protected, the implicit minimum value of the ecological and/or possibly cultural values for the site is the foregone income from development. In other words, the opportunity costs of withholding the area from development constitute a form of direct cost (see also Chapter 6). Financial settlements from environmental-related litigation might possibly reflect some elements of direct costs and hedonic pricing, while being largely based on some form of contingent valuation.

It is probably best to view the options for putting a monetary value on unpriced environmental impacts as being: first, partial rather than comprehensive; and second, indicative or suggestive rather than definitive. In other words, while such techniques are useful, one must keep in mind the significant limitations that often exist on our ability to *fully* monetize environmental values, and to fully and directly incorporate environmental impacts into standard benefit cost analyses. Chapter 11 presents more detailed examples of some of the techniques presented here.

THE MARGINAL BENEFITS AND COSTS OF
MONETARY VALUATION FOR DECISIONMAKING

The *efficient level of action* is where the marginal benefits of the next increment of action equal the marginal costs of taking that incremental step (see Chapters 2 and 3). Clearly, this rule is relevant to a wide range of situations, including decisions about the appropriate level of monetization in a policy assessment or project appraisal. Development of reliable and convincing measures of the monetary equivalent value requires resource inputs, such as time, money, and expertise, each of which has a cost. The decision-making process is improved when as many inputs and outcomes as possible are measured in a common unit of value, such as money. It should also be clear that the monetization process should continue only so long as the value to decisionmakers of additional precision in the benefit-cost analysis (BCA) is greater than the cost of attaining that degree of added precision.

The basic issue is, what is the cost of developing additional monetized estimates of value, and, noting the conceptual limitations of the various techniques, what are the resultant benefits in terms of added precision in assessing the problem? Even when the conceptual limitations of the techniques are not sufficiently serious as to undermine the credibility of estimates which might be produced, the costs of conducting adequately designed studies to quantify and put a money value on such impacts tend to be high. Yet the value of the added precision to decisionmaking when a particular impact is monetized may be quite modest unless such information significantly changes the level of net monetized costs or benefits. In other words, in assessing the desirablity of undertaking the next step in monetization of specific unpriced values, the analyst needs to consider both the likely benefits to the precision of the decision-making process and the costs of obtaining that increment of added precision.

Since the value of additional information for decisionmaking is subjective, objectively determining the appropriate level of monetization for any particular case is generally not possible. However, as with much of economic theory, a basic concept may prove to be quite useful even when it cannot be precisely applied. So even if we cannot determine a specific answer, it is important to ask the question, how much more precise does the decision-problem become if the value of this particular impact is monetized?

As noted previously, there typically will be some residual non-monetized (and often non-monetizable or non-quantifiable) impacts that necessitate some form of tradeoff assessment between the net monetized values and the non-monetized impacts as part of the BCA. The basis of that assessment is the response to the question, *is the value of the non-monetized impacts greater than or less than the monetized net costs?* If yes, the intervention is justified. Such implicit valuation of minimum (or maximum) valuation for the non-monetized impacts may not be as precise as analysts would like, but it may be precise enough for the needs of a policy decision. The issue is how extensive the residual non-monetized impacts should be. The appropriate level of valuation needs to be determined for each specific case, through a comparison of the marginal benefits and costs of increments of database development and the value to decisionmaking.

CONCLUSION

This chapter stresses the usefulness of monetizing, as far as is feasible, unpriced environmental values. It also sets out a taxonomy of different types of value that should be considered, and outlines various general classes of techniques for calculating a monetary value for various types of unpriced environmental values. Appendix 7.A gives the definition for each broad category of monetary valuation, along with a brief review of the major advantages and limitations of each. In conclusion, we note that monetization can be quite useful as long as the following points are acknowledged:

1. The available techniques typically do not produce highly credible estimates of the full range of environmental values.
2. The marginal benefits and costs of monetization need to be carefully weighed.
3. In the end, there will nearly always be some residual non-monetized set of impacts whose implicit minimum or maximum monetary equivalent values will need to be determined by a decisionmaker in a tradeoff assessment rather than through a formal monetization process.

Chapter 8 concludes our benefit-cost analysis review by examining more fully the matter of time-dependent valuation and the controversies that continue to surround standard discounting procedures.

APPENDIX 7.A

MONETARY VALUATION TECHNIQUES &
ADVANTAGES AND LIMITATIONS

Direct Cost Approaches

Definition: Estimation of actual expenditures required to mitigate at least in part the effects of or to prevent some form of environmental damage.

Examples: Pollution-related health expenditures, travel costs, the costs of maintenance or defensive activities.

Advantages: Provides market-based relatively reliable and sometimes are easy to estimate.

Disadvantages: Gives only minimum indication of the particular environmental/ health value of concern.

Hedonic Pricing Approaches

Definition: Examination of market transactions for indications of the willingness to pay for (or to be compensated for) differences in environmental, health, or safety conditions.

Examples: Property values, wage differentials.

Advantages: Provides a market-based indication of the value people are willing to pay in order to obtain some environmental, health, or safety benefit.

Disadvantages: At best indicates what the market requires people to pay for these values rather than an indication of consumer surplus; estimates may be questionable due to confounding factors and problems with insufficient disaggregation of data.

Contingent Valuation Approaches

Definition: Estimation of willingness to pay (or to be compensated for) differences in some feature of environmental quality based on surveys or games.

Examples: Tradeoff games, costless choice, priority evaluation questionnaires.

Advantages: Provides potentially comprehensive indication of the full level and range of environmental, health, or safety values.

Disadvantages: Potential for considerable uncertainty with regard to the honesty and accuracy of the responses.

NOTES

1. As noted in Chapter 8, issues for those values we may be reluctant to apply standard discounting (for example, the value of stewardship of the earth) might be dealt with through such approaches as constrained benefit-cost analysis or a tradeoff

assessment. However, where we are willing to assign environmental values a monetary equivalent measure of value, then it is difficult to argue that it should not be discounted along with other monetized values.

2. In any market situation the actual price paid indicates that the purchaser values that good at least as highly as the price. However, as discussed in Chapter 2, there tends also to be a consumer surplus because the buyer might value the good or service more highly than the price he had to pay to acquire it.

8

Time-Dependent Valuation

A basic consideration in economic analysis is how to value future benefits and costs.[1] Consider a bag of rice. A bag to be delivered to us next year might be indistinguishable from another delivered today, but do we value both bags the same? At first it might seem that a bag of rice is a bag of rice, and if market conditions do not change, why would we place a different value on the one compared to the other? But when we consider the value of something for which we have to wait twenty or one hundred years, then it becomes clearer: market conditions aside, not all bags of rice are the same. Those available in the future are worth less than those we can use right now.

The issue goes beyond uncertainty and its associated risk. Even when a particular benefit or cost is virtually certain to occur, there remains the question of how to compare the time-dependent value we place on a specific impact (*return*) coming next year, in five years, or in a thousand years, with the value we place on that same impact when it occurs in the near-term. This question has nothing to do with inflation. Consider a barter situation in which we would willingly trade one sack of corn for three cooking pots received today. Would we so willingly trade our sack of corn today for three cooking pots to be delivered ten years from now? Perhaps not.

We all make comparisons of present and future values in our everyday decisionmaking. Would you rather receive a $1,000 bonus now or $2,000 in five years? Would you rather pay for your education now or after finishing your study? Your answer depends, of course, on your own personal preferences. But in general, most of us individually, and collectively as a society, prefer to receive benefits in the near-term and postpone costs to the future. In other words, both a future benefit and a future cost are usually worth less than the same benefit or cost in the present. This type of time-dependent adjustment to the value we place on something is referred to as the process of *discounting future value,* or simply discounting.

Some readers may disagree and argue that every time we make an investment we violate this rule. That is, you might invest money and time, both of which are costs, today in your education so that you will have better employment opportunities and other benefits in the future. Likewise, a business may invest $1 million today (a present cost) in order to produce goods for sale next year and for some time thereafter (future benefits). Clearly, we frequently do accept costs today in expectation of future benefits. Yet in general we do this because it is necessary (and not because we prefer it), or because it will enable us to make a profit. In other words, we are willing to make such investments only when the expected future benefit is greater than the present cost. In some cases, such as when we obtain a certificate of deposit, this higher return might be quite certain; in other cases it is quite speculative, as with futures markets. Whether certain or speculative, some level of reward typically is expected before we willingly incur a cost today in order to receive a benefit in the future. In other words, we demand compensation for having to wait to receive benefits, or for incurring costs sooner than necessary.

There are several reasons why benefits today are typically preferred over ones postponed into the future. One is simple human nature. We desire good things and would rather have them sooner than later. Another consideration is the opportunity costs of resources. Near-term monetary benefits may be invested to yield greater returns in the future, and they offer greater flexibility in near-term decisionmaking. For example, a $5,000 bonus this year might be invested to bring even greater monetary benefits in the future (for example, if invested at 10%, the amount would have grown to $5,500 by this time next year). If general price inflation was only 5%, then we have clearly gained something for waiting this year for the money ($5000 x (1.10)/(1.05) = $5,238). Alternatively, you might decide that it is best to use the $5,000 to make a repair to the roof of your home which, if left unattended, could lead to a cost of $7,000 in damages next year. Hence, in this alternative investment the benefit is $2,000 in avoided costs next year. In both cases, for reasons that go beyond simple time preference, it is preferable to have resources available today instead of having to wait until they become available later.

An additional factor is that some types of uncertainty increase with time. If a benefit is postponed long into the future you might not be alive to enjoy it, or your tastes and preferences might change. Likewise, what a society prefers today may not be something a future society values highly.

Similarly, there are several reasons why we tend to prefer costs to come in the future instead of today. Again, simple human nature plays a large part. How often do we postpone going to the dentist or put off anything unpleasant? We know that we are simply postponing and not actually eliminating the costs, but we may do so anyway, because we generally prefer to postpone costs whenever possible. Also, postponing monetary costs may allow us to buy something before we have the money to pay for it.

If a student must borrow money to pay tuition, he or she is paying for both the tuition and the interest on the money borrowed. If, however, the school gives a deferment on paying the tuition until graduation, then the value that the student places on the tuition bill is lower, even if there is no inflation. And, if the student has the money today to meet his tuition bill, it would be in his financial interest to postpone paying the tuition and invest the funds so as to collect an interest payment. In other words, it is important to remember that costs faced today have a higher negative value than those faced at some point in the future.

IMPORTANT EXCEPTIONS TO DISCOUNTING FUTURE VALUE

As just noted, typically we prefer to have benefits sooner rather than later, and prefer to incur costs later rather than sooner. We expect compensation when the receipt of benefits is willingly postponed or costs are voluntarily incurred sooner than need be. There are, however, some noteworthy exceptions to this set of normal preferences. Persons without a secure retirement pension, for example, may save today simply to have a source of income when they no longer are able to work. While people in that position surely would prefer to receive compensation, such as an interest rate higher than the rate of general price inflation, they might save even if no such compensation were offered. Indeed, a similar set of preferences operating at the social level lies behind such things as long-term food storage programs designed to meet future emergency food shortfalls. Rather than earning interest in these long-term storage programs, some of the food might actually spoil before it is used, if indeed the stored food is ever used. The compensation here, as generally in the case of insurance programs, comes not in the form of an absolute growth in the level of the invested resource. Rather, compensation is provided in the form of a greater sense of security about the future.

In a similar manner, setting aside certain areas as nature reserves to provide a legacy for future generations may be viewed as providing compensation to the present generation. Here, the compensation takes the form of the satisfaction experienced by the present generation in knowing that future generations will enjoy this particular ecological heritage, whether that be for its beauty, its genetic legacy, or something else.

The implications of these exceptions for environmental issues are considered later in this chapter. However, while these exceptions are important, we stress that they are exceptions to the normal preferences reflected in the process of discounting. In the cases noted in the preceding paragraph, we postpone the use (consumption) of some present benefit in order to ensure that the same, or perhaps even somewhat smaller, level of benefit is available in case we need to meet an unexpected future supply shortfall. We usually would do this only when we are concerned about meeting *minimally* acceptable quality of life standards in the future. Once we have taken action to insure against unacceptable resource shortfalls in the future, if indeed we undertake such insurance steps in the first place, the general preference for discounting future returns would tend to take precedence once again. The role of this type of concern for decisions with respect to inter-generational transfers and discounting is considered later in this chapter.

The standard practice in economic and financial benefit-cost analysis is to discount future benefits and costs including those for the environment. If we did not discount future costs and benefits it would presumably distort people's time preference, as well as ignore the opportunity cost of resources. Basically, we need to recognize two facts. First, while we may care about the future, we, as individuals and collectively as a society, typically do not value future impacts as highly as we value present ones. And second, resources have productive potentials that we can tap only when they become available to us.

CALCULATION PROCEDURES FOR DISCOUNTING

If we agree that the value of future benefits or costs are not the same as those occurring at present, exactly how should future values be adjusted downward? In standard practice, economists attempt to put near-term and longer-term benefits and costs on an equivalent value basis. If it is possible to do this accurately, then people today would be indifferent between x dollars worth of benefits or costs today and x + y worth of benefits or costs in a specific future year.

In benefit-cost analysis (BCA), this is done by applying a selected single discount rate to calculate the present value equivalent of the expected value of the future benefit or cost. The farther the benefit or cost is postponed into the future, the lower its present value. The specific difference between the nominal value of something expected to occur in the future and its present value depends on when it occurs, and on the particular discount rate employed.

As shown in Chapter 6, the standard procedure for calculating the present value of a future benefit or cost is admittedly rather mechanical: the present value of a future return declines exponentially as it recedes farther from the present; at any positive discount rate, the present value asymptotically approaches zero. Discounting is typically done on a year-by-year basis. The present value (PV) calculation we use here is:

$$\text{PV (for benefit or cost in year t)} = (\,B_t \text{ or } C_t\,)\,/\,(1 + i)^t$$

Where,
   t = year when the benefit or cost occurs (t_0 = present year),
   i = the discount rate

Table 8.1 shows the present value at various discount rates of a return of $1. We see that a return of $1, occurring in seven years, has a present value of $0.87 at a discount rate of 2%. At a discount rate of 14% that same return coming seven years from now has a present value of only about 40% of its nominal value. We can also see from the table that except for rather low

Table 8.1
Present Values

Year in the future	Discount Rate					
	0%	2%	4%	6%	10%	14%
1	1.00	0.98	0.96	0.94	0.91	0.88
2	1.00	0.96	0.92	0.89	0.83	0.77
3	1.00	0.94	0.89	0.84	0.75	0.67
4	1.00	0.92	0.85	0.79	0.68	0.59
5	1.00	0.91	0.82	0.75	0.62	0.52
6	1.00	0.89	0.79	0.70	0.56	0.46
7	1.00	0.87	0.76	0.67	0.51	0.40
8	1.00	0.85	0.73	0.63	0.51	0.35
9	1.00	0.84	0.70	0.59	0.42	0.31
10	1.00	0.82	0.66	0.56	0.39	0.27
15	1.00	0.74	0.56	0.42	0.24	0.14
20	1.00	0.67	0.46	0.31	0.15	0.07
25	1.00	0.61	0.38	0.23	0.09	0.04
30	1.00	0.55	0.31	0.17	0.06	0.02
40	1.00	0.45	0.21	0.10	0.02	—
50	1.00	0.37	0.14	0.05	—	—
100	1.00	0.14	—	—	—	—

Note: — indicates that the present value is less than 0.01

discount rates, for instance, under about 4%, returns postponed past about 40 years (roughly two generations of people) count for relatively little in present value terms. This is despite the fact that many people who are alive today are expected to be alive in forty years time.

The effect of discounting is perhaps made even more dramatically when we consider the present value of a large return postponed into the moderately distant future. For example, at a discount rate of 14% a return of $1 million, occurring fifty years in the future, has a present value of only $1,482! Even at a discount rate of 4%, a $1 million return for which we wait fifty years has a present value of only about $141,000.

Table 8.2 shows the cumulative present value of a stream of annual returns of $1 each year. At a high discount rate, such as 14%, the total value of a series of returns, such as might occur in the case of crop production where profits are made annually, increases very slowly after about fifteen years. It makes little difference to the overall benefit-cost calculations if the evaluation period is thirty years or fifty, or by extension, a hundred or a thousand years. Even at a relatively low rate of discount of 2%, it makes only a rather modest difference whether the evaluation period is thirty or fifty years. Hence agricultural returns several generations from now count little in present value terms.

Figure 8.1 shows a set of benefits and costs over a project evaluation period of twenty years. In part A, returns are undiscounted and total benefits

Table 8.2
Cumulative Present Values: The Present Value of an Annuity
(how much $1 paid of received annually for x years is worth today)

Year in the future	Discount Rate					
	0%	2%	4%	6%	10%	14%
1	1.00	0.98	0.61	0.43	0.91	0.88
2	2.00	1.94	1.89	1.83	1.74	1.65
3	3.00	2.88	2.78	2.67	2.49	2.32
4	4.00	3.81	3.63	3.31	3.04	2.80
5	5.00	4.71	4.45	4.21	3.79	3.43
6	6.00	5.60	5.24	4.92	4.36	3.89
7	7.00.	6.47	6.00	5.58	4.87	4.64
8	8.00	7.33	6.73	6.21	5.33	4.64
9	9.00	8.16	7.44	6.80	5.76	4.95
10	10.00	8.98	8.11	7.36	6.41	5.22
15	15.00	12.85	11.12	9.71	7.61	6.14
20	20.00	16.35	13.59	11.47	8.51	6.62
25	30.00	19.52	15.62	12.78	9.08	6.87
30	30.00	22.40	17.29	13.76	9.43	7.00
40	40.00	27.36	19.79	15.05	9.78	7.11
50	50.00	31.42	21.48	15.76	9.91	7.13
100	100.00	43.10	24.50	16.62	10.00	7.14

are greater than total costs. At a discount rate of 4% (part B), the present values of both benefits and costs decline, but the effect is greater in the case of the benefits because more of these returns occur later in the evaluation period. Nonetheless, net benefits are still positive at this discount rate, and so the project would be acceptable. However, if we use a 14% discount rate as shown (part C), the discounted stream of benefits is much smaller than the discounted stream of costs. Since the net benefits of this project investment opportunity are negative when evaluated using a 14% discount rate, the project would be rejected if this were considered the appropriate discount rate.

Discount rates employed in project evaluation can be as low as 2%, a level chosen when future impacts are considered a priority, and can reach up to perhaps 20%, in situations where near-term costs and benefits are more important. The more typical range is about 3% to 12%.

In theory, discounting may be applied to anything that has value, whether or not it is expressed in monetary terms. However, in order to compare precisely the time-dependent values of different types of things, their respective values must be expressed in a common unit of value (e.g., money). In practice, precise discounting tends to be limited to those benefits and costs with a dollar value assigned to them. Indeed, the computational limitations that come into play when we cannot put all benefits and costs into a common unit of value provide the strongest impetus for developing monetized surrogate measures described in the preceding chapter. In benefit cost analysis the summarizing of

Figure 8.1
Discounting over the Near to Mid-Term

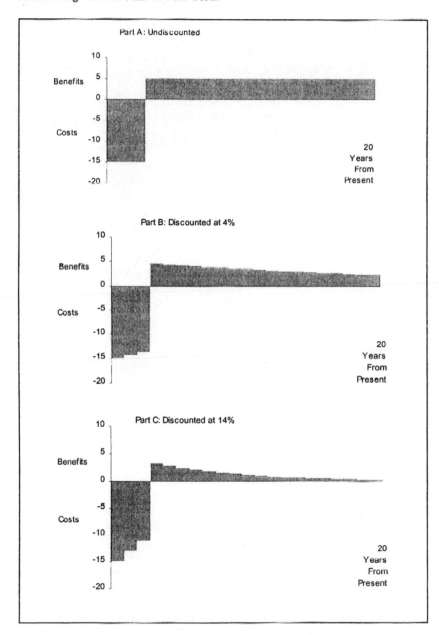

benefits and costs into a single time-dependent measure of value applies only to *monetized* values. We will return to this point later in this chapter.

SELECTING THE DISCOUNT RATE

Pure Time Preference and Opportunity Costs

In considering their own personal consumption decisions, individuals often employ rather high discount rates, perhaps as high as 20% or 30%. We prefer to have things now, and their value decreases markedly as they recede farther into the future. But are such rates appropriate for collective decisions, such as when evaluating public sector projects? Probably not. Pure time preference discount rates, which typically are presumed to range from 1% to 3%, would generally be considered more appropriate for social decisions, particularly when we consider the effect of higher rates on the value of benefits and costs coming at least one generation in the future. Pure time preference would tend to set the lower minimum for any discount rate selected. Once the discount rate for pure social time preference is determined, we then consider the opportunity cost of the resources required for a particular investment to determine if this is higher.

The opportunity costs of resources clearly depend on the particular economic circumstances. In times of relative economic expansion, the opportunity costs of resources might be rather high (8% to 15%), while in times of relatively slow growth, we might be fortunate to find investment options that provide returns of more than 2% or 3%.

Risk

All decisions involving an element of risk inspire controversy, and the question of incorporating risk into calculations of the present values of future returns is no different. Some economists argue that the discount rate should reflect only the time value of returns and the opportunity costs of funds, in order to be "risk-free." Proponents of this argument believe that uncertainty about future benefits or costs should not influence the rate at which we discount future values. Instead, they say, if the future benefits and costs are uncertain, we should lower their expected value directly, by decreasing the probability and hence the "mathematical expected value" of the future benefit or cost, rather than accounting for such uncertainty through a higher discount rate. On the other hand, it is clear that since uncertainty tends to increase as a return is postponed farther and farther into the future, some types of risk do increase with time. Financial markets add a risk premium on the discount rate applied to various types of investments.

There are two options for incorporating risk in the present value calculations. We can lower the value of the numerator (the mathematical expectation of the nominal value of the future benefit or cost), and divide this by the risk-free discount factor. Alternatively, we may decide that it is acceptable to leave the expected nominal future value unaltered, and add a risk premium to the discounting factor by raising the value of the denominator. The drawback of this latter approach is that it implicitly assumes that risk increases steadily as returns occur farther and farther in the future.   While this characterizes many forms of risk and uncertainty, it would be inappropriate for others. The treatment of risk is explored in greater depth in Chapter 9. Here we note that to the extent that there is uncertainty that projected returns will occur exactly as expected, such risk must somehow be incorporated into the present value.

Government-Set Discount Rates for Project Evaluation

The above debate aside, in practice, the government sets discount rates for public sector projects. For mature economies growing relatively slowly from a large base, typical real discount rates range from 2% to 10%, while in more quickly growing economies growing from a smaller base, a range of 8% to 15% is more likely. No matter which discount rate is chosen, it is axiomatic that the rate should not fall below a reasonable pure time preference level (typically 1% to 3%). Estimates of the opportunity costs of funds in the economy should be backed up by evidence to the extent possible. Nonetheless, just as the judgments of reasonable and informed people may differ, so do decisions about the most appropriate discount rate.

DISCOUNTING AND INTER-GENERATIONAL TRANSFERS

Although in general it is safe to assume that individuals prefer near-term benefits as noted earlier, the long-term effects of some projects may lead us to behave in ways not entirely consistent with this principle.   Consider the example of a project in which the benefit and cost time streams look like those in Figure 8.2. You may notice that the time period shown (60 years) is much longer than the 20-year period of Figure 8.1 (i.e., three generations rather than one).   Perhaps this is an agricultural improvement project in which the most important impacts, such as soil stabilization, are expected to come after years or decades. Is the project in Figure 8.2 a good one (i.e., does the value of the benefits outweigh the value of the costs)?

Let us at first assume there is no issue of non-monetized benefits or costs. In other words, for simplicity we assume that the money values we are discounting and comparing capture *all* of the value, from the perspective of the present generation (those making the decision).   The project would not be accepted with standard discounting, since even at a modest discount rate of 4%, discounted benefits are somewhat less than discounted costs. In Figure 8.2 much of the benefit side comes late in the project's life, 12 to 60 years in the future, and the costs are entirely borne by the present generation! At a discount rate of 14% future benefits nearly vanish in comparison to the costs.

Figure 8.2
A Project with Long-Term High Future Benefits

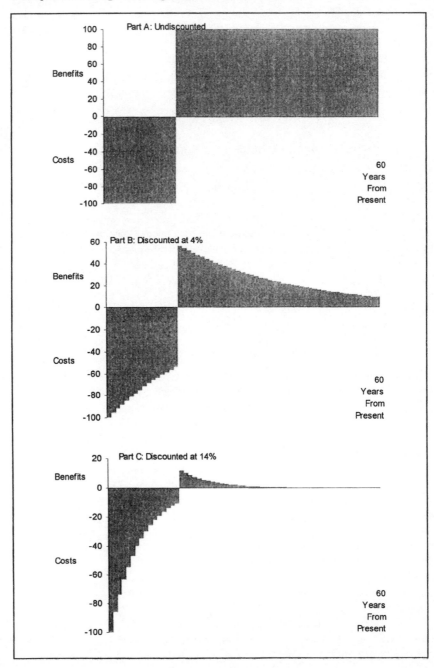

Yet this project may be intended to stop erosion and reverse ongoing soil degradation, so that people can continue to farm a certain area for generations to come. Indeed, it is possible and even likely that this project is intended to reverse the impacts of the past and current activities that led to the soil degradation in the first place. Does the present generation have the right to impose high costs (e.g. in the form of environmental damages) on future generations, and then justify the failure to take corrective action by showing that net value from the standpoint of the present generation is negative?

Consider another example of a project with the benefit-cost time stream shown in Figure 8.3. Here let us say that the project would produce valuable items for near-term consumption, but would also result in deadly soil contamination with long-lasting effects, hence precluding the land from further use. Again, consistent with our narrow focus in these examples, we are considering future costs only in terms of the *monetary value* of foregone food production or other commercial uses of the land. Yet, even so, undiscounted costs are far greater than the benefits. If we apply a 4% discount rate, the costs are still somewhat larger than the benefits. However, at a 14% discount rate, the future costs nearly vanish and the present value of the benefits outweighs the present value of the costs. Should we apply normal discounting procedures in this and similar cases? If not, how do we compare future and present values?

There is no consensus on the answer to these questions. Some economists argue that since incomes in most of the world are rising, we should expect future generations to be wealthier than ours. Thus, it would be foolish for us to incur costs today to enable our rich descendants to receive benefits. If we follow this logic, we should apply normal discounting procedures to every situation. Implicit assumptions of this argument are that the current rise in income around the world from technological advances and the accumulation of man-made capital can offset losses in environmental quality, and that there is no reason to believe that such advances will not continue into the future.

Other analysts argue that much of the recent increase in wealth has been based on the current and recent past generations' exploitation of finite material resources, particularly fossil fuels and minerals, and on the over-exploitation of many renewable resources such as fisheries and forests. In other words, they argue that we are living off our natural capital. Thus, some and perhaps much of the recent increase in income is transitory and unsustainable. According to this argument, technology and man-made capital may well help people in the future just as they have enabled us, and our parents and grandparents, to make better lives. Nonetheless, if we lose too much soil to erosion, if most forests have been logged and much biodiversity has been lost, if the prime reservoirs of high quality, readily available energy are exhausted, then future improvements in technology and growth of man-made capital may only partly offset the forces likely to lead to a decline in global incomes. With fewer resources to exploit and continuing growth in population, future generations may well be less wealthy than we are. Given this possibility, they argue that we must do what we can to maximize the natural resource legacy passed to

Figure 8.3
A Project with Long-Term High Future Costs

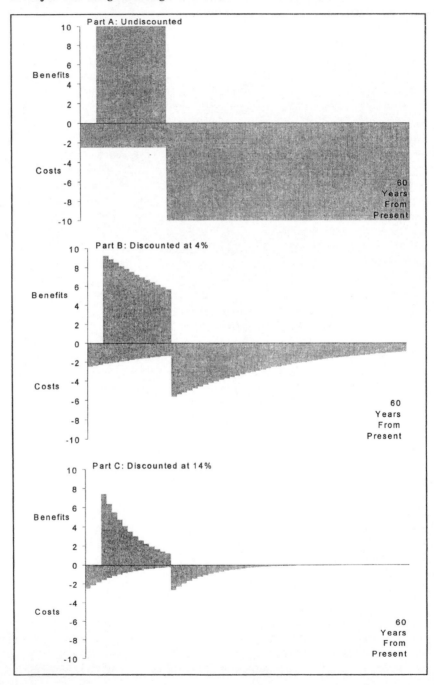

future generations.[2] The proponents of this view might recommend that we either apply a very low social discount rate, even as low as 1%, or that we should somehow remove certain types of long-term or environmental impacts from the process of discounting in the first place.

Of course, we might wish that people in past times had invested their resources in more massive projects with benefits lasting into the twentieth century—such as the pyramids, the Great Wall, or the ancient Yangtze River diversions. But would a decision to proceed with these monuments, at the expense of other projects with greater near-term benefits, have been economically rational from their perspective? Probably not. It is often hard to justify giving priority to the long-term. Yet the decisions of our ancestors that resulted in the preservation of highly valued parts of the natural environment, such as great national parks have had a marked effect on the wealth of our generation, and we should remember this when faced with decisions of a similar nature. How might we reconcile the fact that it would not have been economical for past generations to sacrifice for our benefit with the fact that, even though we are richer than they, we nonetheless treasure the monuments and legacy they did pass on to us and might regret their destructive exploitation of many other natural resources (e.g., completely destroying Europe's old forests, decimating the vast herds of American bison).

We can make one important distinction between the two types of activities. Investing in a *man-made* project (such as space exploration) solely on the basis of benefits likely to come only far into the future is probably not an economical decision for the present generation, though we might still decide to do so for other reasons (e.g., to stimulate technological development, to advance knowledge, or as a form of insurance). However, if we fail to undertake such investments as a space exploration program, this probably does not represent an ethical issue. In contrast, the irreversible destruction of something of natural significance, such as an important ecological system (e.g., fisheries and rainforests throughout much of the world), arguably does present a serious ethical issue and our decision should be based on an information that goes beyond the strict benefit-cost present value calculation. If we accept this distinction, then when we deal with matters such as species extinction, which the present generation is causing at a level completely unprecedented in human history, we should consider the irreversible effects (irreversibilities) and their implications for inter-generational transfers. We should recognize that such consequences probably should be evaluated outside the framework of normal present value calculations.

A PRAGMATIC COMPROMISE

It is probably fair to say that at the time of this writing, there has arisen no general consensus on how to treat irreversibilities and inter-generational transfers. Clearly, it would be presumptuous of us in the extreme to casually view the world as being the sole heritage of the present generation. Yet, the simple fact is that much of what we do, and of what generations before us have done, is in effect irreversible. We simply cannot avoid every possible irreversibility or always attempt to transfer as much as possible of our natural resources to future generations.

At a discount rate above about 10, environmental benefits occurring in the next twenty to forty years have comparatively little weight in the net present value calculations. Even at very low discount rates, such as 1% to 2%, impacts one hundred or one hundred and fifty years from now simply do not count for much in present value terms. Yet, if the environmental impacts have been appropriately monetized, then on what basis should we treat them differently from other monetized benefits and costs? After all the basic reason for using money as a unit of value in the first place is to be able to directly compare and sum different types of value. If we are willing to monetize environmental impacts, then by what rationale should they not be treated as the other values in money terms?

Chapters 6 and 7 reviewed basic discounting techniques and noted that often we can monetize certain aspects of environmental value, but that such monetization typically captures only a portion of the full range of unpriced values. Yet, it is essential that such non-monetized residual values somehow be taken into account in the decision-making process. Earlier in this chapter we noted that in principle discounting could be applied to non-monetized values, but that for the purposes of project evaluation, only monetized project impacts enter into the net present value calculations.

We now see why such an assumption may not only be unrealistic, but may also present us with a dilemma when it comes to time-dependent valuation. Once we take the step of monetary valuation, it becomes difficult to argue that the next step of time-dependent valuation should not be taken for some things, such as, in the above example, soil erosion, while it is taken for all the other things we value in money terms.

If we wish to keep selected potentially monetizable environmental impacts, such as long-term crop yields, out of the standard discounting process, we might simply refuse to accept a monetary measure as the full indicator of value for them. Alternatively, we might put some of environmental value in money terms and discount them, but stress the point that in such cases the monetized values (in this example, the market value of future crops) constitute only one element in a larger set of social values. We then would deal with these other aspects of value, such as, to continue the example, the importance of preserving productive farmland in the tradeoff assessment stage of the BCA, or through a constrained BCA as outlined in Chapter 6. Indeed, arguments of this sort are sometimes used for governmental support to small traditional farmers, even when making the land available to other uses might be justified on a strictly financial basis. Perhaps more to the point of environmental management, matters of insurance value (i.e., protecting the stratospheric ozone layer) need to be dealt with through some type of tradeoff assessment rather than strict present value based assessments of the benefits and costs.

As noted in Chapter 6, when we argue that some important aspect of an environmental impact should not (or cannot) be monetized, the decision turns on the answer to the following question: Does the decisionmaker value the monetized (and discounted) net benefits highly enough to accept the net non-monetized costs? If yes, then he or she implicitly values the non-monetized impacts less than the net monetized benefits. If no, then he or she implicitly values them more than the level of the net monetized benefits.

While a purist might argue that even the non-monetized future impacts should be formally assigned a time-dependent discounted value, such as one based on the weights as shown in Table 8.1, in practical terms there is not a strong impetus for this. Indeed, even if we say that a "large sum" is only 20% of that in present value terms, what does that mean? It means whatever the decisionmaker says it means! By its nature the tradeoff decision between the monetized net benefits and the non-monetized impacts is indeterminant except as the decisionmaker is willing to make an implicit assignment of minimum or maximum values for the non-monetized impacts by declaring his or her willingness to forgo or incur the monetized ones. While the decisionmaker should consider time-dependent values for environmental impacts, is there a compelling reason to make this part of the decision a rigorous and explicit one? Perhaps not.

In some situations it may be possible simply to sidestep time-dependent valuation issues. If project benefits and costs are relatively uniform from year to year, then the rate of discount does affect the NPV but not the benefit to cost ratio.[3] And we can use the B/C to determine if the project is acceptable. Even where the investment requirements are not uniformly distributed over time, often the money to pay these costs will be borrowed and repaid in uniform annual installments. Hence, when the benefits are relatively uniform from year to year, we may then judge the project on the basis of whether annual benefits are greater than annual (*amortized*) costs and this ratio will be the same irrespective of the discount rate. While this approach of looking only at annualized (uniform) benefits or costs may be applicable in some important project evaluation cases, it clearly is a special case with restricted potential for avoiding time-dependent valuation issues more generally.

CONCLUSION

As a practical matter, we recommend that standard discounting at normally accepted rates, such as 3% to 15%, be applied to project evaluations, including those with monetized environmental impacts. However, where the benefit or cost stream extends more than a few decades, or the project involves significant irreversibilities (or even the substantial risk of these), and in all cases where there are important values which remain non-monetized, then it is essential that these concerns be *addressed outside of rigid discounting procedures*.

How might this be done? In addition to the type of tradeoff decision described, we might agree to set constraints on project impacts so as to ensure that certain levels of damage for selected environmental impacts are not exceeded (see also Chapter 6). For example, a project might be approved subject to the constraints that soil erosion is kept below some specific level, and that other measures to maintain the site's future productivity are undertaken. In other situations, for instance when the main concern is the preservation of biodiversity, we might set up separate projects to meet explicit environmental goals. For example, one area of old growth forest might be opened for logging with a requirement that another area of similar ecology be permanently preserved.

In closing, we note that although it is probably inappropriate to formally discount every future environmental impact, it nonetheless remains important to ask how the *time* when an impact (environmental or otherwise) occurs affects the value we place on it. Such adjustments might be vague rather than precise (in economic terms, they might be part of the tradeoff assessment rather than reflected in the NPV), but it would be inappropriate to simply assume that all environmental impacts have the same value regardless of when they occur.

In the end, rational decisionmaking requires a recognition that the values of most types of benefits and costs are at least partly dependent on when these returns occur. In evaluating our planning options, we should recognize that benefits and costs delayed into the future generally are valued less than those that occur today. When we decide that this is not appropriate in a particular case, we must recognize that this decision has its own costs in terms of forgone monetized present values (opportunity costs). And, of course, if we begin doing this explicitly in a large number of cases, we may rather quickly come up against the limits of the present generation's willingness to sacrifice for future generations. Still, it would be best to make the costs of inter-generational transfers as explicit as possible. Unfortunately, under normal narrowly defined BCA project evaluation procedures, in which every type and level of future impact is monetized and then discounted, inter-generational transfers are subsummed and tend to be lost from sight. This is despite the fact that the present generation may care about these consequences if explicitly reminded of them.

If the environmental legacy we pass on to future generations were made an explicit part of the policy discussion and project evaluation, perhaps we would be less likely to simply ignore future generations or to say that we care as much about them as we care about ourselves. Neither of these extremes is likely to be an accurate reflection of our values, nor how we really value the heritage we pass on to posterity.

NOTES

1. In this chapter we will be dealing exclusively with real (i.e., constant purchasing power) future monetary values. The treatment of nominal future prices and general price inflation is covered in Chapter 6.

2. It may be useful to note here that this issue cannot be definitively answered through analyses of the composition of gross national product (GNP). The on-going debate about the appropriateness of national income accounts makes clear that what we can readily measure in monetary terms is not necessarily what is most important to the sustainable well being of a society or a nation.

3.

$$B/C = \sum_{t=0}^{T} [B_t / (1 + i)^t] / \sum_{t=0}^{T} [C_t / (1 + i)^t].$$

The term $(1 + i)^t$ in the denominator and numerator cancel out when the benefit and cost streams are the same each year (i.e., if $B_1 = B_2 \ldots = B_n$ and $C_1 = C_2 \ldots = C_n$.

9

Dealing with Risk and Uncertainty

Although there is disagreement about the exact distinction between risk and uncertainty, a widely used convention is that risk is usually associated with numerical probabilities. These probabilities might be estimated objectively, such as an engineer would calculate the risk of a dam failing or of an environmental control technology not working. Probabilities also can be specified subjectively through one's own personal best guesses and hunches. In contrast to risk, uncertainty is often associated with socio-economic factors, such as the vagaries of consumer tastes and preferences, physical phenomena (e.g., the long-term effect of specific weather events), the transport and fate of effluents and emissions in the environment, the response of the environment to stresses (e.g., increased CO_2 concentrations), or the impacts of pollutants on human health. The important point is that uncertainty is said to exist when our understanding is limited and probabilities of occurrences cannot be readily estimated.

Dealing with risk and uncertainty is of fundamental importance for the environmental economist. For many decisions or project evaluations, we cannot be sure what the outcomes of a decision will be. For example, what will be the effect on a population's exposure to a certain kind of chemical of a policy limiting its use? What is an acceptable exposure to a toxic or hazardous material? In terms of a project implementation decision, we might need to consider what the reliability and operating costs are likely to be of a piece of equipment designed to limit pollution levels to some government-mandated standard.

Most environmental decisionmaking takes place under considerable uncertainty concerning key factors and effects. This chapter discusses the sources and significance of various types of uncertainty. The importance of recognizing and describing risk and uncertainty is stressed, as is the need to make decisions on the basis of the best available information, even when that information is incomplete. We discuss various approaches for doing this, with some of these approaches being extensions of benefit-cost analysis, discounting, and valuation discussed in the preceding chapters.

UNCERTAINTY, BCA AND COST-EFFECTIVENESS

Some techniques that can be used for handling risk and uncertainty in benefit-cost analysis and cost-effectiveness analysis include adding risk premiums to discount rates, or lowering the expected value of future returns, setting minimum thresholds for measures of project worth, conducting sensitivity analysis, and undertaking probability analysis.

Risk Premiums

As we discussed in Chapter 8, discounting is used to account for time-dependent valuation. That is, future benefits and costs are usually worth less than the same benefits or costs received or incurred today. We also noted that a risk premium is nothing more than adding some percentage to the "riskless" discount rate that would otherwise be used. Adding this risk premium has the effect of discounting the future more highly and lowering the value of future benefits and costs. For example, if our risk free discount rate is 6%, we might add 2% to account for the fact that we are not entirely sure that the benefits and costs will occur in the future exactly as expected.

There are two major objections to adding risk premiums to discount rates. First, doing so combines all variables involving elements of risk and uncertainty into one factor, the discount rate. Second, and perhaps more important, adding a percentage to the discount rate implies that risk/uncertainty increases steadily over time (i.e., the effect of compounding). Although it is generally more difficult to predict events ten years in the future rather than five, many environmental decisions or projects may, in fact, become less uncertain in the future. For example, in the case of deciding on an environmental restoration project, the time of greatest uncertainty might be the initial years, when technologies used to clean-up wastes are being tried and tested. Adding a risk premium to the discount can also introduce selection bias if the decision at hand is to choose among a group of projects to implement, since adding the risk premium to the discount rate has the effect of favoring projects with shorter time horizons.

Minimum Thresholds

Another simple technique that incorporates project risk and uncertainty into decisions is to establish minimum thresholds for measures of project worth. The use of minimum thresholds is often associated with projects that are very risky from a private financial perspective, usually involving relatively large sums of investment capital. Typically they are not used in public sector decisions. For example, a private firm contemplating investing in a country with an unstable political structure might require as a condition of the investment a relatively short payback period, perhaps three years or less. The requirement of a short payback period tends to preclude projects in which benefits (or revenues in the case of a private firm) are more or less uniform and extend well into the future. Minimum thresholds favor projects that limit exposure of investment capital. Minimum thresholds are most often used with the payback period, but can also be used with the benefit-cost ratio and internal rate of return.

Sensitivity Analysis

Sensitivity analysis is the most common technique for considering risk and uncertainty. In fact, sensitivity analysis is often a requirement in public sector environmental benefit-cost analysis and cost-effectiveness analysis. It is a way to understand how, for example, the net present value changes (i.e., is sensitive to) a given change in one or more decision variables. Properly used, sensitivity analysis can identify which variables are most important, thus allowing the engineer or biologist to focus on these in order to reduce uncertainty, or to better understand the nature and source of the uncertainty.

Let us consider a private firm that is contemplating investing in a power plant in a developing country. The country is having trouble meeting demands for electricity in rural areas and is looking toward the private sector for help in solving its power needs. The project will involve growing wood on managed plantations on land that currently has little alternative use value. The land was stripped of its trees years ago and exploited for agriculture until the nutrient-depleted soils, which were exposed to the harsh effects of the monsoon climate, made food farming uneconomic. The power project offers numerous local economic and environmental benefits. Growing trees helps stabilize erosion and reduces siltation of streams. It provides local employment, and the power would help to satisfy the needs of rural households and agro-industrial users. Of course, the private firm is only interested in whether it can make money from growing trees and selling the power to the local utility. Since these local economic and environmental benefits do not directly profit the private, they are likely to be external to the financial analysis.

This investment project is relatively complicated. It first involves identifying land to grow trees; assessing specific planting sites (e.g., soils, rainfall, slopes, etc.) and their productivity potential; evaluating appropriate tree species and cultural management practices with respect to this particular piece of available land and its soil resources; assessing fuel supply logistics, handling, and storage; evaluating local and regional power demand issues; and deciding on electric generating technology (e.g., size, efficiency), including operating issues (e.g., load factors, fuel supply assurances) and integration to the local distribution grid. Any one of these involves considerable uncertainty and an evaluation of what variables are most important for the project's financial performance measures. In conducting a sensitivity analysis, the first step is to establish and document the base case and calculate measures of project worth. The base case should reflect the analyst's best estimates of various variables. Let us assume that the results of the base case yields an internal rate of return of nearly 31%. This is high, but not abnormally high given the uncertainties and potential project risks.

The sensitivity analysis begins by selecting important variables and shifting the value of each by a given percentage and noting how the primary measure of project worth, the internal rate of return in this case, changes as a result. For this illustration the important variables are the sales price for the power, the cost of supplying wood to the power plant, the investment cost for the power plant, and the discount rate. These variables and parameters are usually selected on the basis of their contribution to project benefits and costs. Table 9.1 summarizes the sensitivity analysis. Each variable was shifted from -40% to +40%, a fairly large range, but not unusual in this context. We find here that the internal rate of return is particularly sensitive to the sales price for power. A 20% reduction in the sales price would have the effect of lowering the internal rate of return by nearly 10 percentage points. The power plant investment cost also turns out to be an important variable. Here, a 20% reduction in the cost of the power plant would increase the internal rate of return from 30.9% to 38.5%.

Sometimes the results of the sensitivity analysis are clearer when presented in graphical form. Figure 9.1 presents these results. We can see that the sales price for power and the investment cost of the power plant are the two most important variables among the four variables. In contrast, even very large changes in wood fuel costs or the discount rate have relatively little effect. The main purpose of the sensitivity analysis is to identify which variables are most important and to determine how uncertainty about these estimates can be lowered and/or estimates made more precise. The importance of sales price to the viability of the project suggests that the private firm should perhaps seek purchase price guarantees before committing to the investment. It also may suggest the need for a survey to ensure that sufficient demand for power exists. The importance of the level of investment capital suggests a closer inspection of these costs is warranted. For example, could capital be saved by using a higher proportion of locally manufactured equipment? Could a less efficient, and thus less costly, boiler be used given that wood fuel costs are so low? Here we might examine this tradeoff between capital costs and operating costs (wood fuel) much more closely. These are just some of the questions that sensitivity analysis might highlight.

Sensitivity analysis is quite useful, but it does have a major limitation. Consideration of the combined effect of simultaneous changes to two or more variables is difficult and often impractical. Moreover, sensitivity analysis may not allow the analyst to take into account very unlikely or low probability events or the probability dispersion surrounding our best estimates; in such

Table 9.1
Sensitivity Analysis of the Internal Rate of Return

Variable	Percentage Change in Variable				
	-40%	-20%	Base case	20%	40%
Power price	11	21	30.9	41.2	51.8
Wood fuel cost	33.6	32.2	30.9	29.6	28.5
Investment cost	50.9	38.5	30.9	25.8	22.2
Discount rate	31.9	31.5	30.9	30.3	29.6

cases, we should consider if it is practical to assign probabilities to alternative outcomes.

Probability Analysis

In probability analysis, we begin by specifying probability distributions for important variables. Next, we select specific values from each variable's probability distribution and then estimate net present value or some other summary measure such as the IRR. By repeated application of sampling, and calculating net present value, the measure of project worth, we could generate a probability distribution for it (i.e., a mean and variance).[1] A limitation of this technique is our ability to develop the information necessary to specify meaningful probability distributions. As noted at the outset, we frequently do not have sufficient information to do this.

Figure 9.1
Sensitivity Chart

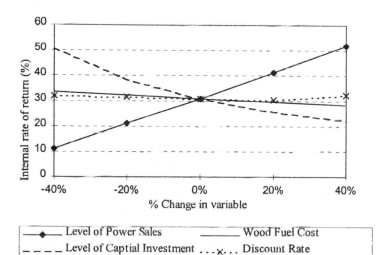

Scenario Analysis

Scenarios are simply alternative views of the future that enable decisionmakers to look at a range of possible events rather than just those that are *most likely* to occur. By design this scenario should be plausible, although some may be more realistic or likely than others. Scenarios account for the unexpected, yet plausible, events not accounted for in standard forecasting. Scenario analysis usually begins by specifying a base case scenario (most likely or surprise free) and a few alternative scenarios each of which correspond to a theme (e.g., faster economic expansion, heightened environmental concerns, or new technology development). Key factors that are crucial to the study are then projected within the context of the base case and modified to conform with the alternative scenarios. Each scenario places different estimates or values on selected variables. The net present value or other summary measure would then be calculated. In energy economics, for example, alternative scenarios are often constructed around different projections of economic growth and world oil prices. Other scenarios could include very different assumptions about the future. For example, rather than normal demand and price levels for petroleum, we might evaluate a scenario in which we learn five years from now that because the link between the use of fossil fuels and global warming has been determined much more precisely, it is decided by governments around the world that steps must be taken immediately to deal with the situation. Our scenario might be designed to allow us to see how rapidly and extensively renewable energy technologies could supplant fossil fuels.

MULTI-OBJECTIVE DECISIONMAKING

In Chapter 6 we briefly touched on multi-objective decisionmaking. This was done in the context of constrained benefit-cost analysis and tradeoff assessment. We discussed situations in which it is nearly impossible to be very precise in estimating values or being able to fully enumerate all sources of value. We mentioned intrinsically non-monetary impacts in which we might feel relatively comfortable in measuring in physical terms, but for which we are hesitant to assign monetary values. Multi-objective analysis is often used in complex environmental decision problems in which alternatives or proposed projects have many important conflicting dimensions including uncertainty that makes explicit monetary valuation impossible.

Here we discuss only the rudiments of multi-objective decisionmaking. We will do this with the aid of a simple example in which alternative locations are being considered for the siting of a facility, say a power plant. To keep the example simple, we will assume that differences between each alternative location can be reduced to two objectives—the level of cost and of environmental impact. Hence, each alternative location for the power plant will result in a different set of costs and a different set of environmental impacts. We summarize the cost objective in terms of dollar per kilowatt/hour ($/kWh) of electricity produced and the environmental objective in terms of an index of environmental impacts.   An index is used because it reduces various environmental attributes into a single measure. The attributes of the index might include water use and quality impacts, flora and fauna impacts, air emissions, noise impacts, land use and soil impacts, aesthetic impacts, and others. In Table 9.2 we show summary measures for cost and environmental impact objectives for five alternative power plant sites.

The cost objective for the five sites ranges from a low of $.049/kWh for location D to $0.063/kWh for location E—the higher cost of generating electricity from a power plant located at site E is attributable to longer transmission lines.   The environmental index (EI) measures a host of environmental attribute impacts. In this example, it is based on a 0 to 100 scale. The higher the number on the scale means greater overall negative environmental impact. The environmental impact scale ranges from a low of 39 for location E to a high of 83 for location D. Location E might involve the draining of a wetland and its location near a major population area. Location D might be far removed from a major population area and have only minimal site disturbance impacts.

The summary results in Table 9.2 illustrate two key factors associated with multi-objective decisionmaking. The first factor is dominance. Oftentimes, the results of a multi-objective analysis will reveal particular alternatives to be dominated by other alternatives. This can be seen by comparing locations A and B. Location B dominates alternative A because it is both lower in cost and lower overall environmental impact. The second factor is that for the four remaining locations we cannot select a preferred location without having "preference" information from the decisionmaker. Because the two objectives are conflicting (i.e., lower cost means higher environmental impact), choosing among alternatives is impossible unless the decisionmaker(s) indicates some preference or willingness to tradeoff the attainment of one objective for another. For example, how much additional cost can be accepted for less environmental impact?

The manner in which decisionmaker's preferences are elicited and incorporated into the solution process distinguishes the many multi-objective

Table 9.2
Illustrative Multi-Objective Decision Problem

Objective	Power plant site				
	A	B	C	D	E
Cost ($/kWh)	0.056	0.053	0.061	0.049	0.063
EI (0-100 scale)	61	60	45	83	39

Note:
$/kWh: dollar per kilowatt/hour
EI: Environmental Index

methods. In many real-world decision settings, benefit-cost analysis is often practised by valuing only those non-monetized impacts for which application of a valuation technique (see Chapter 7) is practical. In such cases, those impacts for which valuation is not possible because of limited understanding and uncertainty are ignored. Where this is clearly inappropriate, we must consider an alternative approach. There is a substantial literature on this topic with literally thousands of applications of the technique to problems of environmental management. The choice of technique depends, in large part, on the characteristics of the particular problem and how well the problem is defined. The choice of method might depend on whether the number of alternative objectives are few or numerous; whether the values of the objectives are known with some degree of certainty or unknown; whether the alternatives are completely known in advance or not; and whether the objectives are explicitly or implicitly defined.

It is beyond the scope of this book to examine the full range of potentially applicable multi-objective decision-making methods. However, we do note that they all share the following operational steps:

1. Defining alternatives and objectives.

2. Evaluating each alternative separately on each objective (scaling).

3. Assigning weights to the objectives (weighting).

4. Aggregating the objective weights and the single-objective evaluations of the alternatives to obtain an overall measure of value or worth.

5. Conducting sensitivity analysis and making recommendations.

There are a number of fundamental or more prominent methods that are particularly relevant for environmental decisionmaking.   The principle differences among the specific methods lie in the choice of procedures used to scale, weight, and aggregate.   One particular method that has appeal for environmental decisionmaking is the simple multi-attribute rating technique (SMART) (von Winterfeldt and Edwards, 1986).   The technique has wide application as it is easily understood and relatively transparent to decision-makers. Table 9.3 summarizes the steps used in this technique. The interested reader may want to refer to Clemen (1991), Cohon (1978), and Keeney and von Winterfeldt (1978) for a more complete treatment on multi-objective decisionmaking.

SOME ELEMENTS OF DECISION THEORY

Thus far we have been dealing with relatively formal approaches to the incorporation of risk and uncertainty into the environmental assessment process. While such approaches can be quite useful in certain situations, in other cases we may simply lack the necessary data, or we may really

Table 9.3
Steps Used in the Simple Multi-Attribute Rating Technique

The SMART Method	
Step 1	Identify the organization(s) (and/or stakeholders) whose values are to be maximized.
Step 2	Identify the issues (decisions) or purposes of the assessment.
Step 3	Identify the alternatives that are to be evaluated.
Step 4	Identify the set of objectives and relevant attributes (i.e., measures of value).
Step 5	Rank the objectives or attributes in order of importance.
Step 6	Make ratio estimates of the relative importance of each attribute relative to the one ranked low in importance. For example, assign the least important objective a value of 10, then consider the next important objective and assign a value based on how much more important it is. A value of 30 would imply the least important criterion is 1/3 as important.
Step 7	Sum the importance weights, and divide each by the sum.
Step 8	Measure the relative value of each alternative on each objective on a purely subjective scale (1 to 9 linguistic scale, etc.), a partly subjective scale, or a numerical scale (e.g., levelized cost). Value scale can either be linearly monotonic (more is preferred to less) or nonlinear scales can be used (use of thresholds).
Step 9	Calculate the overall values using a simple weighted addictive function.
Step 10	Rank and choose among the alternatives according to value.

Source: Van Winterfeldt and Edwards (1986)

be concerned with developing a more intuitive feel for the nature of the risk and uncertainty. When we must choose from among a number of possible courses of action, a decision box can be useful as a way of organizing information and presenting overviews of the possible consequences of specific decisions. In a decision box decisions are broken down into three elements: possible *states* of the world, *acts* that we are capable of undertaking, and *outcomes* that are the consequences of a specific act and particular state of the world proving to be true. The states are defined in a way that captures the major uncertainties of concern to the problem at hand. They must be defined such that they are mutually exclusive and complete.

For example, as you leave your home you may ask yourself "will it rain?" Your scope of action (the *acts*) might simply be to take an umbrella or not. (You do not have the option of taking an act to make it rain or not rain.) The *outcomes* here would be something like the combination of rain and the act of not taking your umbrella resulting in you getting very wet, or taking your umbrella and it not raining meaning that you have needlessly carried your umbrella.

Often it will be possible to assign at least rough probabilities to the various states of nature and a numerical value, or at least a rank order of preference to the value of the outcomes. For example, there may be a 20% chance of rain, (and 80% chance of no rain), and you might value the possible outcomes: "rain and no umbrella" gives very negative utility; "rain and umbrella" gives moderate negative utility; "no rain and no umbrella" results in neutral utility; "no rain and umbrella" gives low negative utility. If we are able to assign numerical values to the outcomes we can calculate *expected values* for each by multiplying its nominal value by the probability and then compare the overall expected value of one act (i.e., the sum of the expected value for each possible state of nature) with that for the other possible acts. If the decisionmaker is playing the odds, then he can identify which act is preferred on the basis of the expected value of the possible outcomes. Sometimes decisionmakers' objectives go beyond that of maximizing the expected value of their action. For example, let us extend our umbrella decision and say we have important documents which we do not want to get wet. In this case we may be concerned with avoiding an act that has even a very small likelihood of that happening. Sometimes, we may simply eliminate from consideration an act that contains a highly negative possible outcome, even if the probability of that outcome is very low.

In Table 9. 4 we show a decision box for an environmental issue. Here we consider the case of a dangerous pollutant, the source of which remains uncertain. Let us say that we are confident enough only to outline the three states as shown. In other words, (i) the factory is the only or the major source of the problem, (ii) it is a significant contributory source but not the only one, or (iii) it is not a significant source. Our acts might be to (a) close down the factory, (b) to severely curtail emissions through expensive control equipment, or (c) simply to take no action.

Let us say that we can roughly estimate the net benefits of each outcome. For example, the outcome of closing the factory and it proving to be that it is the only or the major source of the problem has a net value of 4. This might be the combination of avoiding the damage which we value at 7, less the cost which we value at 3. Where costs exceed the benefits, the net benefits take on negative values.

Now let us assume that we believe the probabilities can be at least roughly estimated and are as shown. (Note that the probabilities must add up to 1.) Here we see that with a 40% probability that the factory is not a source of the problem, the expected value of the outcome of imposing strict controls on the factory under this state is -0.8. Overall, the expected value of closing the factory is negative as is the course of taking no action. Imposing strict controls is only slightly favorable. However, another advantage of imposing strict control is that the worst possible outcome is only - 2 compared to a - 3 for the act of closing the factory and a - 7 for taking no action.

Table 9.4
A Decision Box

ACTS	Factory is the only or major source	Factory is a significant contributory source	Factory is not a source	Overall Expected value of the act
	P = .2	P = .4	P = .4	
Close the factory	+4	-1	-3	
	(+0.8)	(-0.4)	(-1.2)	(-0.8)
Impose Strict Controls	+3	+1	-2	
on Factory	(+0.6)	(+0.4)	(-0.8)	(+0.2)
Take no action	-7	-2	0	
	(-1.4)	(-0.8)	(0)	(-2.2)

Note:
( ): Expected value
P : Probability

One interesting exercise is to use a decision box to assess possible actions about global climate change. Here the states might be something like: (i) the climate is changing but this is not induced by human activity, (ii) the climate is changing and is caused by human activity, and (iii) the climate is not changing. Possible acts might be to (a) undertake a major program of reducing emission of greenhouse gases, (b) undertake a limited program, or (c) wait and see. Most outcomes (under any of the acts) are likely to have a negative net present value, and the effort might be one of identifying the action with the lowest net expected cost. Another consideration is that of discounting, since the benefits will tend to come in the future and much of the costs in the near term. We leave such an exercise for the reader to pursue. However, even from the very brief description given above, it may be evident why the political process finds it so difficult to come to a workable agreement on addressing climate change concerns.

NOTE

1. Computationally this can be quite daunting. Fortunately, there are a variety of computer software programs that will automatically repeat random sampling and do the associated calculations.

10

Policy Instruments for
Environmental Management

This chapter introduces and reviews a number of basic approaches to the design of environmental policy instruments. One fundamental distinction is between policy instruments that place requirements on parties responsible for environmental damage to change their behavior, and instruments that provide inducements for such changes in behavior. We further distinguish between inducements based on priced market incentives and those for which the incentives are market-oriented but not explicitly priced.

The requirements approach includes measures that most texts label "command and control," and we refer to as *direct controls*. Examples of direct controls include emission standards and requirements to employ a specific technology. What other texts often refer to as "market-based measures" or "economic incentives," we term *priced market incentives*; this is in order to distinguish measures such as emission taxes and permits from market-oriented, though unpriced, inducements to voluntary self-regulation. In addition to emission taxes and permits, examples of priced market-based incentives include deposit/refund programs and government procurement programs. Examples of unpriced market-oriented incentives include exemption from some reporting requirements as a reward for implementing a certified voluntary regulation program, and the dissemination of information about emitters' performance to potential customers and other interested groups.

While a number of factors influence the choice of policy instrument, the most basic consideration is the need for policy instruments that are both effective and efficient. This chapter describes and illustrates the impressive theoretical advantages of priced market incentives. It also notes the significant practical limitations on their application in a number of common environmental management situations. While describing the inherent inefficiency of most forms of direct controls, the persistent appeal of such measures is also considered. With regard to inducements for voluntary self-regulation, we show how these potentially can have the same basic advantages in terms of economic efficiency as do priced incentives, and note their strengths and weaknesses relative to priced incentives.   Separately, the polluter pays principle is considered with regard to the elasticity of demand to engage in environmentally damaging activities; and the ability of the regulatory agency to monitor such activity and enforce compliance.

SEEKING EFFECTIVE AND EFFICIENT POLICY INSTRUMENTS

Optimal Environmental Quality

Achieving optimal environmental quality is one of many goals. In a world of limited resources and competing demands, there are more opportunities for, and areas in need of, environmental improvement than we are able or willing to pursue. To attain the best overall environmental quality, we must use available resources as efficiently as possible. This means we must first properly set environmental goals and then apply the policy instruments that meet the goals, while requiring minimum resources to do so.

The optimal level of overall environmental quality is definable in concept, but often difficult to specify in practice. In principle, the optimal level is where the incremental (marginal) costs of environmental improvement equal the incremental (marginal) benefits of that improvement.   This matching of incremental costs with benefits must be determined *individually* for each situation. For example, where two factories emit the same effluent, the damage caused by each may be quite different, if their locations differ. Even if the individual damage functions could be specified (a daunting task in itself), the conceptually more difficult problem remains of putting an appropriate value on such damage, in order to compare the costs of the practice's effects with those of preventing them.

As Ronald Coase (1960) demonstrated, in a world without transactions costs, those who damage the environment and those concerned about such damage could come to a negotiated agreement on the appropriate level of damage, regardless of how the environmental property rights are assigned. By extension, interests of the natural environment and future generations could be represented in such negotiations by concerned members of the present generation. Yet, as Coase pointed out in his original work and later reiterated (1990), in the real world transactions costs, such as information barriers, are significant impediments to effective negotiated solutions on the environment.

We may view environmental quality standards set by government as an attempt to overcome the limitations of individually negotiated agreements on the appropriate level of environmental damage.   Nonetheless, while government's involvement may lessen institutional barriers to negotiation, the major problems of information availability remain, for instance about who is causing what specific damage, and the valuation of that damage.

In the face of such obstacles to the determination of demonstrably 'optimal' standards for environmental quality, Baumol and Oates (1988) recommend accepting the ambient environmental quality standards set by the government and then attaining these as efficiently as possible,[1] They refer to this as "efficiency without optimality." With this point noted, we also would argue that *a priori* if firms are willing to go beyond the standards and if regulators or the public are willing to compensate them for doing so, then the existing standards probably are too lax.

Criteria for Comparing Policy Instruments

In a specific context some environmental policy instruments will be more effective and efficient than others. Effectiveness may be viewed as the combined result of the strength of the policy instrument in affecting changes in behavior, the ease of its implementation, and its robustness – how effective it is under changing conditions. Here, we stress that efficiency assessments should be aimed at that subset of policy instruments that are generally agreed to be reliably effective in meeting an explicit environmental goal. In other words, conceptual advantages mean little if the policy instrument that embodies such advantages is impractical in the real world setting.

In practice, the choice of instrument is based on more than effectiveness and efficiency. The most obvious consideration is how the cost burden will be shared. The incidence of cost among different groups may be quite different under a charging scheme for waste disposal compared to a recycling requirement, for example. Likewise, some instruments, such as a mandate to employ a specific effluent clean-up technology, may have greater effect than others, such as fuel regulations, on the relative competitive position of one type of firm to another. Well-financed multinational corporations may be able to undertake voluntary in-house pollution reduction measures that might be burdensome or simply beyond the capacity of poorly capitalized, locally based enterprises. While policymakers hopefully look to what is good for society as a whole, in the real world powerful interest groups often are able to block policies that would result in a heavy cost burden for themselves.

Control measures that leave the affected party as much flexibility as possible tend to be more efficient than those that dictate specific actions. A related matter is a policy's adaptability to changing conditions. The need to alter controls frequently in order to keep pace with technological or economic changes may undermine effectiveness. Administrative costs, for instance to monitor compliance, must also be considered. A regulatory agency with a tight budget may avoid policy instruments that involve high administrative costs, even if such instruments have significant advantages in other respects. To the extent that environmental policy instruments differ with regard to these and other criteria, the appropriate choice of instrument to address a particular problem requires assessing tradeoffs among multiple objectives.

While practical decisionmaking generally considers the need for such tradeoffs, theoretical arguments tend to have a more narrow focus. Economists sometimes seem to focus on efficiency in environmental management, to the virtual exclusion of other objectives. Typically, such arguments relate to the inherent efficiency advantages of market-based environmental policy instruments over direct controls. Indeed, the case in favor of market-based approaches often is presented so forcefully that readers may find it difficult to understand how market-based measures could possibly remain the exception, while direct controls remain the norm in the real world. Here, we examine the potentials and limitations of different types of policy instruments for achieving environmental goals. We note the importance of efficiency, but consider factors such as effectiveness in environmental protection, administrative requirements, and the incidence of costs.

Targeting Specific Process Stages

Before selecting an environmental policy instrument to deal with a particular problem, and perhaps even before deciding what type of approach to employ, it is important to consider at what stage to target the policy instrument within the cradle to grave system of production, consumption/use, and disposal. All else being equal, it is generally best to implement controls as close as possible to the process stage at which the greatest environmental damage occurs. For example, when attempting to limit the emission of a particular industrial pollutant, targeting the pollutant emissions themselves through performance-based standards is likely to be preferable to targeting material inputs into the production system, the process technology employed, or the sale of final products produced through the polluting process.

Yet, in the real world, other things often are not equal. It may be very expensive to measure emissions from numerous sources, and more practical to require changes to the production process. Similarly, it may be far more practical to mandate changes in the composition of a product than to control its disposal. Clearly, compliance monitoring considerations may strongly favor controls aimed at process stages other than that of direct concern.

A CLOSER LOOK AT REQUIREMENTS VERSUS INCENTIVES

Regardless of which process stage is targeted, another fundamental question is whether to employ a policy instrument that mandates specific actions on the part of those subject to them, or encourages desired changes by altering incentives. While some policy instruments may have features of both philosophies, and sometimes a package of instruments of various types may be applied, often the basic choice is between a requirements and an inducements approach. The terms *direct controls* and *market-based inducements* represent broad categories, each encompassing a wide variety of possible management tools. Indeed, these categories are defined not so much as a fixed set of instruments, but rather the attributes of a particular policy instrument which might be designed.

We first consider the requirements philosophy. What type of mandates might such measures entail? One example is a pollutant concentration limit (emissions standard) applied to the effluent streams of factories emitting a certain pollutant. An upper limit might be set on the allowable concentration (e.g., micrograms per cubic meter), or on amounts emitted over some period of time (e.g., tonnes per day). Sometimes in combination with an emissions standard, and sometimes separately, a regulatory agency may mandate the use of a specific process input (e.g., low sulfur fuel), or a certain technology (e.g., flue gas desulfurization [FGD]).[2] Other policy instruments within the category of direct controls might include location or time restrictions on activities (e.g., industrial zoning, time-of-day noise controls) and health and safety regulations.

In theory, direct controls could be tailored to match the particular situation of each polluter. In practice, however, the information and administrative requirements for such individual treatment typically are prohibitive. Hence, the specific requirements tend to be applied uniformly to all those subject to the measure.

In contrast to direct controls, market-oriented measures *influence* rather than *dictate* specific behavior by altering the incentives faced by those engaging in environmentally damaging activities.[3] As the United States Environmental Protection Agency (U.S. EPA) notes, the freedom of action allowed for with market-based incentives comes only after "correcting the incentives faced by private parties to reflect important social costs" (U.S. EPA 1993).

As with direct controls, the category of market incentives is potentially quite broad. Examples include emission taxes, taxes on polluting inputs, credits for emission reduction, permits to emit a specified amount of a pollutant, waste disposal charges, and deposit/refunds (for materials that may be recycled or for hazardous substances to be isolated from the common waste stream). More positive inducements might involve government procurement policies, exemptions from certain direct controls as a result of implementing voluntary environmental management, and information disclosure to encourage better market functioning.

The Inefficiency of Requiring Uniform Requirements

While market-based controls have much to recommend them, economists' preference for such instruments is strongly reinforced by inherent drawbacks in the use of direct controls. At the heart of what economists dislike about direct controls is that they tend to be applied uniformly to all affected parties, while those parties themselves tend to differ with regard to the costs each faces to reduce environmental damages. When affected parties face different costs for compliance, a uniform requirement applied to each emitter is inherently inefficient; total compliance costs are greater than necessary to achieve the desired improvement in environmental quality.

Table 10.1 and Figures 10.1 and 10.2 illustrate the inefficiency of a uniform emissions standard. Here, the inefficiency of concern stems not from differences in the impact of the pollutant emissions from different sources, but because the emitters face different costs in curtailing emissions.[4] Consider the case of two factories in similar locations, each emitting 100 tonnes per hour of the same pollutant. To simplify the illustration, let us assume that changes are possible only in increments of 20 tonnes per hour. In practice, it is not uncommon to find that changes in operating technology or procedures are somewhat lumpy, that is, involving rather large units of change. The smooth cost curves typically used by economists are stylized abstractions and we avoid there here in the interest of at least somewhat greater realism. Table 10.1 shows the incremental cost of each tonne per hour removed from the waste stream in increments of 20 tonnes, and the cumulative cost to each firm of successively higher levels of removal. These data are used to develop the incremental pollution abatement cost functions in Figure 10.1 and Figure 10.2.

In Figure 10.1, each firm is subject to an emissions limit of 40 tonnes per hour. Although the first increment of 20 tonnes reduction (from 100 to 80 tonnes per hour) costs both firms the same ($100,000 per tonne), Firm A faces a more steeply rising incremental (marginal) cost than does Firm B for further reductions. Firm A's cost is $300,000 per tonne of pollutant removed as its emissions are reduced from 80 to 60 tonnes per hour. This increases to $700,000 as emissions fall from 60 to 40 tonnes per hour and to $1.1 million per tonne if the level of pollutant releases were to fall from 40 to 20. As we see in Table 10.1 and Figure 10.1, Firm B also faces rising incremental costs, but its pollutant removal costs rise more slowly. Faced with an emissions limit of 40 tonnes per hour, Firm A incurs a cumulative in-house compliance cost of $22

Table 10.1
Hypothetical Marginal Cost and Cumulative Cost Schedules for Pollutant Removal from Emission Stream (in million $ per tonne removed per hour)

	EMISSION REDUCTION	From 100 to 80t	From 80 to 60t	From 60 to 40t	From 40 to 20t
FIRM A					
	Cost $/tn	$ 0.1	$ 0.3	$ 0.7	$ 1.1
	Step Cost	$ 2.0	$ 6.0	$14.0	$22.0
	Cumulative	$ 2.0	$ 8.0	$ 22.0	$ 44.0
FIRM B	**Cost $/tn**	$ 0.1	$ 0.2	$ 0.3	$ 0.5
	Step Cost	$ 2.0	$4.0	$ 6.0	$10.0
	Cumulative	$ 2.0	$ 6.0	$12.0	$22.0

Figure 10.1
Uniform Emission Standard

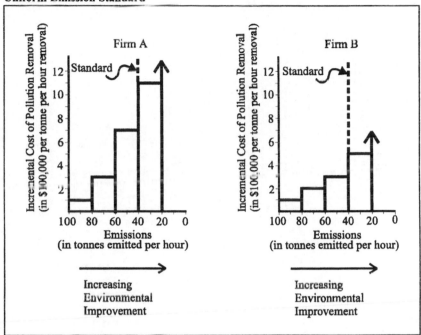

million, while Firm B incurs an in-house compliance cost of $12 million. Hence, the combined cost for reducing emissions from 200 to 80 tonnes per hour is $34 million.

Figure 10.2 illustrates how this same result (i.e., limiting combined emissions to 80 tonnes per hour) could be achieved at a lower combined cost by setting individual emission standards. Here the two firms still emit the same combined total, but more efficient Firm B removes more than it did before, with an off-setting change by Firm A. Firm A now removes only 40 tonnes per hour and so continues to emit 60. Firm B now removes 80 tonnes per hour, emitting only 20. With conditions as shown in Figure 10.2, Firm A now faces a cumulative in-house pollutant control cost of $8 million, while Firm B faces a cumulative cost of $22 million. Combined costs to industry for meeting the overall emissions reduction is now $30 million (instead of $34 million), a savings of about 11%. Since we are using step functions here, the incremental costs of the two firms are not equal when we reach the minimum combined cost (i.e., Firm A faces an incremental removal cost of $300,000 per tonne per hour, while Firm B faces $500,000). If the technology exists for very small changes in the level of clean-up, then emissions trading could continue until the two firms faced the same marginal removal costs (i.e., where A emits between 40 and 60 tonnes per hour and B emits between 20 and 40).

Figure 10.2
Individually Set Emission Standards

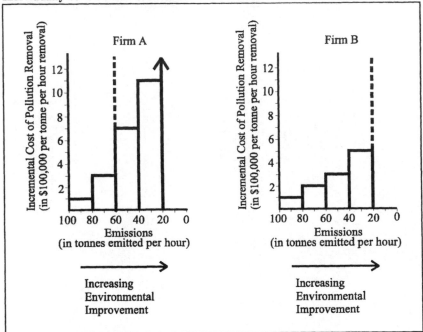

This result has its direct counterparts in daily life. If a certain amount of work is to be accomplished by two individuals, and one is more efficient than the other, it obviously requires less combined effort when the more efficient person increases his contribution beyond half and the less efficient one reduces his contribution correspondingly.

Of course, the use of individually determined emission standards raises several issues. The first is equity. Presumably, the more efficient firm should not be penalized by having to bear the full cost of its greater efforts, while the less efficient firm is rewarded with a lower compliance cost. Hence, some mechanism would be required for an income transfer between the firms.

Another problem is information availability. If government sets standards for each source, how does it acquire the necessary information on the costs of pollutant removal? Those subject to the controls may not be fully forthcoming with the necessary data. And, instead of only two firms, a more typical situation would involve tens, hundreds, or perhaps even thousands of emission sources.

Uniformly applied emission standards are not the only forms of direct control to have significant drawbacks. Consider, for example, industrial sulphur dioxide (SO_2) controls. Emissions may be reduced in various ways, including low sulfur fuel and flue gas desulfurization (FGD). In other words, we may reduce the pollution problem by limiting the input (sulfur) of the material which eventually becomes a pollutant (SO_2), or through end-of-pipe clean-up. Which of these methods should be employed, assuming that either alone would be sufficient to bring a group of emission sources into compliance with a given emissions SO_2 standard?

Regardless of which particular technique for pollution reduction is mandated, if that measure is applied across the board, it is likely to be inefficient. If the firms are heterogenous, some probably would find it cheaper to switch to low-sulfur fuel in order to achieve the required reduction in emissions, while others could comply more cheaply by using FGD. Hence, the uniform application of either measure will result in a higher total compliance cost for the affected group of emitters compared to a system allowing flexibility of response.

The Efficiency of Market-Based Incentives

Whereas direct controls fail to discriminate among dissimilar firms (or at best, result in the regulator making such distinctions), market-based measures naturally exploit such differences to attain the most efficient, overall least-cost solution. And they do this without discouraging technological innovation, or otherwise unduly interfering in private decisionmaking.

In addition, if applied to all increments of an environmentally damaging activity, priced market-based policy instruments make engaging in such activities a restricted privilege for which one must pay. Hence, under many forms of market-based measures, "emitters" (those who emit pollutants or otherwise damage the environment) see *all* of their environmentally damaging activity as a cost, rather than simply that component that is above a threshold level.

Consider a tax on pollutant emissions imposed on the two firms represented in Figures 10.1 and 10.2. The uniform standard (Figure 10.1) does not lead to the least-cost solution. The information costs of individually determined standards (Figure 10.2) tend to be prohibitive. But when faced with an emissions tax, the firms will naturally respond in a manner that minimizes overall compliance costs.

Each firm compares the cost of the emissions tax against its own cost of pollutant removal, and lowers emissions until the in-house cost of doing so equals the tax rate. After that point, it would be cheaper for the firm to pay the tax on remaining emissions rather than do more in-house emissions reduction. When two firms face the same pollution tax but have different in-house costs for pollutant removal, they arrive at different *optimal* levels of removal, just as happened in Figure 10.2. And this will be the combined least-cost approach for achieving the overall emission reduction. Under the tax system, firms will also have an incentive to lower future costs for pollutant removal through technological and operational changes.

To illustrate, in Figure 10.3 we use the same cost data as in the earlier figures. Note that here the control is not imposed as a vertical line (on the "pollutant output" or x axis), but rather as a horizontal line on the cost (y axis). Let us say that the tax is set at $600,000 per tonne emitted per hour. We can see in Figure 10.3 that Firm A will find it efficient to emit 60 tonnes per hour, while Firm B will find it efficient to emit 20. Firm A will pay $36 million in emissions tax (60 tonnes per hour times $600,000 per tonne/hour), while Firm B will pay $12 million in tax for its 20 tonnes per hour. Of course, compliance costs for each firm are higher than each would face under the individual standards approach. However, the costs of in-house clean-up are the same as with the individual standards approach and this is the crucial point. From the perspective of *economic* efficiency (as distinct from the financial perspective of the polluters), the emissions tax paid is a transfer payment from one part of society (the industrial sector) to society at large (represented by the government). While transfer payments are seen as costs or benefits to those affected, such payments do not directly change the welfare of society as a whole.

Another priced market-based measure is the use of tradeable pollution permits. Normally, a limited number of permits would be issued for some fixed amount of pollutant emitted or other environmentally damaging activity, and for a fixed time period. When permits are tradeable, the holder has an incentive to look for ways to curtail emissions when the costs of doing so are below the market value of the permits. The permits become an asset to be used or sold, whichever is more profitable. To deal with issues of the local concentration of impacts, the validity of the permits might be restricted to a specific geographic area.

When a permit system is instituted, the way in which the initial stock of permits is distributed determines the overall economic impact on the industry (though not necessarily the impact on individual firms). One strategy is to auction permits to the highest bidder. This results in cash transfers to government roughly equivalent to those that arise under an effluent tax system. Alternatively, the government may offer the permits at a fixed price. More often, in order to reduce opposition to the program, the government may distribute permits at no cost to existing pollutant emitters, who each receive a number proportionate to its current emissions. Variations on these ideas are possible. For example, the government may issue some permits free of charge, then auction the remaining ones. The important point is that all permit markets, regardless of the method of initial distribution, function in the same general manner. Once a permit is received by a firm, it acquires a market value, and the firm is motivated to reduce emissions until the capitalized value of its incremental in-house emission control cost is equal to the permit's market value.

Under the permit system, emissions are allowed only to the extent that permits have been issued for them, and because they may be sold pollutant emitters have the incentive to look for ways to free permits for sale rather than

Figure 10.3
Emissions Tax or Tradeable Permits

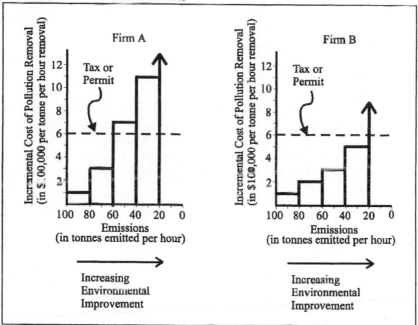

use. Compared to tax schemes permits have the advantage of keeping the overall level of pollution strictly under control, hence avoiding concerns over price inelasticity and general price inflation.

For the situation illustrated in Figure 10.3, the regulatory agency might issue 80 certificates, each good for one or several years and allowing the holder to emit one tonne per hour of the pollutant. Let us say the government decides to sell the certificates for $250,000 each. Firm A would lower emissions to 80 tonnes per hour and seek to purchase all 80 permits. Meanwhile, Firm B would find it efficient to reduce emissions to 60 tonnes and bid for 60 certificates. Of course, with the two firms seeking a total of 140 permits when only 80 are available, the price would be increased as a result of active bidding.

How much would the firms eventually bid? If the price reached $400,000, Firm A would want only 60 certificates and Firm B would seek 40, leaving a smaller shortfall relative to demand, but a shortfall nonetheless. In a situation of perfectly divisible units of emission control, the final bidding price would be where the cost of a certificate equals the marginal cost of in-house clean-up, and both firms face the same marginal costs for additional in-house emission reduction. In our less idealized example in Figure 10.3, a market price of $600,000 per certificate (the same as for the emissions tax) would clear the market.

Priced Market-Based Measures and Income Redistribution

We now return to the point about pollutant emitters' higher costs under market-based policy instruments. As shown in Figure 10.3, the cost of the tax or permit is *in addition to* the in-house emission reduction costs. Firm A now faces a total compliance cost of $44 million ($36 million in pollution tax or permit cost, plus $8 million for in-house actions). Meanwhile, Firm B now faces a total cost of $34 million ($12 million in tax or permit cost, plus $22 million in-house).

When taxes or permits are applied to all aspects of the emissions stream, emitters face a higher total compliance cost. Yet, as noted from the perspective of society as a whole, rather than only industry, this tax is not a social cost. After accounting for internal transfer payments, as a whole society saves $4 million in compliance costs, just as it would if the individual emission standards approach were feasible.

Yet, what some analysts might rather casually refer to from a social cost perspective as a mere *transfer payment* is, from the financial perspective of affected emitters, a very real private cost indeed. One approach for dealing with the opposition such added financial costs might engender is to reduce other industrial taxes. This possibility would, of course, need to be considered within the larger context of overall industrial and tax policy. Another option for limiting the extent of the transfer payment from industry to the rest of society might be to apply the tax to emissions above some threshold. (Likewise, tradeable permits might be issued free-of-charge for emissions up to a threshold). This approach may be expedient, but it has implications for the implied assignment of environmental property rights. If compensation to industry to offset the higher financial costs to pollutant emitters is deemed appropriate, it should be done in a manner that has minimal effect on the incentive for each one to look for his own least-cost solutions for controlling all pollution not just that above some threshold.

This raises the point of the effect of environmental management on innovation. Some forms of direct control mandate use of specific technology. Such measures tend to stifle technological change, and intrude on private decisionmaking. In contrast, the market-based measures tend to involve minimal interference in such decisions. It is important that such advantages are not inadvertently lost through attempts to compensate emitters for their higher financial costs under market-based policy instruments.

Emission Taxes Versus Emission Permits

The effectiveness of a pollutant tax depends on the price elasticity of demand to engage in environmentally damaging activities. Such elasticity is often unknown in advance, and it may be difficult to iteratively seek the appropriate level of tax to bring about the desired behavior. Industry would argue that a frequently changing tax level unfairly complicates corporate planning. Tradeable permits avoid this problem, since the permits limit overall emissions.

While the tax system tends to encourage adoption of improved environmental control technologies as these become available, the number of permits may set a floor for emission reductions, since the market price of their permits would tend to fall as the alternative of employing control technology becomes cheaper. Over the longer term, this problem could be overcome by issuing fewer permits to replace expired ones or by buying back some. Hence, while both taxes and permits offer appealing efficiency advantages, it is important to consider which of these two options is more appropriate for a particular situation. Taxes are likely to be considered more attractive than permits when one or more of the following conditions holds:

1. The price elasticity of demand to emit pollutants can be estimated with some confidence, and demands are likely to be price elastic under politically feasible tax rates.

2. It is expected that the costs of pollution control technology will fall in the future.

3. Tax levels are easy to change in order to account for any initial misjudgments about the price elasticity of emissions or to compensate for general price inflation.

Permits are likely to be more attractive than taxes under conditions in which one or more of the following holds:

1. It is essential that a limit be placed quickly and reliably on pollutant emissions to protect human health or fragile ecosystems.

2. The price elasticity of demand to emit a pollutant is highly uncertain or may be price inelastic at politically feasible tax rates.

3. General price inflation is expected to be relatively high and tax levels are not easily changed with sufficient frequency to compensate.

4. There is a potential to gradually reduce the number of permits offered to reflect improvements in emissions control technology.

5. The incidence of the cost burden can be manipulated through the initial distribution of permits.

OTHER EXAMPLES OF PRICED MARKET-BASED INSTRUMENTS

The number of different types of environmental controls that are included under the rubric of "market-based" is relatively large. Here we outline a few more commonly discussed ones.

Environmental taxes or permits need not be limited to emissions. Taxes could be imposed or permits required for the use of environmentally damaging materials, equipment, or processes. Yet, as noted above, the key to economic efficiency is to leave the polluter as much flexibility as possible. As we move back from the emission of pollutants (already one step back from attempting to deal directly with the damages these cause), we leave less scope for the polluter to find his own least-cost solution to deal with his most damaging behavior. Hence, in general, we should employ taxes or permits on polluting inputs or processes only where significant limitations exist on our ability to implement market-based measures targeted more directly at the environmentally damaging activity.

Deposit/refund schemes for recyclable or hazardous materials provide consumers with incentives to re-use a material, such as aluminium, or to separate it from the common waste stream items such as aluminium cans or items, which require special disposal or handling (e.g., some types of batteries). A deposit is required of the manufacturer, the distributor, or the buyer for each unit produced or sold. This deposit is returned only when the unit is returned for reuse or proper disposal. Each user is free to decide if the value of the refund is sufficient to warrant his or her effort to return it. The value of the refund does not necessarily need to be enough to attract the effort of the product user. So long as the material is easily identifiable and separable, other persons may find it attractive to undertake such separation to obtain the refund.

Government procurement policies may be used to help create or strengthen a market for environmentally preferred goods or services by increasing demand. A common example is recycled paper; some government agencies commit to purchase recycled paper even if it is not the lowest priced option in the market, thus providing a reliable and sizable demand. In principle, this approach could be quite comprehensive. It could extend to such things as particular types of plastic, photocopier maintenance services, or even selection of dry cleaning services. In practice, however, such policies may face practical limitations, such as requirements to take low-cost bids and controversy over the environmental benefits of specific products. There also is the possibility of political opposition from those who lose out in government contracts under such a procurement approach.

Incentives for Voluntary Self-Regulation: Regulatory Relief

We have focused so far on market-based environmental policy instruments involving price signals. In addition to these, there are policy instruments that work through incentives but are not directly priced. Here we consider two basic forms of such measures. First, those that involve exemption from some form of direct control as a reward for implementing an in-house environmental management system; and second, those that involve the dissemination of information regarding environmental performance to an emitter's customers and other interested parties. Incentives for voluntary self-regulation, in principle, retain one of the major arguments in favor of priced incentives: the flexibility offered to emitters so that each may respond in the way that best reflects his own cost structure.

Voluntary measures or self-regulation may involve formal certification programs by industry associations such as Responsible Care (Association of International Chemical Manufactures) or ISO 14000 (International Standards Organization). Alternatively, they might involve individual agreements between one or more selected firms (or even a single plant) and regulators in a certain jurisdiction. Typically, such programs include specific steps, such as implementing sound in-house environmental management programs, and in some cases they may involve pledges to employ a specific process or production change. While voluntary measures are often undertaken in the absence of explicit agreements with the regulators, in general, the emitters would argue that such steps warrant serious consideration by regulators of ways to reduce the cost burden to industry of complying with existing standards. Such cost saving might be in the form of less burdensome reporting requirements or greater flexibility in the manner in which emission reduction targets are to be met.

Why might some emitters be interested in opportunities for self-regulation? Largely because they believe that they possess options for in-house improvement that could be undertaken if they received sufficient compensation. Why are they potentially efficient? Like priced market incentives, such as emission taxes, in self-regulation each emitter evaluates his own cost of internal clean-up versus an externally imposed cost (e.g., reporting requirement), and then chooses the least-cost option.

Incentives for Voluntary Self-Regulation: Information Dissemination

Another basic incentive for self-regulation is the potential value in terms of image. For organizations that sell directly to consumers, the value of a "green" (environmentally friendly) image, and the negative value of a particularly bad environmental image, might be quite high. Even firms engaged in primary or intermediate product production can face a knock-on effect from demands made by environmentally conscious consumers of the final products. In addition, producers tend to be conscious of potential opposition from the community in the general proximity (or downwind/downstream) of large production facilities. Information about an emitters' environmental standing (in absolute terms and relative to the performance of similar facilities elsewhere) could have a significant effect on how much trouble or support the local community is likely to offer. This, in turn, will affect the industry's costs of operation, or even the viability of operation at a particular site. A government program of publicizing the environmental performance records of individual emitters could potentially serve as a spur to greater self-regulation. As with the potential for regulatory compensation, the value a firm places on its green image will often be quite different from one emitter to another. Each would decide for itself if additional self-regulation is more cost effective than the financial risk associated with a poor environmental image.

We illustrate such unpriced incentives for voluntary self-regulation through a marginal benefits step function shown in Figure 10.4. We assume that emissions are strictly limited through direct control to 60 tonnes per hour and that the marginal cost associated with a failure to meet that emission ceiling is undefined but unacceptably high. Let us assume that if the firms go beyond the standard, for instance from 60 to 40 tonnes per hour, then they would receive compensation in the form of reduced environmental reporting requirements and greater flexibility in the choice of emission control technology. In this example, such a step would have a marginal benefit to each firm of $800,000 per year. Let us further assume that a new environmental information dissemination program will be started in the coming year, and records of this year's environmental performance are expected to affect future profits. For the sake of illustration, let us assume that if a firm went even further to reduce emissions, for instance from 40 to 20 tonnes per hour, its green image would be enhanced such that the present value of the marginal future profits is estimated at $600,000 per year.

Using the same emission reduction incremental cost function used in Table 10.1 and Figures 10.1 through 10.3, and the incremental benefit information in Figure 10.4, we show in Figure 10.5 the decision situation for our two firms. In this case both Firm A and B find it in their own interest to undertake self-regulation to reduce emissions from 60 to 40 tonnes per hour. However, only the lower cost Firm B finds it in its interest to take the next step of reducing emissions from 40 to 20 tonnes per hour. In the real world, the value different emitters place on such benefits might vary considerably. For example, reporting requirements are likely to be a greater relative burden to a smaller firm, or one with numerous emission discharge points, than for a larger firm with fewer points of discharge. Yet, even if this is the case, the same efficiency potential exists when each firm decides on its action by comparing its own incremental benefits and costs in determining the level of pollution to discharge.

Thus, emissions are reduced from a combined total of 120 tonnes per hour to 60 tonnes, and achieved at a lower net cost than if it had been attained without compensation (in this case, lower administrative costs and an improved image). Firm A saves $100,000 and Firm B $600,000, when compared with a situation in which they were each mandated to reduce emissions by a further 60 tonnes per hour. To the extent that the compensation to these firms is a result of improved efficiency in regulation and a better-functioning, better-informed market, then it represents a true efficiency gain for society.

Clearly, self-regulation requires trust, and a willingness and ability on the part of regulators and the regulated community to form a true partnership. Unfortunately, throughout much of the world and for much of the history of environmental policy, relations between regulators and the regulated community have tended to be rather confrontational. Creating a context of sufficient trust generally is an iterative process, in which experience with a

Figure 10.4
Perceived Benefits of Voluntary Measures

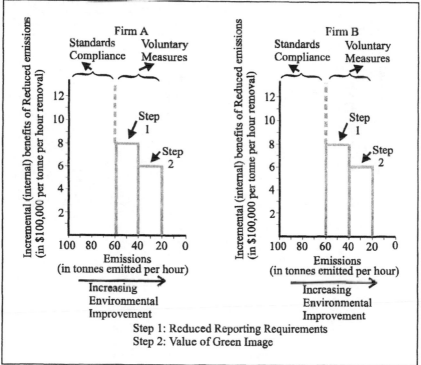

Step 1: Reduced Reporting Requirements
Step 2: Value of Green Image

relatively modest scope for self-regulation forms the basis for the design and level of more ambitious efforts. An important part of this process is the role of the public, both those who experience the impacts of the pollutant emissions most directly and those who purchase the products produced.

We note that unless the community in the vicinity of the plant (or down wind/down stream of its pollutant emissions) is somehow brought into the process of negotiating voluntary steps, then any *quid pro quo* the regulators might want to offer may be viewed with considerable suspicion or even resistance. Basically, what each of the three players (regulators, emitters, community) will desire is some form of adequate safeguards to insure that any agreements, once made, are honored.

Increasingly throughout the world firms are conscious of the value of a green image and the potential costs to corporate profit of the opposite image. At the time of this writing, certainly not all, and probably not most, consumers or stockholders care greatly about the public perception of a firm with regard to its impact on the environment. Yet, often even limited concern expressed by such groups will be enough to induce a firm at least to avoid an exceptionally environmentally unfriendly reputation, and even in some cases to promote an

Figure 10.5
Costs and Perceived Benefits of Voluntary Measures

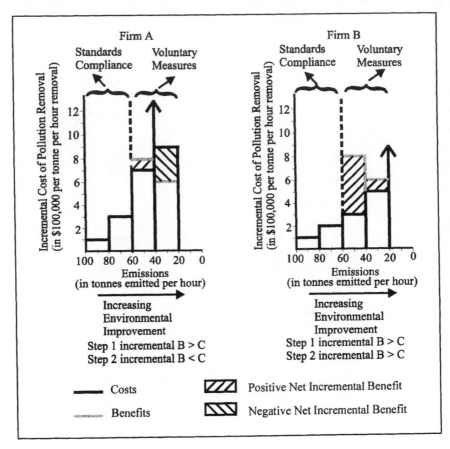

environmentally friendly one. Hence, greater dissemination of information on a particular firm's environmental record may help industry to meet the standards or even go beyond them. As the world economy has become increasingly integrated, large firms have become conscious of how the environmental records of suppliers and distributors throughout the world affects their own reputation in major consumer markets.[5] While information dissemination can be an effective tool in both higher income economies and developing ones, it should be recognized that the effects may be transitory. Consumers often have a short attention span, and the many firms that deal more with other members of industry than with the public are usually less susceptible to public pressure of this sort. Nonetheless, information dissemination can be a useful supplemental tool.

LIMITATIONS OF MARKET-BASED MEASURES

Administrative Considerations

The greatest practical limitation of emissions taxes and permits is the need for point-of-discharge monitoring to determine the amount of tax or compliance.[6] Point-of-discharge monitoring is feasible in situations with relatively few emitters, or when emitters can be relied on for self-monitoring. Often, however, adequate monitoring is physically impossible, prohibitively expensive, or simply administratively unappealing. More generally, it is necessary to keep in mind that enforcement costs may partly or fully offset the potential efficiency advantages of market-based incentives.

A problem with the emissions tax is the difficulty in estimating responsiveness to the tax (i.e., the price elasticity). If the rate is set too low, pollution remains too high to meet ambient environmental quality targets. If the tax is too high, it could harm the economy to such an extent that this cost outweighs the value society places on that degree of pollution reduction. And it is important to get the rate right with a minimum of adjustment, as frequent changes in the tax rate are likely to meet with strong opposition.

With regard to tradeable pollution permits, competitive trading of permits, an important feature for attaining overall least-cost, is likely only when the number of bidders is sufficiently large; and emitters differ significantly among themselves with respect to compliance costs. If geographic restrictions are placed on trading to avoid undesirable pollutant emission concentrations, the conditions for attractive trading opportunities may become harder to meet.

As for deposit/refund schemes, it is important to recognize that such schemes often involve complex and expensive administrative requirements. In the case of recycling, the costs of the recycling process itself can be prohibitive. If the main obstacle to private sector recycling is the cost of material cleaning or reprocessing (rather than the cost of the material separation and collection) then deposit/refund schemes are of little value.

With regard to inducements for voluntary self-regulation, these avoid the administrative costs typical of emissions taxes and permits, but unlike the priced measures, self-regulation will only work in a context of sufficient trust. Information dissemination will only be effective in specific circumstances. If regulators offer emitters compensation for undertaking self-regulation, and it is later learned that this trust was violated, then the costs to the regulators in terms of their own public image could be quite high. Because of the risk involved, direct compensation to emitters for self-regulation is likely to be offered only gradually and it is likely to proceed only as experience is gained in forming an effective partnership between the regulators and the regulated community.

Information dissemination to induce self-regulation avoids the need for a context of trust between the regulators and the regulated community, but it has other drawbacks, primarily that of uncertain effectiveness. Basically, some firms will care sufficiently about their environmental image and others will not.

Figure 10.6
Administrative Considerations in Implementing Incentive Measures

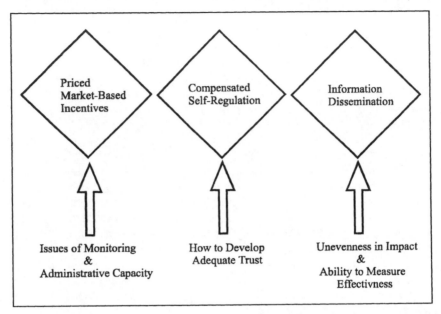

Even where an information dissemination program might be effective initially, it may lose effectiveness over time as consumers lose interest. Information programs are likely to play a secondary or supporting role as part of a larger set of environmental policy instruments to promote self-regulation. Figure 10.6 outlines the major administrative considerations with regard to a range of market-based policy instruments for environmental management.

INCOME DISTRIBUTION IMPACTS: IMPLICATIONS OF MARKET-BASED MEASURES

Under some emissions tax or permit systems, emitters face costs for *all* their emissions, rather than receiving the free-of-cost right to emit up to a level set by the standard. Hence, groups subject to the tax or permit system are worse off under such an approach, even though society as a whole gains. As one would expect, this lessens the appeal of market-based measures to affected groups, when they believe that their own financial costs would increase.

Beyond the immediate concerns of the polluters, some groups may object to these market-based approaches on the grounds of equity. Priced market-based policy instruments allow those who can afford to pay the tax or to out-bid others for permits to continue to engage in environmentally damaging activities, while those less financially well-off are prevented from doing so. This raises the question of whether anyone has the right to buy the privilege to damage the environment. The answer is simply that market-based measures make damaging the environment activity for which one must pay (i.e., rather than a "right to pollute" it represents a restricted "privilege granted to pollute" for which one must pay). And those who cannot afford to pay and so must reduce their environmentally damaging activities benefit in the form of the taxes or permit fees which others have paid in. Of course, for some groups the objections might be most fundamental: that humans have no right to damage the environment at all. As noted in Chapter 1, the perspective taken in this book is that humans will use the environment in ways which inevitability cause some type and level of damage and the task at hand is to prevent excessive damage and to do so as efficiently as possible.   Yet, even if one accepts that some level of environmental damage is appropriate—in other words, that in some cases an appropriately set value of damage is less than the costs of preventing it, then the debate continues over the acceptability of using the market to allocate access to environmental services.   Our position is that the market is appropriate for allocation of environmental resources so long as basic equity goals of society including inter-generational ones are not thereby threatened.

THE APPEAL OF DIRECT CONTROLS

In addition to the limitations of the market-based policy instruments, direct controls have their own appeal to regulators, environmental advocacy groups, and affected parties by virtue of one or more of the following features:

1.   Compliance requirements can be made unambiguous and often can be defined in ways that are easy to monitor.

2.   They may be applied evenly, requiring everyone without exception to adhere to specific requirements.

3.   With the exception of outright bans and some other types of direct controls, direct often controls allow those engaged in an environmentally damaging activity to continue to engage in some level of that activity without cost.

Perceived Effectiveness

While efficiency in meeting environmental quality goals is clearly desirable, the overriding criterion is generally *effectiveness* in attaining these goal. Direct controls have the advantage of being unambiguous with regard to the required response on the part of those subject to them, and this tends to appeal to regulators and to environmental advocacy groups. In contrast, the effectiveness of environmental taxes depends on the price elasticity of demand to engage in environmentally damaging activities.   In the case of tradeable permits, the trading may result in an undesirable concentration of pollution damage at certain locations. Yet geographic restrictions can undermine trading potential if zones have too few emitters to provide sufficient differences in abatement costs to make trading attractive. Hence, some regulators and environmental advocacy groups may deem self-regulation simply too risky.

From the regulators' perspective, effectiveness in limiting environmental damage in large measure depends on the ability to monitor compliance. Mandates for the use of specific technologies may minimize monitoring and enforcement requirements to occasional checks to confirm that the technology is in place and being used. For example, if a reliable technology exists for end-of-pipe treatment of an exhaust gas, for instance catalytic converters for gasoline-fuelled vehicles, the regulatory agency might simply require that all new gasoline vehicles employ that technology, since monitoring and enforcement for such a vehicle technology requirement is likely to be far lower than for a tax on measured vehicle emissions.

Likewise, restrictions on inputs, such as type and quality of fuel, may be monitored through the smaller and more concentrated group of wholesale suppliers rather than retail distributors or end users. Even where emissions monitoring is technically feasible, data collection and analysis represent an ongoing regulatory cost, with associated administrative commitments. Regulators may prefer a one-time requirement to employ a technology or specific process input on the simple grounds of fewer administrative costs to themselves. Regulators are, after all, an interest group with their own set of perceived benefits and costs separate from their designation or being responsible for looking out for the interests of society as a whole.

Even Handedness

Conceivably, direct control measures could be tailored for each party; however, in practice, this is generally administratively infeasible. While it may be making a virtue of necessity, the uniform application of a given mandate does have the appeal of appearing to be equitable: rich and poor alike are treated equally and all those damaging the environment must change their behavior in a prescribed manner. In contrast, market-based or permit tax schemes allow some affected parties to continue environmentally damaging behavior so long as they are willing (and able) to pay for it.[7]

Another potential advantage of many forms of direct control is that compliance costs are relatively easy to predict. This is in contrast to transferable pollution permits, the price of which changes with market conditions. Some businesses may find the ability to predict future environmental compliance costs an attractive feature for long-term planning.

Cost Burdens

When pollution is only regulated with regard to emissions above some amount, in effect this assigns environmental property rights in favor of those engaging in externality-generating activities up to that level. Those whose actions damage the environment might argue that since economic activity is essential and some degree of tradeoff between economic activity and environmental quality is inevitable, such a limited free "right to pollute" (or otherwise degrade the environment) is simply common sense. However, from Chapter 4 we know that when environmental damage is treated as an externality, there will likely be excessive pollution, because the value of avoiding such damage is seen as virtually zero by the one causing it. In other words, any private prevention cost is unattractive when there is no private value attached to the benefits of pollution abatement. In order for the assessment of pollution abatement actions to be appropriately specified, the one causing the externalities must see associated costs.   Thus, except where compliance monitoring costs are prohibitive, it is not valid to argue that a "right to pollute" free-of-charge up to some level is consistent with economic efficiency.

CHOOSING BETWEEN INDUCEMENTS AND REQUIREMENTS

The choice between an *inducements approach* and a *requirements approach* to the selection of environmental policy instruments largely comes down to:

1. Faith that market-based measures are likely, in practice as well as in theory, to be adequately designed and implemented to ensure attainment of environmental quality goals.

2. An assessment of the relative administrative costs and complexity of implementation between the two approaches.

3. Decisions about how environmental property rights and associated cost sharing should be allocated among different parts of society.

The polluter pays principle is one way to assign environmental property rights. The principle is consistent with pollution charges for all increments of environmental damage, even those that society might deem "acceptable," and it is the subject of the penultimate section of this chapter.

The Polluter Pays Principle

The ethical principle that the polluter should pay for the environmental damages he or she causes is an appealing one. Assuming that the rights of people to high quality environmental services outweigh the rights of others to dispose of unwanted waste products, this principle is consistent with the logic of internalizing externalities. The polluter pays principle is not, of course, limited to market-based measures. For instance, a manufacturing establishment subject to a requirement to employ a certain type of process technology is being made to "pay" for its pollution through restrictions in the choice of technology.

Elasticity Considerations. The question of the price elasticity of demand to generate wastes or to engage in other environmentally damaging activities is important when considering what we hope to accomplish through application of the polluter pays principle. For reasons outlined in Chapter 2, in some cases the price elasticity is likely to be relatively high (e.g., in the case of recyclable or easily recoverable materials). In other cases, it may be relatively low (e.g., sewage). The elasticity of demand to generate various other forms of industrial, transport, agricultural, commercial, and household wastes falls in between the two extremes. Basically, if the polluter finds his marginal cost of abatement to be relatively low, then his price elasticity of demand to generate pollution will tend to be quite high. Likewise, if it is very difficult to reduce the generation of pollutants, then the price elasticity of demand for doing so is likely to be relatively low (i.e., inelastic).

When the demand to pollute is highly price *inelastic*, making the polluter pay provides revenues for measures to mitigate associated environmental damages, though it probably will not lead to a significant reduction in the amount of pollution. Nonetheless, as it is relatively easy to forecast pollutant output, it is a simple task to set the level of charges so as to cover the cost of treatment facilities or post-emission clean-up.

When the demand to pollute is highly price *elastic*, then making the polluter pay significantly reduces the amount of pollution generated. However, unless we know the degree of this price elasticity in advance (and usually we do not), the tasks of sizing treatment facilities for the residual wastes and setting charge levels may be problematic.

Monitoring Pollutant Discharges and Other Damages. The question of the price elasticity of demand to engage in environmentally damaging activities raises another issue: the ability of the authority to monitor pollutant releases, and to enforce compliance with requirements such that all wastes be treated in-house or sent to the central treatment facility. If the generators of the waste are charged substantial amounts for collection and treatment, and if it is not possible to fully monitor the generation of waste, then there may be clandestine disposal. In other words, sometimes it may be rather risky to make the polluter pay. We should be careful to attempt to do so only when we are reasonably confident that the rules will be adequately enforced. Where pollutant discharges cannot be adequately monitored, it may even be appropriate to subsidize waste treatment or safe disposal.

A PRAGMATIC ASSESSMENT OF OPTIONS

This chapter has noted a number of limitations for both direct control and market-based environmental policy instruments. Fortunately, individuals and societies are usually able to make decisions and manage their affairs even in the face of severe limitations. We sometimes simply cut the Gordian knot, instead of allowing ourselves to be stymied by our inability to untie it. Rather than waiting for full information before acting, it may be appropriate to make first approximations of the costs and benefits associated with specific environmental improvements and set our ambient environmental quality standards accordingly. Even though it is often impossible to determine optimal environmental tax rates or emission standards, we may deem it useful to set one or the other so that we may begin moving toward a higher level of environmental quality, however imprecise our assessment of benefits and costs may be. The *theoretical* advantages of market-based control measures are impressive. Yet as also noted, in many practical situations such measures work only in a severely constrained fashion, or are simply impractical.

One recommendation is that environmental managers first carefully evaluate the potential use of market-based environmental policy instruments. They can then move on to technology or input restrictions or other forms of direct control, where it is clear that in the particular circumstances at hand, market-based measures are not practical—in other words, where monitoring costs are prohibitive or the prospects of effective enforcement are uncertain.

And even if emission standards, technology requirements, or other direct controls are employed, it is important to look for ways to:

1. Encourage desired changes through price signals whenever possible. Use direct controls, if necessary, to attain some minimum level of environmental protection, and then use market-based measures to encourage further improvements.

2. Give affected parties as much flexibility as possible while keeping the risks of failing to meet environmental goals within acceptable limits.

Although there is growing interest in market-based environmental policy instruments, these remain the exception rather than the rule for environmental management throughout the world. There are a number of likely explanations, including the limitations of market-based measures themselves, as well as the perceptions and the private interests of waste generators, government regulators, and environmental advocacy groups.

For those cases in which market-based environmental policy instruments are feasible, it would seem that potentially powerful opposition to their use comes from rather basic concerns:

1. When administrative requirements for compliance monitoring and enforcement are considered along with efficiency, the *net* advantage of using a market-based policy instrument may be less than a direct control alternative in certain specific cases.

2. Market-based measures reduce the scope of and power of the regulatory bureaucracy.

3. Market-based measures potentially make those damaging the environment liable for *all* of their damaging activity, rather than only for that above some designed excessive level. This may make emitters oppose them.

4. Market-based measures also may be seen by emitters as an *additional* set of measures to be put in place along with the exiting direct controls rather than as a replacement for them. Hence they may see them simply as an added cost.

5. In capital intensive industries firms with old technology may oppose a regulatory system that rewards innovation.

6. The use of regulatory incentives for self-regulation requires a context of partnership and mutual trust, and its creation often will require initiatives on the part of the regulated community.

7. Emissions and effluent permits are quite literally a license to pollute and hence regulators may face difficulty in convincing the public that such approaches are not only potentially more efficient, but that they do not constitute an unfair privilege granted to the wealthy.

Figure 10.7
Attaining and Exceeding Goals with Different Policy Instruments

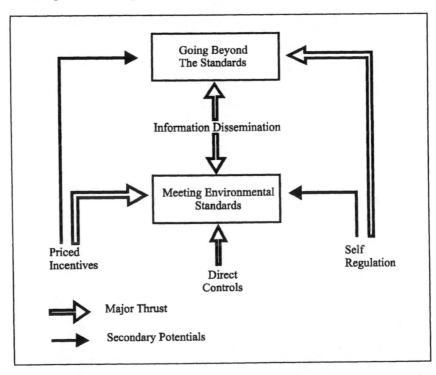

The basic recommendations of this chapter are that environmental managers thoroughly examine possibilities for using market-based policy instruments, and move on to direct controls only where they offer clear and compelling advantages. Even when a direct control approach is utilized, opportunities may exist to improve efficiency through supplemental incentive measures, and by framing the requirements in a manner that allows as much flexibility as possible in response. Allowing such flexibility (where it does not undermine potential effectiveness) may not only be more efficient; it may also lead to greater support for the environmental intervention.

Figure 10.7 shows how we characterize different types of policy instruments with regard to attaining minimum standards and going beyond these. Appendix 10.1 summarizes the major advantages and disadvantages associated with selected direct controls and market-based measures.

APPENDIX 10.1

SUMMARY OF ADVANTAGES AND LIMITATIONS OF SELECTED POLICY INSTRUMENTS FOR ENVIRONMENTAL MANAGEMENT

Ambient Standards

Definition: An environmental quality goal, usually in the form of an upper limit on the average concentration of a specific pollutant in the air or water.

Advantages: It sets a relatively objective and measurable indication of certain types of environmental quality against which actions to protect the environment may be judged.

Limitations/Drawbacks:

The optimal level of the standard is very difficult to determine.

The specific compliance measurements may be flawed due to such factors as local variations in concentration.

It may be difficult or impossible to associate violations of an ambient standard with any particular discharger's actions.

Emission Standards

Definition: A legal limit on the amount of a pollutant an individual source may emit under specified conditions (e.g., discharge per unit of time).

Advantages: It allows the regulatory agency to set clear and explicit limits on pollutant emissions.

Technology-based standards can be developed that achieve the standard at demonstrable costs.

Limitations/Drawbacks:

It is difficult to determine optimal standards (i.e., where the marginal benefits of the standards equal the marginal costs of attaining them).

If the standards are applied uniformly, they will result in excessive compliance costs.

If standards are set individually for different sources, the information requirements are likely to be excessive.

Technology-based controls discourage technological innovation.

Input- or Technology-Related Requirements

Definition: These are requirements to employ specified processes, equipment, input materials, or end-of-pipe emission stream clean-up systems.

Advantages: They provide those subjects to the controls with explicit, specific directives on the actions each needs to take to be in compliance.

They provide the regulators with considerable flexibility in deciding which parts of the production, end-use, and disposal stream to target for control.

Limitations/Drawbacks:

Such approaches may retard the search for and introduction of new technology.

The imposed control method typically will not be the most cost-effective solution for all those subject to them.

There may be no incentive for polluters to look for lower cost ways of achieving the same level of environmental quality; therefore, it may inhibit technological progress.

If the requirement is not to become technologically out-dated, it must be periodically reviewed and revised.

The regulation must have access to considerable information on production technology and technology choices.

Emission Taxes (Charges)

Definition: This is a fee levied on each unit of pollution (e.g., a tonne of ash, a liter of untreated waste water).

Advantages: It tends to lead to the least-cost solution.

It encourages development of improved technology.

If technological improvements result in falling abatement costs, this leads to higher levels of emission reduction.

It makes firms face the costs for all pollutant emissions and not just those above some specified limit set by a standard or technology-based control.

It raises revenue for government.

Limitations/Drawbacks:

Like emission standards, monitoring becomes a matter of *discharge measurement* and in some cases it may be that adequate monitoring of individual emissions is impractical.

The initial tax rate might be set either too high or too low. In principle, the level may be changed over time, but in practical terms this often may be difficult;

General price inflation will erode the effectiveness unless the charges are periodically revised upward.

Some persons/organizations may feel that it is unjust for polluters to simply pay a fee for pollution, rather than being compelled to stop. (This type of feeling might be particularly strong against foreign firms or those unpopular for various reasons).

Higher total cost for polluter (i.e., abatement costs, plus the tax on remaining emissions).

Tradeable Emission Permits

Definition:

Here, emitters of the subject pollutant must purchase a permit for a specified allowance of emission. Permits can be traded (sold) on an open market. Total emissions are limited by the number of permits issued. Firms exceeding permit levels are severely penalized.

Advantages:

As with pollution charges, permits tend to promote the least-cost solution for emission control.

It encourages the search for more efficient means of pollution control (since firms can make money by further reducing their own emissions and selling the unneeded permits to others).

It is flexible with regard to economic growth, that is, new firms entering the market must purchase pollution permits from existing firms or bid for those available the next time they are issued.

It makes firms face costs for all units of emission and not just those above some specified limit set by a standard or technology-based control.

Possible to control income transfers by choosing the means of initial distribution of the permits.

Limitations/Drawbacks:

As with emission charges and emission standards, monitoring becomes a matter of *discharge measurement* and it may be that adequate monitoring of such discharges is infeasible.

Compared to a system of emission taxes, broadly falling costs of pollution abatement will lower pollution control costs, but not increase the level of emission reduction; however, with generally cheaper emission's control, the market value of the permits would fall, and this would make it easier for government or NGOs to buy-up (and retire) some permits, thus reducing aggregate emissions.

Some persons and organizations may object that the permits grant a "licence to pollute."

Input and Process Charges or Permits

Definition: Fees or permits applied to polluting material inputs or processes to discourage their use.

Advantages: May allow use of market-based incentives in situations where emissions monitoring is not practical.

Other advantages similar to emission taxes/permits.

Limitations/Drawbacks:

They leave the polluter less flexibility in determining the least-cost method of control and hence are likely to be less efficient than emission-based charges or permits.

Charges versus Permits

Charges may be preferred when limiting the total cost of pollution abatement is more crucial than exact control of pollutant emissions, or when the cost of pollution abatement is expected to decline.

Permits may be preferred when the ability to strictly limit total pollutant emissions is considered more important than strict control over the total costs of abatement.

Deposit/Refund Schemes

Definition: In such schemes, a fee is paid on potentially polluting materials, and a refund is paid for the return of that material; the purpose is to facilitate and encourage recycling, reprocessing, or safe disposal of waste material.

Advantages: Makes it in the financial interest of purchasers or scavengers to maximize recycling, reprocessing, or collection of material that otherwise would end-up in the general waste stream and be difficult to separate.

Where the demand for a certain product is relatively price elastic, it may reduce demand levels for that product and hence lower associated pollution levels for the fraction of the product which escapes the refund collection process.

Limitations/Drawbacks:

Works best with solid wastes and certain types of other materials (e.g., CFCs), but in general limited application for many types of air and water pollution.

Must be adaptable to the existing product sales and distribution systems.

Possible implications for trade (i.e., a form of trade barrier).

Regulatory Compensation for Self-Regulation

Definition: Through formal or informal assurances, emitters who institute effective voluntary self-regulatory programs so as to exceed standards can expect some form of compensation from regulators (e.g., reduced reporting requirements, greater flexibility in the method used to attain standards compliance).

Advantages: Provides the potential for efficiency gains whereby additional increments of environmental quality could be attained at least cost.

Could serve as a supplement to other policy instruments. Has some of the potential advantages of priced market-based measures such as emission taxes and tradeable permits, but without the drawbacks of requiring point of discharge monitoring.

Limitations/Drawbacks:

Requires a context of sufficient trust which is often lacking.

Information Dissemination to Encourage Self-Regulation

Definition: Information on a firm's environmental record would be disseminated to those in the vicinity of production facilities and to consumers and the public at large. Firms concerned about their green image would presumably institute additional self-regulation to enhance that image for consumer or stockholder appeal.

Advantages: Relatively low cost measure.

May serve as a supplement to other policy instruments.

Limitations/Drawbacks:

Effectivness may be difficult to determine and changeable over time.

At most would serve as a supplement to other measures.

When Should the Polluter Pay?

The polluter pays principle is most applicable when

i.   the polluters can be clearly identified and pollution levels from each can be directly or indirectly measured to a reasonable degree of approximation, and

ii. the imposition of a quantity-dependent charge is not expected to lead to serious illicit disposal or by-passing of waste collection/processing channels.

NOTES

1. The term *environmental standards* is a common one. However, it is important to distinguish between *ambient standards*, which are concerned with overall environmental quality, and *emission standards*, which limit pollution outputs from individual sources.

2. Technology requirements are often specified through such terms as Best Practical Control Technology (BPT), or Best Available Technology (BAT) which have formal definitions in the United States and in some countries. For example, in the US, BPT is the *average* of best existing effluent treatment performance within a certain industrial category, while BAT is the *best example* of existing technology performance within an industrial category.

3. Here we focus on *dis*incentives, although much of the discussion would apply to positive incentives as well. The choice between a strategy of punishment versus reward depends on such factors as administrative costs and political/social acceptability, and as noted in Chapter 4, most basically on how environmental property rights are assigned

4. Differences in the damage caused by various emitters are also an issue of considerable theoretical importance. Since problems of measurement are often paramount, it is usually impractical to specify damages from individual emission sources.

5. In a similar fashion, labor conditions for suppliers and distributors may affect sales as much as conditions among a firm's own direct-hire employees.

6. Some forms of direct controls also may require point-of-discharge monitoring. However, in general, direct controls offer greater flexibility with respect to the level and extent of monitoring (e.g., through spot checks instead of continuous monitoring).

7. That argument is not valid, however assuming that the tax or the number of permits has been properly set, the overall effect on the environment is not altered by this behavior. Market schemes require that the possible profligacy of the few be offset by increased abatement efforts of others. For example, under the permit system, if some firms elect to buy permits rather than reduce discharges, the remaining firms must adjust their discharges to reflect the reduced number of permits available.

11

Applications of Environmental Economics: Illustrative Examples

We conclude with a number of examples that illustrate the application of a variety of techniques and approaches stemming from economic theory and its use in environmental assessment. The studies presented cover only selected applications of environmental economics. Nonetheless, we hope that readers will find these examples useful in seeing how some of the topics covered in this text are applied.

In keeping with our stress on the practical use of environmental economics while also noting its commonly encountered limitations, each example presents: a summary of the study, a review of the techniques employed, comments on techniques that might potentially have been employed but were not, the major findings of the study, and the manner in which the results fit into the larger environmental decision-making context.

EXAMPLE 1: VALUING THE HEALTH BENEFITS OF AIR QUALITY IMPROVEMENTS IN SOUTHERN CALIFORNIA

Context

In Chapter 7 we discussed the advantages of monetizing external costs for both market and non-market values so as to assist decision-makers in comparing benefits and costs of some particular policy option. We also described various techniques for doing this to a full or partial extent. In the United States, Jane Hall and Victor Brajer, along with a number of co-authors, carried out assessments of the health effects of exposure to excess levels of ozone (O_3) and respirable particulate matter (PM_{10}) and attempted to place a dollar value on some of the resulting damages. The results of their work are reported in Brajer, Hall and Rowe (1991) and in Hall et al. (1992). The following descriptions are based on these sources.

Air pollution is a serious problem in southern coastal California with ozone and respirable particulate matter being among the major concerns. The purpose of the analysis was to estimate the economic benefits that would accrue to the twelve million residents within the South Coast Air Basin (centered on Los Angeles) if ambient levels of ozone and respirable particulate matter were brought into compliance with air quality standards. The researchers based their estimates of current exposure on hourly monitoring data for O_3 and 24-hour average data for PM_{10}.

Since exposure and dose are not necessarily the same (e.g., due to differences in activity levels in different groups of people), the researchers employed a regional exposure model (REHEX) which estimated the number of persons subject to higher than average pollution exposure due to such factors as type of employment, location of residence, and age. These estimates of dosage were related to adverse health effects through dose-response functions measured in earlier clinical and epidemiological studies. Taking O_3 into the lungs causes a variety of upper respiratory symptoms such as sore throat, cough, headache, chest congestion, and eye irritation. PM_{10} is a complex pollutant with the damage it causes being determined in large part by associated contaminants (e.g., heavy metals attached to the particle). High PM_{10} levels also tend to be associated the presence of other air pollutants.

For O_3, it was the value of alleviating the upper respiratory symptoms that was the researcher's focus for monetization. Noting that "epidemiological studies cannot prove causality," Brajer, Hall and Rowe use PM_{10} levels as a surrogate measure "strongly associated with a constellation of systematic effects, including increased mortality." The authors noted that,

> results from the REHEX model showed that during the period 1984-86, 98 percent of the Basin's nearly 13 million residents were exposed at least once a year to ozone concentrations exceeding the federal standard of 12 parts per hundred million (pphm). About 6.5 million people were exposed to ozone levels above the stage I alert level (20 pphm), more than 200,000—all in Los Angeles county—still experience at least one stage II alert (36 pphm) each year. About 10 million exposures to PM_{10} levels exceeding the federal 24-hour standard also occurred in the Basin. (1992:88)

Overall, "the adverse health effects of polluted air were widespread, and almost no one escaped such effects. Children were impacted more than other groups largely due to the amount of time they spend outdoors and their higher levels of physical activity" (Brajer, Hall, and Rowe, 1991:88).

Tables 11.1 and 11.2 show the effects for ozone by age and symptom and for respirable particulate matter by location and level of risk. On average each resident of the air basin experiences ozone-related symptoms up to seventeen days per year and faces a one in ten thousand risk of premature death due to elevated PM_{10}.

Table 11.1
Reduction in Number of Ozone-Related Symptom Occurrences (Annual) by Demographic Group with Attainment of Air Quality Standards

			Symptoms		
GROUP	Cough	Headache	Eye Irritation	Sore Throat	Chest Congestion
Infants	27	24	1,392	40	14
Toddlers	24,472	21,592	26,866	35,987	12,955
School aged Children	52,873	46,653	77,100	77,755	27,992
College Students	3,543	2,244	3,974	3,740	1,346
Adults Non-working	10,487	9,253	19,706	15,421	5,552
Adults working Indoors	17,043	15,038	37,669	25,063	9,023
Adults working Outdoors	11,580	10,218	15,228	17,029	6,131
Adults working In-transit	987	870	1,601	1,451	522
Elderly Adults	1,744	1,539	8,079	2,565	924

Source: Brajer, Hall, and Rowe (1991:89).

Economics Techniques Employed

The value of the adverse health impacts was estimated through the cost of illness (COI) and contingent valuation (williness to pay) on the part of the public to avoid these dangers. The COI measures such things as the value of lost work time, cost of doctor visits, and related expenditures. In this case, the analysts used values from available data on actual health care expenditures and

Table 11.2
Annual Reduction in Number of PM_{10}-Related Effects

Effect	Basin
RAD	14,630,000
Premature Death	1,617
Increased Risk of Death	1/10,000

Source: Brajer, Hall, and Rowe (1991:90).

Table 11.3
Adjusted Values for Ozone Symptoms (in 1990 U.S.$)

Effect	Low	Medium	High
Cough	$0.50	$ 1.50	$ 4.50
Headache	1.00	2.75	7.25
Eye irritation	0.75	1.75	4.00
Sore Throat	1.00	2.00	4.25
Chest Congestion	1.50	3.25	6.75
MRAD	14.50	23.00	37.25
MMSD	7.50	16.75	37.25
RAD	---	53.00	---

Source: Hall et al. (1992:815).

wage levels. As the authors note, "the COI cannot capture all the benefits of better health, since it fails to include such costs as the value of lost leisure, of general misery, or non-reimbursed child care or home care." They go on to note that, "theoretically, the CV [contingent valuation] method would yield the best estimate of value, but carefully conducted CV studies had not been carried out for all the effects to be valued" (Brajer, Hall, and Rowe, 1991:84).

The researchers use the COI as the lower bound for value and estimates of willingness to pay (WTP) as the upper bound. The specific COI costs and WTP levels used in their analysis were taken from other studies. The values employed by the authors for minor restricted activity day (MRAD), multiple minor symptom day (MMSD), and restricted activity day (RAD) for the ozone-related symptoms are shown in Table 11.3

Limitations of the Analysis

The authors stress that their estimates of the value of reducing ozone and particulate matter reflect only specific aspects of the full values. For example, "the study did not consider reduced lung capacity—a known result of ozone exposure. Nor did the study account for ozone damage to forests, agriculture and materials" (Brajer, Hall, and Rowe, 1991:82). Reduced lung function was left out, because "no values for reduced lung function existed in the economics literature"; in addition, "significant pollutants were dropped from the analysis," for example carbon monoxide (CO), "since the REHEX model could not reliably calculate CO dose" (83).

Conclusion

Table 11.4 shows the summary dollar benefits estimated by the researchers. They note that while the mortality values dominated the totals, the benefits of reduced RADs were also large. "The total annual value of attaining the federal

Table 11.4
Basin Total Annual Dollar Value Benefits of Attaining Federal
PM_{10} and O_3 Standards (in billions, 1990$)

Effect	Low	Mid	High
RAD[a]	$0.77	$0.77	$0.77
Averted Mortality[b]	2.94	6.39	14.86
Symptoms[c]	1.25	2.68	5.84
Total Benefits	4.97	9.84	21.47

Note:
[a] is restricted activities days related to PM_{10}.
[b] is averted mortality related to PM_{10}.
[c] is minor restricted activities days, minor multiple-symptom days, and residual single-symptom
  occurrences related to ozone.
Source: Brajer, Hall, and Rowe (1991:90)

ozone and PM_{10} standards in the basin range from $5.0 billion to $21.5 billion. With a best estimate of $9.8 billion" (Brajer, Hall, and Rowe, 1991:90). They also note their study made "significant advances in several areas: human exposure modelling, quantification of ozone dose and symptoms, and economic valuation" (90). The 1992 article, while still stressing the importance of the findings of the study, adds a cautionary note: "Benefit estimation has not yet reached the maturity that policy makers would like and cannot yet provide definitive answers to difficult economic questions ... This work, and that of others shows that some progress is being made and that the foundations for such analyses are becoming stronger ... Continuing work on valuing reduced risk to life narrows uncertainty" (Hall et al.1992:816). Finally, the 1992 article underscores the fact that

> some questions are inherently political; although we settle on a mid-range value of life, a broader range is provided, reflecting our belief that the political process must decide which value is appropriate. Finally, available information shows that important benefits (including preservation of lung function) are not yet quantifiable in dollars and that current benefit estimates are therefore likely to be underestimates. We conclude that it is prudent to continue pursuing a policy of attainment for the O_3 and PM_{10} NAAQs [National Ambient Air Quality standards] in Southern California. (816)

EXAMPLE 2: BENEFITS AND COSTS OF AN
AIR QUALITY IMPROVEMENT IN HONG KONG

Context

A survey of children's respiratory health conducted by the Department of Community Medicine of the University of Hong Kong in 1989 found significant differences in some health indicators among school children aged eight to eleven living in a heavily industrialized area characterized by poor air quality compared to a control group living in a non-industrial area of Hong Kong with much better air quality. In July 1990 the Hong Kong government imposed regulations on the sulfur content of industrial fuel. This resulted in substantial lowering of ambient sulfur dioxide (SO_2) levels, and a moderate lowering of particulate concentrations in industrial areas. A follow-up survey of respiratory health for the same age children in the same schools conducted in 1992 found a decline in the estimated avoidable health risks of living in the more polluted area. The two respiratory health surveys (RHS) served as the starting point for a study of the costs and *some* of the near term benefits associated with the ban on high sulfur fuel oil by industry in Hong Kong, published in Barron et al. (1995).

The industrial district of Kwai Tsing was the focus of the RHS. As one of Hong Kong's most industrialized areas, Kwai Tsing was seriously affected by the air quality intervention (the mid-1990 ban on high sulfur fuel), both in terms of the costs to locally based industrial plants and the local benefits from improved air quality for the people resident there. Monthly average ambient sulfur dioxide levels ranged between 100 and 140 $\mu g/m^3$ for the first five months of 1990 and then fell to under 20 $\mu g/m^3$ following the imposition of the regulations on July 1. Average concentrations of respirable suspended particulates (RSP) for the first half of 1990 were 51 $\mu g/m^3$ and fell to 40 $\mu g/m^3$ for the second half of the year. In contrast, the control area in Southern District was little affected (either in terms of costs or benefits) as there are few industrial establishments in that district and for much of the year the area enjoys cleansing fresh winds coming from the South China Sea, making it among the cleanest parts of Hong Kong in terms of ambient air quality.

Economics Techniques Employed

The analysts started with estimates of direct costs and benefits (i.e., avoided direct costs). The banning of high sulfur fuel oil resulted in an estimated annual increase in fuel cost to industry in the Kwai Tsing District of about U.S.$8.3 million. From the 1989 health survey the estimated attributable excess risk for a doctor consultation in the industrial area was 23%, while the 1992 survey showed that this excess risk had fallen to the point where it was not statistically significant at the 95% confidence level. Unfortunately, the RHS only asked whether the child had visited a doctor for the relevant symptoms at least once within the past three months. Hence, there was uncertainty with regard to how to annualize the responses. In addition, while the sampled schools were believed to be representative, some caution had to be taken with respect to boundary effects. After a review of the literature and locally gathered information, the researchers used a range of 570 to 6,900 annual cases of avoidable doctor visits due to sulfur dioxide and RSP for all Kwai Tsing children aged eight to eleven.

While the RHS dealt only with children age eight to eleven, it would seem reasonable to assume that some excess risk exists for younger and older children as well. Perhaps the risk would be higher for younger children and lower for older ones, but there was no available data to support this. As a working approximation, the analysts preliminarily assumed that the excess risk for doctor consultation for these other groups of children was the same as for the study group.

A further assumption was made that the scale of industrial activity, the contributions from other sources of air pollution, and population levels in Kwai Tsing did not change greatly within the relevant planning horizon. Hence, for at least the near term the approximate scale of the benefits and costs were assumed to remain the same. This allowed the authors to calculate average annual costs for avoided symptoms. Taking this short- to medium-term perspective made it possible to sidestep issues of deciding what would be an appropriate discount rate for the valuation of improvements in human health.

In an area such as Kwai Tsing many people rely on government supported health clinics. However, there are also many private doctors in the area and their unsubsidized fee of approximately U.S.$15 per consultation (in 1990 US$) was used as the market value in Hong Kong of the cost of such visits. Adding locally developed direct cost estimates for transport and medical prescriptions, each doctor consultation was estimated to cost a resident in Kwai Tsing roughly U.S.$30 in out-of-pocket expenses. Since the doctor consultation involved children, virtually every such visit would require adult supervision. Each doctor consultation was assumed to take one half day of an adult's time and the opportunity cost of that was taken from typical wages in this lower income industrial area (i.e, $15 for a half day). Hence, the total cost of each doctor consultation was valued at $45. Applying the range of avoidable doctor consultations for the targeted age groups gave an estimated direct cost savings of $25,700 to $311,000.

Limitations of the Analysis

In concept, it is possible to extend the monetization much further, particularly if one is able to estimate impacts on adults, where the value of lost work time for doctor consultations or sick leave would be directly monetizable. In addition, it might be possible to estimate hedonic property price differences between the industrial and non-industrial areas and possibly even pre- and post-intervention differences in Kwai Tsing. Contingency valuation techniques might be applied to estimate willingness to pay for the value of feeling better, while direct cost estimates of corrosion and other effects of sulfur concentration could conceivably be made as well.

Yet, as the authors note, the costs of conducting adequately designed studies to quantify and put a money value on such impacts of an intervention would be high, while the actual value of the added precision to decision-making when a certain impact is monetized may be quite modest, unless that piece of information really significantly changes the level of net monetized costs. Since the resources to carry out further monetization were unavailable to the analysts, they limited the detailed monetization to direct costs of doctor consultations for children and showed only a likely range of values from other studies which are applicable.

Table 11.5
Tradeoffs Between Monetized Net Cost and Non-Monetized Net Benefit

Monetized Benefits			
Costs of avoided doctor visits for children 8-11	Avoided doctor visits for all children	Estimates of avoided doctor visits for adults	Estimate of value of avoided symptoms
Annual Gross Cost Less Monetized Benefits (millions $)			
8.0 to 8.3	7.1 to 8.2	6.8 to 8.1	3.5 to 7.3
Remaining Non-Monetized Benefits			
Avoided symptoms in other age children			
Value of avoided doctor visits by adults	Value of avoided doctor visits by adults		
Avoided symptoms for which no doctor visit	Avoided symptoms for which no doctor visit	Avoided symptoms for which no doctor visit	
Long-term health impacts of cleaner air	Long-term health impacts of cleaner air	Long-term health impacts of cleaner air	Long-term health impacts
Productivity (on the job and school) impacts	Productivity (on the job and school) impacts	Productivity (on the job and school) impacts	Productivity (on the job and school)
Reduced defensive expenditures	Reduced defensive expenditures	Reduced defensive expenditures	Reduced defensive expenditures
Others	others	others	Others

Table 11.5 summarizes the situation with regard to costs of the fuel oil regulations in Kwai Tsing, the estimated direct costs for doctor consultations for children, and a preliminary listing of other expected benefits from the attained improvements in air quality in Kwai Tsing.

Conclusion

The ban on high sulfur fuel oil was quite controversial before it was implemented, yet was viewed as a great success afterwards. In large part this was probably due to the ban's relatively low cost and to the obvious near-term benefits. The authors note that their study showed that "at least a moderate portion of the intervention costs have been offset simply through the near-term health impacts with respect to symptom relief. It would also appear reasonable to argue that if one measured Hong Kong people's willingness to pay for avoiding such symptoms, much of the intervention costs have been offset" (Barron et al. 1995:116).

The analysts also stress that the high cost of data gathering often limits the ability to fully exploit economic tools to help better define the nature of the tradeoffs. Yet, even when the monetization process is only carried out only to a limited degree, such steps hopefully provide "policy makers with a more rational and precise basis for decision-making and hopefully encourages them to be more open in indicating the minimum or maximum value they would have society place on specific environmental and health impacts" (116).

EXAMPLE 3: AUDIT OF THE ECONOMIC VALUE OF PUBLIC LANDS IN NEW SOUTH WALES, AUSTRALIA

Context

Public lands of the upper northeast region of the state of New South Wales, Australia, make up nearly half the total land area and contain a significant portion of the resources that drive the region's economy, including forest products, fish, minerals, agriculture, tourism, and water resources. Between 1993 and 1995 the Natural Resources Audit Council (NRAC) of the government of New South Wales (NSW) conducted a series of regional audits for this region. Attempts were made to do an economic valuation of commercial products and resources associated with public lands, recreation and tourism, and the non-use values for these public lands. These studies were published in December 1996 by the Resource Conservation and Assessment Council (RCAC) of the NSW government. As the published report noted, "while these studies do not constitute a conclusive or definitive work on the area, they do, however, combine previous knowledge with recent research and expose gaps in current understanding and available data" (RCAC, 1996: Preface).

Table 11.6
Public Lands Products Contributions, 1992-93

Product	Output Value ($)	Composition (%)
Timber & forest products	23,005,188	5
Fish	24,276,256	5
Minerals	8,659,828	2
Water	150,000	0
Agricultural products	3,659,383	1
Recreation	149,000,000	30
Tourism	288,000,000	57
TOTAL	496,750,655	100

Source: Jensen et al. (1995) and Centre for Tourism (1995) reported in RCAC (1996).

Table 11.7
Value Added Commercial Products, Upper Northeast NSW, 1992-93

Product	Value added/output (%)	Value added ($)
Timber & forest products	87.99	19,996,442
Fish	79.22	19,231,650
Minerals	52.58	4,553,337
Water	52.43	-
Agricultural products	51.43	1,918,781
TOTAL		45,700,210

Note: Estimated value of water was based on the costs of production and hence does not involve a component of value added.
Source: Jensen et al. (1995) reported in RCAC (1996).

Table 11.8
Recreation and Tourism Consumers' Surpluses, 1992-93

Site type	Per Unit Consumers' Surplus	Consumers' Surplus ($m)
Terrestrial	$91 per visitor day	280
Beach	$1.19m per km of coast	360
Boating	-	26
Diving	$50 per dive	7
Fishing	$33 per angler day	9
TOTAL		682

Source: Jensen et al. (1995) reported in RCAC (1996).

Economics Techniques Employed

The NRAC commissioned a series of studies employing a variety of techniques including the tracking of revenues and expenditures related to economic activities in the study area, an input/output study of the area's economy, and an estimate of the net benefits that accrue to the community as a result of using the resources of the public lands through an estimation of the consumers' and producers' surpluses for both marketed and non-marketed goods and services.

Table 11.6 shows the revenue and expenditure associated with products from the public lands, with tourism and recreation being the most significant. Tables 11.7 and 11.8 show, respectively, estimates of the value added for commercial products and estimates for consumer surpluses for various activities. The value added figures in Table 11.7 were developed using an input/output model which estimated the direct value added and that generated through flow-on activities. For the consumer surplus estimates in Table 11.8 the benefits transfer approach was used with the assumption that "the conditions applying when the original estimation study was performed are approximately replicated in the current circumstances." It was assumed that, for example, "the per user surplus generated from boating on the Great Barrier Reef is the same as that enjoyed by the Upper North East Region boaters" (RCAC, 1996: 11).

Limitations of the Analysis

The benefit transfer method was considered as a means to estimate the consumer surpluses associated with non-use activities. In other words, an attempt was made to determine if such techniques as travel cost estimates and contingent valuation would be applicable in this case to non-use values (e.g., bequest or option value). However, the main author, J. Bennett, concluded the task could not be carried out with an acceptable level of accuracy and reliability. Because "there are simply too few studies estimating non-use values across too great a variety of ecosystems and populations for their findings to be extrapolated in any statistically rigorous fashion" (RCAC, 1996: 11). The report goes on to note that, "while it is inadvisable for a figure to be placed on the non-use environmental values of the public lands of the upper North East Region, it is likely to be substantial" (12).

Conclusions

The report concludes that the public lands of the study region give rise to 17% of the region's total economic activity in terms of output and 20% of its jobs, predominately though tourism and recreation. It also noted that consumers are substantially better off because of their use of public lands (i.e., as reflected in the estimated consumer surpluses from recreation and tourism). Finally, the report notes that the non-use values of the area, although very difficult to estimate, may be even higher than those given in the foregoing tables.

EXAMPLE 4: FISH CONSUMPTION ADVISORIES AND SPORT FISHING IN TENNESSEE

Context

In the United States, there are a number lakes, rivers, and coastal water bodies that are contaminated with heavy metals, polychlorinated biphenyls (PCBs), dioxins, and other toxic compounds. Fish advisories are usually posted to warn anglers of the potential health problems that could result from the consumption of contaminated fish. These posted advisories account for about 15% of U.S. lake acreage and 4% of total river miles. Advisories vary according to the level of contamination and can include outright prohibitions, or consumption guidelines on the number, size, species, and frequency of meals.   Fish consumption advisories are issued when contaminant concentrations of sampled fish exceed specified threshold limits set by the U.S. Environmental Protection Agency (U.S.EPA).   These advisories are considered to be much more cost-effective when compared to the actual cost of removing the contaminant. However, the effectiveness of these advisories depends on fishermen heeding the warnings.   The effectiveness of the advisories also depends on the availability of substitute fishing sites so that the losses in consumer surplus of prospective fishermen are small. Jakus et al. (1997) attempted to determine whether sport fishermen are likely to respond to a fish advisory warning by changing the location of where they fish.

Economics Techniques Employed

The authors estimate fishing site choice using travel cost and reservoir-specific quality measures, including the presence of a fish consumption advisory, as explanatory variables to determine if fishermen adjust their behavior in response to the advisories. Their study is based on data collected as part of a long-term monitoring project to examine the behavior of sports fishermen at Tennessee reservoirs. Their empirical results suggest that these fishermen are less likely to choose a contaminated reservoir over a reservoir that does not have a posted fish advisory. The implication is that advisories appear to be an effective way to discourage consumption of fish from contaminated reservoirs.

The model by Jakus and his co-authors also allows calculation of economic losses associated with advisories and reservoir choice decisions by looking at differences in travel costs with and without advisories. For example, they estimate an average consumer surplus loss due to the existence of the contamination (as reflected through the advisories) of about $2.90 per trip or about 6% of the total trip cost in the eastern Tennessee region. An important policy aspect of their study is that these estimates can be used to compare consumption advisories with environmental remediation options. For one particular reservoir, which covers over 2,000 hectares of lake bottom, the cost of dredging and removing contaminating sediments, was estimated at $16 billion. The per capita annual benefit estimate for that particular reservoir over an entire fishing season was calculated at $28. Multiplying this by the number of fishermen (146,000) and capitalizing this estimate at a 5% real discount rate, yields total losses (in perpetuity) to fishermen of about $81 million, which is only one half of one percent of the cost of environmental remediation (dredging and removing the sediments).

Limitations of the Analysis

A fundamental limitation of this type of valuation study is whether the preferences of the individual fishermen, as expressed in travel costs, accurately reflects society's value. This is especially true in this example since the impacts from the contaminated sediments are long-lived and will continue to impact future generations. The total consumer surplus loss ($81 million for that particular reservoir) could therefore represent only a minimum estimate of value for the lake bottom sediment contamination.

Studies of this type are also plagued by questions of data quality. The survey instrument only measured averting behavior in terms of choosing an alternative reservoir. Jakus et al. mention that fishermen have other responses available to them, including fishing for different species, changing the way fish are prepared prior to consumption, or decreasing the overall consumption of fish in their diet. They also point out that their survey does not distinguish consumption fishermen and pure sport fishermen. For sport fishermen, consumption advisories may actually increase the fishing experience by relieving fishing pressure from those who fish with the intention of eating what they catch.

Conclusions

The study by Jakus et al. provides a good example of how a relatively simple valuation technique can be used to determine or measure the effectiveness of an institutional approach in lieu of a environmental remediation to clean-up a resource. Recall from our earlier discussion that we need to look at foregone opportunities when considering environmental problems. If the advisory warnings are effective in limiting fish consumption and the bottom sediments create no other damages, then the resources that would have been used in remediation (dredging and removal) can be used for other purposes.

EXAMPLE 5: LIFE-CYCLE ANALYSIS OF RECYCLING DECISIONS

Context

In Chapter 6 we included a short appendix on life-cycle analysis. In this example, we extend our discussion on the use of life-cycle analysis for evaluating disposal and recycling decisions. The U.S. Department of Energy (DOE) is involved in numerous environmental clean-up and restoration activities. One such activity is the decommissioning of buildings and facilities once used for uranium enrichment. A key question facing the DOE is how to dispose of radioactive scrap metal in a cost-effective manner without endangering the public and harming the environment. A large number of potential alternatives exist for the disposition of radioactive scrap metal. Among these alternatives are: on-site burial in a low-level waste repository, packaging and transporting of the radioactive scrap metal to a permanent DOE disposal site, decontamination of the metal with subsequent unrestricted release once radioactivity guidelines are met, melting and fabrication of restricted use products (e.g., low-level waste containers), and a combination or hybrid mix of two or more of the alternatives.

Disposal and/or recycle decisions are very complicated because they not only involve different kinds of metal, such as copper and nickel, but different categories of metal. For example, metals that can easily be decontaminated, metals that are inaccessible and cannot be surveyed for levels of contamination, process metals that are highly contaminated and cannot be easily decontaminated, and metals that have been painted or have some type of coating. These decisions also are complicated because of the potential impact decisions can have on the public health and safety and the environment. A life cycle analysis methodology was developed by Yuracko et al. (1997) to help decisionmakers compare and select among competing alternatives for the disposal and/or recycling of radioactive scrap metal. As discussed in Chapter 6, life-cycle analysis is a framework that allows for explicit consideration of all relevant factors in evaluating competing alternatives allowing decisionmakers to make informed choices that take into consideration all potential impacts of a decision.

Economics Techniques Employed

From a benefit-cost perspective, the appropriate question about whether to recycle material is: Do the benefits of recycling and producing new products from contaminated scrap metal outweigh the costs? Because of the complexities of the decision, a life-cycle analysis approach was employed to provide a fuller perspective on the benefits and costs of recycling and to more explicitly evaluate the external effects. The methodology described by Yuracko et al. takes into consideration direct benefits and costs (i.e., the financial perspective of the DOE), as well as socio-economic impacts, including regional impacts, environmental impacts, and health and safety impacts. Since some components of the life-cycle analysis are difficult to value, results are generally not cast in a simple summary measure (e.g., choose the alternative with the greatest NPV)

The methodology is divided into two phases—the life-cycle analysis phase where the possible impacts of each candidate alternative are assessed, and the decision phase. In the first phase, the objectives and boundaries of the evaluation are identified, criteria are specified and performance measures defined, and the impacts of the alternatives are described in terms of the performance measures. In the second phase, the methodology is used to aid the decisionmakers in the comparison of alternatives and the selection of a preferred alternative. That is, the specific analytical approach is defined for each of the performance measures, values are estimated for each alternative, and the results are summarized for use by the decisionmakers. These two phases are linked. Especially important is feedback from the end of the second stage to the first phase to emphasize that performance measures may be further refined, the system definition and process flow model revised, alternatives redefined, and additional analyses performed, if necessary. The decision methodology steps are outlined in Table 11.9.

Limitations of the Analysis

As practiced, benefit-cost analysis suffers from three major shortcomings: it does not explicitly identify affected populations (i.e., those benefited and those harmed); it reduces everything to a single dimension, usually net benefits; and it can hide the degree of uncertainty in various estimates (Dorfman, 1996). Life-cycle analysis attempts to obviate some of these inherent shortcomings. However, because countless external effects can be identified (as is typically done in life-cycle assessment), reduced form models are needed to separate what is and what is not important in the particular context of the problem, to determine what external effects are small or insignificant and do not require further investigation, and to identify what are the priority external effects that need to be explicitly evaluated in detail.

Conclusions

As summarized by Yuracko et al., life-cycle analysis has several advantages —it allows the consideration of numerous factors in environmental decision-making (e.g., potential threats to health and safety; socio-economic impacts, including local and regional economic impacts; and short-term and long-term ecological impacts). By making a complex decision more understandable and open to scientific and public scrutiny, life-cycle analysis fosters greater public participation in the debate about complex environmental problems.

EXAMPLE 6: OPPORTUNITY COSTS: WATERSHED PROTECTION VERSUS TIMBER PRODUCTION IN MALAYSIA

Context

Typically, a land area will offer a number of use opportunities, some of which will be in whole or large part mutually exclusive. Hence, the evaluation of the net benefits of any particular action should go beyond the particular benefits and costs associated directly with a potential project and compare these against the net benefits associated with *foregone alternative uses* for the land. Assessment of such tradeoffs for watershed protection versus timber production for a particular area of Malaysia is the subject of a study by Modh Shahwahid et al. (1997).

The authors examined two land use options for four interrelated water catchments in the Hulu Langat Forest Reserve (HLFR), Selangor, Malaysia. They looked at the total protection of the area, and the reduced impact logging (RIL). The major benefits of the total protection option are associated with the generation of hydroelectric power, the level of municipal water supply, tourism (camping), and low intensity sustainable use of local peoples (e.g., the collection of non-wood forest products). The major benefits associated with RIL are the timber production and local processing of the timber. The purpose of the study was to assess the benefits and costs (including external costs) in allowing reduced impact logging in the catchments.

Economics Techniques Employed

This study focused on developing direct cost estimates for the physical impacts associated with the reduced impact logging versus total protection. Table 11.9 summarizes the types and approximate level of expected conditions under the two options. Sedimentation was projected using a mathematical model which was detailed enough to incorporate specific information related to RIL, such as leaving a buffer zone of undisturbed vegetation 20 meters from the stream and riverbanks. Table 11.10 shows the estimated effects of the two options in terms of sediment runoff and loggable area.

The second step in the evaluation was to assess the value of the environmental and direct economic effects of the two options. The project evaluation period was set at thirty years to coincide with a thirty-year timber harvest cycle and the real discount rate was 10%.

Of course, as noted in Chapter 6, distributional impacts are often of considerable importance. While some economists prefer to leave distributional issues aside and focus on how society as a whole is impacted, a prudent analyst concerned about influencing policy- makers will also attempt to assess how the benefits and costs are apportioned among different groups in society. Mohd Shahwahid et al. considered how the incremental net benefits associated with the low impact logging option would likely be distributed among different

Table 11.9
Hypothetical Physical Impacts of Alternative Land Use Options in Selected HLFR Catchments

Land Use Option	Sedimentation[a]	Timber Harvest	Loss of Dam Storage	Loss of HEP
Total protection	Low	None	Normal	Normal
Reduced impact logging	Medium	Medium	Medium	Medium

[a] Results from the Berembun and Tekam river's experimental catchments (Abdul Rahim 1988) revealed that sedimentation rates increased remarkably in the first year after catchment disturbance, but recovered to background level within three to five years. Degradation in the quality of stream water was observed especially for suspended solids, turbidity, and iron concentration. However, the impacts on water quality were short-term and manageable. The magnitude of impacts generally depends on the intensity of disturbance and harvesting technique.

Table 11.10
Harvestable Forest Area and Sediment Yield

Item	Reduced Impact Logging	Total Protection
For Langat Dam		
Total area (ha)	3,551	3,551
Loggable area (ha)	2,871	-
Buffer area (ha)	680	-
Sediment yield (m^3)	497,244	106,530
For HEP Pond		
Catchment 2	473.0	473.0
Total area (ha)	387.8	-
Loggable area (ha)	85.2	-
Buffer area (ha)	39,903.0	14,190.0
Sediment yield (m^3)		
Catchment 3	265.0	265.0
Total area (ha)	217.4	-
Loggable area (ha)	47.6	-
Buffer area (ha)	22,369.6	7,950.0
Sediment yield (m^3)		
Catchment 4	455.0	455.0
Total area (ha)	373.0	-
Loggable area (ha)	82.0	-
Buffer area (ha)	38,380.2	13,650.0
Sediment yield (m^3)		

Table 11.11
Distribution of Timber Resource Rent Among Interested Parties

Stakeholder	Non-tender	Concession	Tender	Concession [a]
	RM	%	RM	%
State government	2,782,072	16.7	13,353,948	80.1
Logging contractor (windfall profit)	11,128,290	66.7	556,414	3.3
Total resource rent	13,910,362	83.3	13,910,362	83.3
Logging contractor (profit margin)	2,782,072	16.7	2,782,072	16.7
Total net Benefits	**16,692,434**		**16,692,434**	

Note:
RM: Million Malaysia Ringett
[a] Timber resource rent based on the tender system of allocating logging concessions in Kedah State, Malaysia (Mohd Shahwahid and Awang Nor, forthcoming).

Table 11.12
Distribution of Water Resource Rent in Hydroelectric Power Production Among Interested Parties

Stakeholder	Total	Protection	Reduced Logging [a]	Impact
	RM	%	RM	%
State government	-	-	-	-
Windfall profit	9,260	0.3	-473,214	-21.4
Total resource rent	9,260	0.3	-473,214	-21.4
Profit margin (HEP Co.)	2,727,659	99.7	2,684,849	121.4
Total net benefits	**2,736,918**		**2,211,635**	

Note:
[a] Negative windfall profit and resource rent imply that the HEP plant fails to obtain a fair and normal profit under the RIL option. This amount is assumed to be 15% for an average industry in Malaysia.

stakeholders. The results of this assessment are shown in Table 11.11 (which considered both tendered and non-tender concessions for the timber harvesting), while Tables 11.12 and 11.13 show the estimates for water resource rents for hydroelectricity and water treatment, respectively.

Table 11.13
Distribution of Water Resource Rent in Water Treatment
Production Among Interested Parties

Stakeholder	Total Protection/reduced impact logging (RIL)	
	RM	%
State government	-	-
Windfall profit	4,107,337	53.4
Total resource rent	4,107,337	53.4
Profit margin (Water Treatment Co.)	3,586,982	46.6
Total Net Benefits	**7,694,319**	

Note: Since treated water production remains constant under both options, the distribution of water resource rent is similar.

Limitations of the Analysis

The authors stress that their findings are site specific. Perhaps just as important is the fact that this single case study did not include some possibly relevant competing uses, such as highland agriculture, which would be needed to "provide a more holistic view of the economic tradeoffs between various land use options in forested catchments." Within the study area itself the economic analysis was limited to the net benefits of timber and water use, leaving out the value of other forest attributes (e.g., recreation, biodiversity, non-wood forest products), the assessment of which would require further research.

Conclusions

The researchers note that, "the present study supports selective logging operation in forested water-regulating catchments. Such an arrangement is feasible since the water from the affected catchment serves to augment water supply only during the dry season... the case of direct intake water supply requires further study" (1997: 37). They further point out that, "since logging causes an increase in sediment yield, state governments are advised to closely supervise the logging activities in forested catchments. Further, despite the imposition of buffer strips, an increase in sediment yield has been shown to be large enough to increase the external costs of HEP [hydroelectric plants]" (37-38).

Finally, they stress that,

since logging is an alternative option to the status quo the Forest Department could incorporate in the licensing a requirement for logging contractors to internalize the external cost of increased sediment yield. This is similar to purchasing the rights to pollute/release sediment. In the event that this policy is accepted, there remains the difficulty of estimating appropriate sediment yield, since sediment yields only return to normal after about six years after the logging. (38)

EXAMPLE 7: LAND DEGRADATION AND THE ECONOMICS OF TREE PLANTING PROJECTS IN NIGERIA

Context

As reported by Bojö (1991), land degradation is considered by some to be one of the most serious global environmental problems, with the potential to impact as much as one third of the earth's land surface. The causes of land degradation can be traced to over-population, over-cultivation, over-grazing, over-forest clearing—and, in some cases, to climatic changes. In Chapters 4 and 5, we discussed the problem of externalities and common property open access resources; that is, resources that have ill-defined property rights with no single person or institution controlling resource use decisions. For land degradation problems, increasing population pressures can bring on the classic "tragedy of the commons"—overexploitation of the resource and lack of long-term investment in the resource.

Anderson (1987, 1989) examined the economics of an afforestation program in the arid area comprising the upper half of the five northern states of Nigeria. The climate in this area is harsh with relatively low amounts of annual rainfall and long dry seasons (8 to 10 months). Tree stocks have been greatly reduced from years of harvesting fuelwood in excess of natural growth. The loss of tree stocks are also attributable to forest clearing and to cattle raising. The consequences of these actions are a marked decline in tree stocks, an increased encroachment on forest resources further south, and a decline in soil fertility (i.e., wind and water erosion, increased surface evaporation and loss of soil moisture, and reduced nutrient recycling with concomitant effects on agricultural productivity).

Economic or project analysis tends to focus on market benefits or the benefits that are easily measured and valued. Meanwhile the non-market and environmental benefits are often excluded because of problems of measurement and valuation. However, excluding the non-market and environmental benefits may significantly understate the viability of investment projects. Anderson asked the question: "what would be the benefits of a tree planting program?" In this area of northern Nigeria, he identified the following benefits: the value of tree products (firewood, poles, and fruit), the value of additional fodder for cattle, and the benefits of improving current levels of soil fertility and curbing future declines in soil fertility. The "market benefits" are the tree products (fuelwood, poles, and fruit) and, perhaps, the increased availability of fodder for cattle. The "environmental" benefits are those associated with improving soil fertility.

Two types of afforestation projects were evaluated—shelterbelts (long, linear plantings of 6 to 8 rows of trees that protect leeward-side farmland) and farm forestry projects (interstitial plantings along field boundaries and near dwellings). Both types of projects have similar environmental impacts but have different costs, risks, and quantitative effects. The costs and benefits were estimated in series of steps involving:

1. Determination of the gross and net farm income,

2. Determining the growth of agricultural productivity,

3. Determining the increase in farm income as a result of the protection trees afford,

4. Calculating the rate of change in soil fertility from the tree plantings,

5. Estimating the value of wood products,

6. Estimating the costs of the afforestation projects, and

7. Computing the value of the land area occupied by the trees.

Economics Techniques Employed

The work of an environmental economist is especially difficult in developing countries. This is because information and data necessary for measurement and valuation are usually non-existent and/or difficult and very expensive to acquire. Anderson faced such a problem in attempting to estimate the environmental benefits of tree planting projects. Normally, we would want to impute values by using willingness-to-pay principles; that is, approaches that rely on estimating a demand curve. Demand curves can be estimated by eliciting preferences through surveys, such as contingent valuation, or they can be estimated indirectly through revealed preference approaches, such as hedonic pricing and the travel cost method.

In many developing country settings, the absence of data for measurement and valuation means that we may need to employ methods that are not based on estimating a demand curve. We discussed one such approach in Chapter 7, direct cost techniques. Although this non-demand curve method is easily applied, it has a major limitation, it measures only the costs to prevent or mitigate environmental damage. In general, non-demand curve approaches do not measure the entire consumer surplus, and hence they only provide a minimum measure of environmental value.

Anderson approached the environmental valuation problem by estimating the direct effect trees would have on agricultural productivity. Although this would be a minimum measure of environmental benefits, it probably captures most of the value. (An excluded value might be the shade and increased comfort for farmers during the extended dry season.) The benefits come from reduced wind damage and erosion, reduced surface evaporation, and increased soil moisture.

Limitations of the Analysis

In the absence of not having local data, Anderson used a forestry rule-of-thumb to come up with the effect tree plantings would have on crop productivity. This says that a 15% to 25% increase in crop yields can be expected from shelterbelts and a 5% to 10% yield increase from interstitial tree plantings, with the economic effects felt 7 to 10 years after planting for the shelterbelts and 8 to 13 years for the farm forestry projects. As another rule-of-thumb some economists have suggested assigning at least as much value to the non-wood products as to the wood products (Tewari et al., 1990). The rationale is that it is simple, easily understood, and appropriate within the context of a developing country analysis where information is, for the most part, non-existent.

With these assumptions about the effects of tree plantings on crop productivity, Anderson was able to estimate the net benefits of afforestation projects. His results show that concentrating on the marketable tree products provides relatively modest returns; however, allowing for environmental benefits raises substantially benefit-cost measures. For example, the benefit cost ratio for shelterbelt projects increases from 0.3 (wood product benefits only) to 2.2 when wood product and environmental benefits are included. The benefit-cost ratio for farm forestry projects also increases by similar factor.

Conclusions

Although Anderson's approach does not attempt to estimate the demand for improved soil fertility, using a surrogate value of increased crop production provides a reasonable approximation. Anderson correctly asks why, if tree planting projects have such beneficial effects, are farmers reluctant to make such investments? The answer, of course, goes back to the issue of ill-defined property rights, the presence of externalities, the propensity of low-income farmers to discount the future very highly, ignorance of the full range of benefits, and government policy failures. These issues would need to be confronted in advance of any efforts to implement the tree planting projects.

WRAP UP

We hope that these examples suggest to readers some of the breath and scope of applications of the theory and analytic tools of environmental economics. For interested readers there are many more examples available in the relevant literature. There are also many books which treat in much greater depth some of the concepts considered in this text. For all readers we hope that this book has provided an informative and perhaps even stimulating introduction and overview of the role of economics in environmental management.

Bibliography

Abdul Rahim, N. "Water Yield Changes After Forest Conservation to Agricultural Land Use in Peninsula Malaysia." *Journal of Tropical Forest Science* 1, no.1, (1988):67-84.

Anderson, D. *The Economics of Afforestation: A Case Study of Africa.* Baltimore: The Johns Hopkins University Press, 1987.

———. "Economic Aspects of Afforestation and Soil Conservation." In *Environmental Management and Economic Development,* ed. by Gunter Schramm and Jeremy Warford. Baltimore: The Johns Hopkins University Press, 1989.

Barron, W. "Energy Related Environmental Controls: Assessing Transport and Industrial Options in Hong Kong." *Energy Policy* 21, no.6 (June 1993): 679-690.

Barron, W.; Lui, J.; Lam, T.; Wong C.; Peters, J; and Hedley, A. "Costs and Benefits of an Air Quality Improvement in Hong Kong." *Contemporary Economic Policy* 13, no.4 (October 1995): 105-117.

Baumol, W. and Oates, W. *The Theory of Environmental Policy.* Cambridge: Cambridge University Press, 1988.

Bernstein, J. *Alternative Approaches to Pollution Control and Waste Management: Regulatory and Economic Instruments.* New York: United Nations Development Programme, 1991.

Boardman, A.; Greenberg, D.; Vining, A.; and Weimer D. *Cost-Benefit Analysis: Concepts and Practice.* Upper Saddle River N. J.: Prentice Hall, 1996.

Bojo, J. "Economics of Land Degradation." *Ambio* 20, no.2 (April 1991): 78-79.

Brajer, V., Hall, J. and Rowe, R. "The Value of Cleaner Air: An Integrated Approach." *Contemporary Economic Policy* 9 (April 1991): 81-91.

Bunn, D. *Applied Decision Analysis.* New York: McGraw Hill, 1984.

Clemen, R.T. *Making Hard Choices: An Introduction to Decision Analysis.* Boston: PWS-Kent Publishing Company, 1991.

Coase, R. "The Problem of Social Cost." *The Journal of Law and Economics* 3 (October 1960):1-44.

——. "Notes on the Problem of Social Costs." In *The Firm, the Market, and the Law*. Chicago: The University of Chicago Press, 1990.

Cohen, J. *Multiobjective Programming and Planning*. New York: Academic Press, 1978.

Dorfman, R. "Why Benefit-Cost Analysis is Widely Disregarded and What to Do About It." *Interfaces* (September-October, 1996): 1-6.

Gittinger, J. P. *Compounding and Discounting Tables for Project Analysis with a Guide to Their Applications*. Baltimore: the Johns Hopkins University Press, 2nd Edition, 1995.

——. *Economic Analysis of Agricultural Projects*. Baltimore: The Johns Hopkins University Press, 1972.

Gonzolez-Caban, A. and Loomis, J. "Economic Benefits of Maintaining Ecological Integrity of Rio Maneyes in Puerto Rico." *Ecological Economics* 21 (1997): 63-75.

Graedel T. and Allenby, B. *Industrial Ecology*. Englewood Cliffs, N.J.: Prentice Hall, 1995.

Graedel, T.; Allenby, B.; and Comrie, P. "Matrix Approaches to Abridged Life Cycle Assessment." *Environmental Science and Technology* 29, no. 3 (1995):134-139.

Hall, J. V.; Viner, A.; Kleinman, M.; Lurmann, F.; Brajer, V. and Colome, S. "Valuing the Health Benefits of Clean Air." *Science* 255 (February 14, 1992): 812-816.

Hardin, G. "The Tragedy of the Commons." *Science* 162 (December 13, 1968): 1243-48.

Jakus, P.; Downing, M.; Bevelhimer, M. and Fly, J. "Do Sportfish Advisories Affect Reservoir Anglers' Site Choices?" *Agricultural and Resource Economics Review* 26, no.2, October 1997.

James, D. *Environmental Incentives: Australian Experience with Economic Instruments for Environmental Management*. Canberra: The Department of the Environment, Sport and Territories, Commonwealth of Australia, 1997.

Johnston, R. *Fisheries Development, Fisheries Management and Externalities*. Washington: World Bank Discussion Papers, Fishery Series 165, July 1992.

Keeney, R. L. and von Winterfeldt, D. *Operational Procedures to Evaluate Decisions with Multiple Objectives*. Palo Alto: Electric Power Research Institute, September 1987.

Maddison, D.; Pearce, D.; Johansson, O.; Litman, T.; and Verhoef, E. *The True Costs of Transport*. London: Earthscan Publications, 1996.

Norgaard, R. B., and Howarth, "Sustainability and Discounting the Future." In *Ecological Economics,* edited by R. Constanza. New York: Columbia University Press, 1991.

Office of Policy, Planning, and Evaluation. *Economic Incentives: Options for Environmental Protection*. Washington: United States Environmental Protection Agency, March 1991.

Ong, S. G., Lui, J.; Wong, C. M.; Lam, T.H.; Daniel, L., and Hedley, A. "Studies on the Respiratory Health of Primary School Children in Urban Communities of Hong Kong." *The Science of the Total Environment* 106 (1991): 121-135.

Organization for Economic Co-Operation and Development (OECD). *Environmental Policy Benefits: Monetary Valuation.* Paris: OECD, 1989.

———. *How to Apply Economic Instruments.* Paris: OECD, 1991.

Panayotau, T. *Basic Concepts and Common Valuation Errors in Benefit-Cost Analysis,* Singapore: Economy and Environment Program for Southeast Asia, March 1997.

Raiffa, H. *Decision Analysis: Introductory Lectures on Choices Under Uncertainty.* Reading, Mass.: Addison-Wesley Publishing Company, 1970.

Resource and Conservation Assessment Council (RCAC). *Economic Studies of Upper North East New South Wales.* Sydney, Australia, RCAC, 1996.

Richer, J. "Willingness to Pay for Desert Protection." *Contemporary Economic Policy* 13, no.4 (October 1995): 93-104.

Sassone, P. G. and Schaffer, W. A. *Cost-Benefit Analysis: A Handbook.* New York: Academic Press, 1978.

Shahwahid, M.; Noor, A.; Zulkili, A.; and Ragame, U. *Economic Benefits of Watershed Protection and Tradeoff with Timber Production: A Case Study in Malaysia.* Singapore: Economic and Environment Program for Southeast Asia, 1997.

Shrader-Frechette, K. S. *Risk Analysis and Scientific Method: Methodological and Ethical Problems with Evaluating Societal Hazards.* Dordrecht, Holland: D. Reidal Publishing Co., 1985.

Society of Environmental Toxicology and Chemistry. *A Technical Framework for Life-Cycle Assessment.* Pensacola: Society of Environmental Toxicology and Chemistry, 1991.

Tam, A. Y.; Wong, C. M.; Lam, T. H.; Ong, S. G.; Peters, J.; and Hedley, A. "Bronchia Responses in Children Exposed to Atmospheric Pollution in Hong Kong." *Chest* 106 (1994): 1056-1060.

Tewari, D.; Nautiyal, J.; and Singh, K. "Incorporating Impacts of Afforestation Projects in Project Appraisal: A Case Study of the Western Himalayas, India." *Journal of Environmental Systems,* 19, no. 4, (1989-90): 339-347.

U.S. Environmental Protection Agency (EPA). *Life Cycle Assessment: Inventory Guidelines and Principles.* EPA/600/R-92/245, Washington, February, 1993.

Von Winterfeldt, D. and Edwards, D. *Decision Analysis and Behavioral Research.* Cambridge: Cambridge University Press, 1986.

Yuracko, K.; Hadley, S.; Perlack, R.; Rivera, R.; and Curlee, T. "Fernald's Dilemma: Recycle the Radioactive Scrap Metal, or Bury It?" *Resources, Conservation, and Recycling* 19 (1997): 187-198.

Index

About the Authors

WILLIAM F. BARRON is Associate Professor of Environmental Management at the University of Hong Kong.

ROBERT D. PERLACK is the leader of a biomass and resource systems group at Oak Ridge National Laboratory.

JOHN J. BOLAND is Professor of Geography and Environmental Engineering at Johns Hopkins University.

ISBN 1-56720-159-8

9 781567 201598

HARDCOVER BAR CODE

90000>

DATE DUE

DISCARD